B&T - 3/66 (Sweringen)

The Economic Thought of Franklin D. Roosevelt and the Origins of the New Deal

NUMBER 586
COLUMBIA STUDIES IN THE SOCIAL SCIENCES
EDITED BY
THE FACULTY OF POLITICAL SCIENCE
OF COLUMBIA UNIVERSITY

The Economic Thought of Franklin D. Roosevelt and the Origins of the New Deal

by DANIEL R. FUSFELD

COLUMBIA UNIVERSITY PRESS
NEW YORK AND LONDON

The Columbia Studies in the Social Sciences (formerly the Studies in History, Economics, and Public Law) is a series edited by the Faculty of Political Science of Columbia University and published by Columbia University Press for the purpose of making available scholarly studies produced within the Faculty.

Library of Congress Catalog Card Number: 55-9065

Manufactured in the United States of America

Acknowledgments

I WOULD LIKE to thank Dr. John M. Clark and Dr. Joseph Dorfman of Columbia University for their assistance and advice as this study developed, and Dr. Basil Rauch of Barnard College for further helpful criticisms.

The entire staff of the Franklin D. Roosevelt Library was most helpful to me, particularly the director, Herman Kahn, as well as George Roach, Edgar Nixon, and William Nichols. I also wish to thank Miss Elizabeth Seanor of the Hofstra College Library for her aid in obtaining needed materials. Many others, too numerous to mention, have helped with time and effort toward the completion of this work.

Finally, I would like to acknowledge that without the help and encouragement of my wife, Harriet Miller Fusfeld, and my father, Dr. Irving S. Fusfeld, this work would probably not have been completed.

DANIEL R. FUSFELD

Hofstra College
May, 1955

Contents

The Economic Thought of
Franklin D. Roosevelt and the
Origins of the New Deal

Introduction

THE INTERPRETATION of Franklin D. Roosevelt's economic philosophy has passed through two stages. During the 1930's partisan opinion dominated, and two conflicting views were common. Supporters of the New Deal argued that Roosevelt had a definite program of welfare legislation and planned capitalism absolutely essential for the preservation of the American way of life, while his political opponents felt that he had deliberately betrayed the American system of free enterprise in favor of a socialistic economy. While there were during the thirties more objective observers whose views of Roosevelt's economic thought were more moderate, the partisan opinions dominated the scene.

In recent years Roosevelt and the New Deal have become raw material for the historian, who has been unable to accept either of the partisan views. The charge of socialism has been found untenable, while the Roosevelt "myth" of the omniscient leader with definite and well-articulated goals and a program to achieve them has become a major target.

Nowadays it is common among historians to assert that Roosevelt had no economic philosophy, knew little about economics, and derived his program of economic legislation either from his advisers or from his ability to grasp the desires of an ever-shifting public opinion. Broadus Mitchell, for example, says that "he had no reasoned design founded in analysis and issuing in deliberated articulated actions." [1] George Soule has made the charge of inconsistency and lack of knowledge:

Mr. Roosevelt had little understanding of or respect for intellectual consistency; his background of scholarship was sketchy and he was not much of a reader. Most of what he learned came from talking with those who appealed to his imagination. What was told him he utilized or discarded with keen political sense of what people are like and how they could be welded into an instrument of power which would enable his administration to keep acting.[2]

Typical of the now generally accepted view of Roosevelt's economic thought is Richard Hofstadter's characterization of him as "the patrician as opportunist." In an impressionistic sketch of his career derived almost wholly from secondary sources, Hofstadter argues that Roosevelt knew little about economics, that he had no definite program or underlying philosophy, and that the legislation of the New Deal was almost exclusively the product of political pressures and facile improvisation.[3]

Some of Roosevelt's close advisers have lent credence to the belief that he knew little economics. Typical is Frances Perkins's much-repeated story of Roosevelt's conference with John Maynard Keynes in 1934. Roosevelt, bewildered by Keynes's mathematical discussion of the unemployment problem, remarked that "he must be a mathematician rather than a political economist," while Keynes was surprised that Roosevelt was not "more literate, economically speaking."[4] Perkins also wrote that he did not read much in economics[5]—a statement that is not borne out by an examination of the voluminous correspondence and other papers at the Franklin D. Roosevelt Library, by the books in Roosevelt's possession, and the testimony of a number of his closest advisers.

Indeed, a careful examination of Roosevelt's education, letters, speeches, and other documents gives a rather different picture of his economic thought and knowledge than that generally held by historians. He had majored in economics in his graduate year at Harvard and was very widely read in current affairs, including current economic problems. When he had to deal with a specific economic problem he read widely in a variety of books and periodicals bearing on the subject, as well as discussing it with experts in the field. His views on basic economic matters were well articulated—par-

ticularly in such areas as labor, big business, welfare legislation, conservation and power, and regional planning—and
were the basis of the policies he advocated as well as the advisers and administrators he chose. In one area—a crucial
one—his knowledge was weak: depression problems. But this
deficiency was shared by most professional economists of his
time. The record shows that Franklin D. Roosevelt had a
well-developed economic philosophy—largely derived from
Progressivism—which was the basis for his political program.
It also shows that he was quite willing to postpone, shift his
ground, and compromise in order to reach his goals. But the
goals were there and Roosevelt knew what they were.

This book is a study of Roosevelt's economic philosophy:
its sources in F.D.R.'s family background and education and
in the Progressivism of Theodore Roosevelt and Woodrow
Wilson; its development under the impact of contemporary
economic problems and their proposed solutions; and its
culmination in the political programs advocated by Roosevelt.
It shows that both the extremes of the Roosevelt "myth" and
the overly critical reaction of present-day historians to that
myth are incorrect interpretations of Roosevelt's economic
philosophy.

In addition to a reevaluation of Roosevelt's economic
philosophy, two important points emerge from this study.
In the first place, Roosevelt's thought was derived primarily
from the climate of opinion of his time, out of which F.D.R.
selected some ideas and rejected others. It was not derived
primarily, or even in any important fashion, from the writing
of intellectuals such as philosophers or economists or political
theorists. Perhaps this is one reason why historians have
concluded that Roosevelt had no economic thought: it has
been impossible to trace his thought in lineal descent from a
preceding generation of thinkers. Since the fashion in intellectual history is still largely to find intellectual antecedents
for a man's ideas rather than to look for their roots in the
contemporary climate of opinion and in discussions of con-

temporary problems, the real sources of Roosevelt's economic thought have been overlooked.

Secondly, F.D.R. was a man with a tremendously complex personality and a highly intricate system of beliefs. Generalizations about such a person are dangerous, and simplified explanations are bound to be wrong. The method used in this study has been to allow Roosevelt to speak for himself, to place his statements in the context of the ideas, political controversies, and problems of his time, and to allow the varied threads of his economic thought to emerge in all their complexity, complete or incomplete, consistent or inconsistent. Generalizations are made and conclusions are reached, but no attempt has been made to impose one single major theme or trend upon F.D.R.'s economic thought. Instead, his ideas are set forth as they actually emerged and gained meaning when applied to the problems of his era.

CHAPTER I

The Roosevelt Family Background

FRANKLIN D. ROOSEVELT's family heritage left its imprint on his economic philosophy in two important ways. In the first place, he was imbued with the spirit of *noblesse oblige* that characterized the landed gentry of the Hudson Valley. This spirit gave him a concern for the poor and the less fortunate as well as a belief that the individual must work for the good of the whole community. In the second place, since his family were landed gentry they did not share the preconceptions and prejudices of the three major economic interest groups of twentieth-century America—business, labor, commercial farming. Roosevelt was able, therefore, to approach the problems of each group without the preconceived notions of any of the three.

When Franklin D. Roosevelt was born on January 30, 1882, his father, James Roosevelt, had already been retired for two years. When James Roosevelt married his second wife, Sara Delano, in 1880, he gave up active participation in the management of his business interests and retired to his country estate. Prior to that time he had been active in numerous banking and transportation enterprises. He had been one of the incorporators of the City Trust Company and a director of the Farmers' Loan and Trust Company in New York City and for a number of years was a director of the Merchants' National Bank in Poughkeepsie. Shortly after the Civil War he had helped organize the Southern Railway Security Company and served as its president; this company took part in the reorganization of southern railroads after the war, including the lines that were to become the Southern Railway and the Louisville and Nashville Railway. His most continuing railroad interest, however, was the Delaware and Hudson Canal Company, of which he was a vice-president and legal adviser for many years, as well as president of one of its subsidiaries, the New York and Canada Southern Railroad. He was also president of the Champlain Transportation Company, which operated boats on Lake Champlain, and was a director of the Maritime Canal Company of Nicaragua. His only important industrial investment was in a small steel property at West Superior, Wisconsin, but he took no active part in the enterprise.

It was his country estate at Hyde Park which was James Roosevelt's major interest. There he created in microcosm the way of life of the English landed gentry that he admired. Purebred cattle were imported to improve the herds, and a fine stable of horses was maintained. He bred the first horse to trot a mile in less than 2:20, the champion Gloster, later selling the horse to Leland Stanford. Fond of trees, he planted many on his 600 acres, and would never permit one to be cut unless it were decayed.

Ostentation was not part of James Roosevelt's creed. The home at Hyde Park was comfortable but not lavish, large but only large enough to provide comfortably for the family. Indeed, James Roosevelt was not particularly wealthy: upon his death he left an estate valued at $300,000.

He took no large part in public life "although he was repeatedly requested to accept the nomination for Congress, the State Senate and the Assembly." [1] A lifelong Democrat, he was said to have been politically important in that party in New York State and an "intimate friend" of Grover Cleveland, whom he visited at the White House in 1887 with young Franklin, then aged five years.[2] Like the other Hudson Valley aristocrats, however, his ideas of *noblesse oblige* caused him to feel a responsibility for community leadership and charities. He served two terms as Supervisor of the Town of Hyde Park, while in the local Episcopal parish he served as vestryman and warden and was a representative to the Diocesan convention. He served on the Board of State Charities and was a manager of the Hudson River State Hospital. "Actively useful as a business man, a philanthropic and public spirited citizen, he was the very ideal of a gentleman of the old school, witnessing by his kindliness and charm of manner to the nobility and honor of his inner Christian character." [3]

Among the Hudson Valley squirearchy were such wealthy families as the Astors, Vanderbilts, and Aspinwalls—and the Delanos. It was from the last family that James Roosevelt chose his second wife, Sara Delano, half his age and one of the belles of the region. She came from much the same background as her husband: her family were landed gentry, owned numerous investments, and were much respected by all who knew them.

The Delano wealth had come primarily from the China trade. Warren Delano, F.D.R.'s grandfather, had been a partner in Russel, Sturgis and Company, one of the leading firms in the tea trade with China, and had lived at Canton for a number of years. He retired to his estate near Newburgh, N.Y., but, losing much of his wealth in the depression of 1857, returned to the China trade, this time specializing in opium. Recouping his fortune, he once more retired, investing his wealth in New York City real estate and mining properties in Pennsylvania, Tennessee, and Maryland.[4] Of this rentier wealth Sara Roosevelt inherited about $700,000 worth of securities when her father died in 1898.

Sara Roosevelt felt very strongly that there was something inherently valuable in the mode of life of the Hudson Valley aristocracy: honor, dignity, tradition, and responsibility were the keynotes of her philosophy. Perhaps these feelings explain, in part, why she married a man twice her age who was a prime example of that mode of life. She expressed her views in a letter to her son after a family argument with him on the subject:

The foolish old saying "noblesse oblige" is good and "honneur oblige" possibly expresses it better for most of us. One can be democratic as one likes, but if we love our own, and if we love our neighbor, we owe a great example, and my constant feeling is that through neglect or laziness I am not doing my part toward those around me. . . . With the trend to "shirt sleeves," and the ideas of what men should do in always being all things to all men and striving to give up the old fashioned traditions of family life, simple home pleasures and refinements, and the traditions some of us love best, of what use is it to keep up things, to hold on to dignity and all I stood up for this evening.[5]

Perhaps typical of Sara Roosevelt's attitude of *noblesse oblige* is the library she endowed in memory of her husband for the town of Hyde Park. Although a free library, it was in part supported by voluntary paid memberships, and she fought very strongly against any tax support for the institution, feeling that it was the responsibility and obligation of the wealthier members of the community to provide for the library.

The attitudes of James and Sara Roosevelt were passed on to Franklin in his education at home. His parents did not enter him in the local public school, but instead hired governesses and tutors to educate him. A number of notebooks and tutorial papers from this period, preserved at the Roosevelt Library, give us a picture of this type of education: emphasis was placed on such basic tools as grammar, penmanship, and arithmetic, languages—German, French, and Latin —and history. Other subjects were taken up: the Bible, astronomy, geography, Wagner's *Das Rheingold,* and so forth. We note a considerable coverage of English history and geography, ancient and medieval history, and foreign languages. An orientation toward England and Europe is fairly obvious.

One of F.D.R.'s governesses, a French-Swiss young lady, had definite sympathies for victims of injustice and exploitation which she passed on to her young charge. Under her influence the nine-year-old boy wrote protestingly about the common people of Egypt in an "Essai sur l'Histoire Ancienne":

The working people had nothing, they lived in the porches of the temples or in little straw huts. The kings made them work so hard and gave them so little that by wingo! they nearly starved and by jinks they had hardly any clothes! so they died in quadrillions.[7]

Or again, his governess dictated to F.D.R., age eleven, the following little essay describing how the unscrupulous businessman takes advantage of the deserving inventor:

No man ever made so many really remarkable and at the same time useful inventions as Thomas Edison. It is somewhat surprising therefore to learn that he has made very little money out of them or at least, very little in comparison with what he might have made ... in a recent interview he said. If an inventor happens to put something on the market that is of real worth and the pirate sees it, the first thing the inventor knows, is that he has a powerful rival which threatens to engulf him at the start. The pirate claims the invention. so does the real inventor but it is the latter who has to prove his wright, and as it takes a long while to even prepare his case, he is disheartened from the beginning. The capitalists draw on the inventors share in the invention and as all the odds are against him, the inventor has very little chance.[8]

Here are two examples of an attitude of concern for the exploited and the underdog that was characteristic of the Roosevelts' feeling of *noblesse oblige.*

F.D.R. felt that his "affluent heritage" should be used as a basis for service to the community, that it was not enough for the well-to-do merely to set an example for others, but that they had to take an active role in community life. He expressed this idea in an essay written, while a student at Harvard, on the subject of his colonial ancestors:

Some of the famous Dutch families in New York have nothing left but their name—they are few in numbers, they lack progressiveness and a true democratic spirit. One reason—perhaps the chief —of the virility of the Roosevelts is this very democratic spirit. They have never felt that because they were born in a good position they could put their hands in their pockets and succeed. They felt, rather, that, being born in a good position, there was no excuse for them if they did not do their duty by the community, and it is because this idea was instilled into them from their birth that they have in nearly every case proved good citizens.[9]

This statement by young Franklin Roosevelt interweaves two concepts, "progressiveness and a true democratic spirit"

with "duty by the community." This combination of democracy and *noblesse oblige* was inherent in the social philosophy of the Hudson Valley gentry. If the individual has a
responsibility to the community, then each must have the
opportunity to take part in community affairs on an equal
basis. Responsible and independent citizenship in a society
of mutual respect and consideration was the ideal, and it was
up to the gentry to set an example which others could
voluntarily follow.[10]

This same combination of democracy and *noblesse oblige*
was found in the Jeffersonian democracy of the early years of
the nineteenth century,[11] and the Hudson Valley gentry
shared in and retained these beliefs. However, these ideas
were no longer in the main stream of American political
thought. Jeffersonian democracy had given way to more
equalitarian ways of thinking in the Jacksonian period, the
Civil War had destroyed the southern landed aristocracy and
started an aristocracy of wealth on its rise to power, and the
conquest of the West had had its influence on new ideas of
democracy. While all this was going on, the Hudson Valley
gentry retained ideals that were at best outmoded: the idea of
aristocracy implied by the concept of *noblesse oblige* was no
longer a part of the American democratic tradition.

The Roosevelts had not always been members of the landed
gentry. The first of the family in America, Claes Martenszen
van Rosenvelt, had come to New Amsterdam from the Nether-
lands in 1644 and seems to have been just an ordinary, un-
distinguished citizen. His son, Nicholas, born in 1658, took
the name Roosevelt and became a merchant in New York
City. His sons and grandsons developed the firm and became
important businessmen in eighteenth-century New York. In
the fifth generation of American Roosevelts, James, F.D.R.'s
great-grandfather, left active business life to become a landowner. Early in the nineteenth century he owned a farm in
Harlem, but in 1819 he bought the Mount Hope estate at
Poughkeepsie and became a new member of the well-estab-

lished group of Hudson River gentry. His son, Isaac Roosevelt, became a doctor but never practiced, and lived permanently at the Poughkeepsie estate. Isaac's son, James Roosevelt, was F.D.R.'s father, and moved to Hyde Park when the state purchased Mount Hope for the Hudson River State Hospital.[12]

When F.D.R.'s great-grandfather acquired his country estate at Poughkeepsie he moved out of the main stream of American economic life into a backwater: the life of the Hudson Valley gentry was more closely akin to that of the English lord than to any American developments of the time. Indeed, the oldest families had held manors in pre-Revolutionary days modeled after their English counterparts, with rents and dues of various sorts paid by the tenants. Of course, the feudal dues had long since been abolished, but this was still the closest thing to landed aristocracy that remained in America. While New York City was becoming the financial capital of America, while fortunes were being made or increased in trade, finance, and real estate, F.D.R.'s grandfather chose the older way of life—he became a country squire rather than a city capitalist.

The Civil War came and went, and the Roosevelts remained country squires. It is true that F.D.R.'s father attempted to gather a bit of the financial spoil of Reconstruction by his participation in railroad reorganization in the South, but he left economic pursuits for his estate at a relatively early age. The great developments of post-Civil War America by-passed him: industry, stimulated by the war, was expanding rapidly; the land and resources of the West were being preempted and exploited; a new aristocracy of wealth had appeared, along with a new working class; the middle-western farm was applying machinery to the prairie lands. In none of these developments did the Roosevelts take part.

It has been said that the America of the post-Civil War era had a dual nature: "Agricultural America, behind which lay two and a half centuries of experience, was a decentralized world, democratic, individualistic, suspicious; industrial America, behind which lay only half a dozen decades of bustling experiment, was a centralizing world, capitalistic, feudal, ambitious." [13]

The Roosevelts, with their English, manorial heritage, were not of either world, but they had interests in common with both. Although landowners, they were not farmers in the sense that the mortgage-ridden homesteader was, nor even the prosperous, independent farmer of the Midwest. They were estate owners, with hired labor and an income from investments. Likewise, although the Roosevelts were not industrialists and had not taken part in the exploitation of the West, much of the family's income was derived from investments in this capitalist side of America. Even the invested wealth, however, had been derived originally from trade and finance and not from industry.

Being neither farmer, industrialist, nor promoter, the Roosevelt family did not have the habits of thought or preconceptions of those groups. They were little concerned, as was the farmer, with cheap money, banker control of wealth, and railroad monopolies; they were not interested in high tariffs and the destruction of labor unions, as was the industrialist; they were not concerned with preemption of public lands and subsidies, as was the capitalist promoter. Rugged individualism —the philosophy of unlimited rights and no obligations with the objective of maximum acquisition of wealth—passed them by. Success, the goddess of America in this age, was not their ideal. Instead, the Roosevelts clung to the old traditions, honor, dignity, and *noblesse oblige*.

The fact that the Roosevelt tradition was not that of industrialist, or farmer, or laborer may well explain, in part, F.D.R.'s greatest political asset, his ability to include in his program the demands of all three groups. Not being associated closely with any of the three, he did not have the preconceived ideas that would prevent an effective compromise program.

Furthermore, the *noblesse oblige* ideals of his family imbued F.D.R. with the principles of community leadership and concern for those less fortunate than himself. But while the concepts of *noblesse oblige* would lead to charity, Roosevelt was to become a spokesman for newer ideas. The belief that government had a responsibility for social welfare and that the individual could claim governmental aid—ideas then taking form in the writings of Ward, Ely, Patten, and others, and in the political agitation of the Populists—went beyond the ideals of *noblesse oblige* of the Hudson Valley aristocracy. The older viewpoint recognized that the individual had a responsibility for others, while the newer argued that the community as a whole had a responsibility for its less fortunate members. Roosevelt was to show that he could move forward from his heritage in the Hudson Valley aristocracy to modern ideas of welfare legislation that were more appropriate to the needs of a complex industrial society.

CHAPTER II

Roosevelt's Formal Education in Economics

IN SEPTEMBER, 1896, at the age of fourteen, F.D.R. was entered in Groton School. The Reverend Endicott Peabody had founded the school twelve years earlier, modeling it after Cheltenham, the English public school where he had been educated. The school had close ties with the Episcopal Church:

This is a Church School indeed; we claim and stand by the term. By it we mean not simply a school to which is attached a system of religion conducted after the manner of the Episcopal Church.... We mean that man and God belong together, and that education alone is worthy of man's nature which enables him to realize and to incorporate into his life this paramount fact.[1]

A religious atmosphere was maintained: sacred studies, taught by Peabody himself, was a required course in all six years, and chapel attendance was required twice daily.

The curriculum was oriented toward the classics and England, in addition to religion. Six years of Latin and four of Greek were required, while French and German were optional. Ancient history was taught for three years, English history for two, American history for only one. The English courses took up English rather than American literature. A good training in mathematics was given—six years' study ranging from arithmetic to trigonometry. Indications of change in the curriculum were present, however: geography was the only required "science," but physics was optional, and political economy, which included current economic problems, government, and foreign affairs, was taught.

In his first year at Groton F.D.R. had the course in political economy. It may seem strange that a private school in the nineties, emphasizing religion and the classics, should teach such a course, but Groton did not consider itself isolated from the world of affairs. In educational circles of the time there was discussion of teaching the subject in secondary schools,[2] and in that respect Groton was in the forefront of educational thinking. Fortunately, F.D.R.'s notebook for this course is preserved at the Roosevelt Library and we can summarize his first contact with formal economics.

The course was taught by the lecture and discussion method, and the instructor was probably Guy Ayrault, who had come to Groton in 1886 after graduating from Columbia College.[3] It began with a discussion of the economic issue of the day: silver vs. gold. This was September of 1896 and a national election would come in a month and the issue of the campaign was "free silver." Altgeld and his supporters had written a platform for the Democrats that took over in large measure the Populist program; Bryan had stampeded the Democratic convention with his "Cross of Gold" speech; the mortgage-ridden farmer had seized upon the issue of free coinage of silver as the answer to his economic problem. On the other side, many business and financial interests felt that free coinage of silver was inflationary and would reduce the value of accumulated wealth and invested capital; they supported McKinley with one of the largest campaign funds in American history in a bitter and hotly contested campaign.

As might be expected in a private school patronized by the wealthy, gold had all the better of the discussion. It is obvious, ran the argument, that a measure must be stable: a yardstick that stretches is of no use. And, since money is a measure of value, a dollar must always be of the same value. Gold is the only suitable standard of value because it is stable, while silver is unstable. Furthermore:

Free coinage of silver means ... a depreciated dollar. The immediate losers from a depreciated currency are those who have laid by a good dollar, and will receive back a depreciated dollar, ... bank depositors, ... members in various insurance concerns, ... pensioners, ... all those that are creditors. But the greatest loser of all is the working man.

The worker finds his real income falling because prices would rise faster than wages. Thus, all groups in the economy would be injured.

The next subject taken up was capital. In a decade that encompassed two periods of business depression, and in a year that was one of the more depressed of the decade, it was pointed out that capital was the means of expanding production, and there could never be too much capital:

A glut of capital is impossible until everyone has everything he wishes, but there may be too much capital invested in a particular business; in that case capital will be withdrawn and will seek investment elsewhere.

And, as far as interest was concerned, it was a reward for abstinence and risk-bearing.

In discussing the value and exchange of commodities it was pointed out that cost of production is the normal price of a commodity, with supply and demand factors causing fluctuations around the normal price. That this doctrine was based on the assumption of competition was recognized:

Of course the laws of Demand and Supply cannot operate unless there is freedom of Competition. A trust or combination to put up prices is in restraint of Free Competition.

But, although the trust was mentioned, nothing was said of the movement toward merger and monopoly that was occurring at the time.

Since cost of production was held to determine normal price, it was necessary to analyze rent, profit, and wages. Rent, following the Ricardian theory, results from differences in productivity: the owner of highly productive land can charge a higher rent than the owner of less productive land, while the owner of the least productive land will obtain no rent. As for profits, they are "that portion of wealth produced which goes as a reward for ability in managing business."

The discussion of wages was a curious mixture. First came a paraphrase of John Stuart Mill that restated the "wages fund" doctrine, a doctrine that had been rejected by most serious economists since 1876: [4]

Wages are paid from capital. The greater the capital of a country, the greater the amount of wages paid. The rate of wages is determined by demand and supply.

There followed an unsure statement of the Malthusian theory that an increase in wages results in a higher level of living and then is followed by a population increase that depresses wages once more.

But if real wages cannot be raised through higher wage rates, what recourse does the worker have? Only an increase in productivity results in higher real wages because it causes price cuts, and with the same money wages the worker can buy more. On the other hand, an increase in money wages in a particular industry does not benefit the worker because profits are reduced below normal and a withdrawal of capital results. Nor is the strike an answer:

A strike is like a war, costly and cruel, and it would seem that boards of arbitration are the rational way of settling differences between Capital and Labor.

Just as the course began with a discussion of a major issue, so it ended, with a long treatment of tariffs. The tariff system of the nineties was described as special-interest legislation benefiting the manufacturer and resulting in high prices. It had been largely formulated in legislation immediately following the Civil War, and each tariff law passed since then benefited more and more manufacturing interests. However, there were no thoeretical criticisms of tariffs and no theoretical arguments for free trade: the discussion, at least as it appeared in F.D.R.'s notebook, was historical and statistical, with much data on prices, tariff increases, and benefits for particular manufacturers.

This was F.D.R.'s introduction to systematic economic thought. The course was in the classical vein, its heart being the theory of value and distribution and its emphasis on cost of production. The main doctrines were derived from Ricardo, Say, Malthus, and John Stuart Mill. Parts of it were outmoded by 1896; its saving element was the extended treatment given the main issues of gold vs. silver and tariff legislation. Like the orthodox economics of the period, there was nothing in the course that might be termed critical of the capitalist order.

Groton provided many extracurricular activities to supplement active study, and in them F.D.R. exhibited interest in public affairs and in charitable activities—as we might expect from his family background of *noblesse oblige*.

He was interested in the visiting lecturers, who were often men of outstanding accomplishments such as Jacob Riis and Booker T. Washington. He wrote to his mother:

Mr. Riis stayed over yesterday and last night gave a most interesting lecture on the poor in New York, with stereopticon views, and there was great enthusiasm over him and the whole school cheered when "Teddy's" picture was thrown on the screen.[5]

The leading events in international affairs aroused considerable interest among the students. The Boer War, which began in October, 1899, caused considerable discussion and F.D.R., sympathizing with the underdog, took the side of the Boers, much to the chagrin of his pro-British mother:

Hurrah for the Boers: I entirely sympathize with them.[6]

I am to debate in two weeks, but I fear I cannot get the Boer question as we debate second, and the first batch will take it.[7]

I think you misunderstand my position in regard to the Boers. I cannot help feeling convinced that the Boers have the side of right and that for the past ten years they have been *forced* into this war. I am sure you will feel this if you only read up on the Boer case. *However*, undoubtedly, now that the war is actually on, it will be best from the humanitarian standpoint for the British to win speedily and civilization will be hurried on, but I feel that the same result would have been surely obtained without war.[8]

F.D.R. took an active interest in the debating society for the four years he was at Groton. The group was primarily concerned with international affairs during this period, and particularly the issues raised by American imperialism in the late nineties: the Nicaragua canal, whether or not the navy should be enlarged, annexation of Hawaii, the problem of China, independence for the Philippines, and the Boer question. F.D.R. spoke on all of those subjects. In the formal debates sides were assigned, not chosen by the speaker, but F.D.R. happened to be assigned the "anti-imperialist" side of all his debates: against the annexation of Hawaii, against an American guarantee of the integrity of China, and in favor of Philippine independence. He also spoke in favor of a large navy (his cousin "Teddy" then being Assistant Secretary of the Navy).

In his speech in opposition to the annexation of Hawaii,[9] F.D.R. stressed the costs of annexation and defense, the lack of value of a colonial empire, the fact that trade could continue without annexation. Any defense considerations could be taken care of by a naval base at Pearl Harbor. But the young man mentioned nothing about the strong business interests entrenched in Hawaii, which were demanding annexation.[10]

Another major activity of F.D.R.'s at Groton was the Missionary Society.[11] This organization was devoted to religious and charitable work of various sorts: it held religious services in various localities near Groton, it supported a Boys' Club in Boston, and it established and ran a summer camp at Squam Lake, New Hampshire, for underprivileged boys. Elected to the society in 1898, F.D.R. and another boy were appointed "special missionaries" to look after an old Negro lady living near the school: they were to visit and talk to her, feed the chickens, see that she had coal and water, and dig her out in case of snow. A little later in the winter F.D.R. was part of a team that held religious services in the neighborhood, F.D.R. being the organist. His interest in the Missionary Society continued after graduation: at Harvard he spent "a good deal" of time at the Boys' Club in Boston, teaching, helping out with entertainments, and participating in sports.[12]

We find F.D.R. at Groton, then, in an environment with the same orientation and ideas as his home, but associating with more young people of his own age. However, the horizons are broader: F.D.R. has come into contact with and entered discussions at second hand of some of the problems of poverty. He remained, on the other hand, a wealthy young man in the company of other wealthy young men. Nor was F.D.R. outstanding either because he was brilliant or different: the Reverend Endicott Peabody writes that

There has been a good deal written about Franklin Roosevelt when he was a boy at Groton, more than I should have thought justified by the impression he left at the school. He was a quiet, satisfactory boy of more than average intelligence, taking a good position in his form but not brilliant. We all liked him. So far as I know that is true of the masters and boys alike.[13]

From Groton Roosevelt went to Harvard College. Entering in 1900, he completed the requirements for the degree in three years, but stayed on for a fourth, partly because he had been elected editor of the school paper and partly to graduate with his class. As an undergraduate his major work was in the fields of English, history, and government, while as a graduate student he concentrated in history and economics.[14]

During the four years at Harvard Roosevelt lived in Westmorley Hall, south of Harvard Yard on Bow Street (Adams House now occupies the site) and just one short block north of Mount Auburn Street. In those days the students at the College were divided into two cliques, the "Yard" clique that lived in the College dormitories and the "Gold Coast" clique that lived in private residence halls on and near Mount Auburn Street. Roosevelt was one of the latter group, and the many invitations to social affairs that remain among the papers at the Roosevelt Library attest to his participation in its activities. But the other side of college life was study, and although Roosevelt was not an outstanding student he took courses and passed them. No study of his economic or po-

litical thought can ignore those four years spent at the outstanding American university.

Roosevelt took Harvard's introductory course in economics
in his second year. Although Frank W. Taussig usually
taught some sections of this course, he did not do so in that
year and Roosevelt's instructor was Assistant Professor A.
Piatt Andrew.[15] The first half-year of the course was devoted
to the classical triad of production, distribution, and exchange.[16] The foundation of the course was the great syn-
thesis of classical economics in Mill's *Principles,* supplemented
by more recent modifications in Hadley's *Economics.* Production was defined as production of useful goods and services, or
utility, and depended upon division of labor and capital accumulation for its increase. Mill's acceptance of the Malthusian theory of population was rejected, as was his theory of
wages, the so-called iron law that wages tend toward a sub-
sistence level unless there are effective checks to population
growth. The wealth produced in the economy was distributed
in the form of wages, profits, and rent. There was considerable discussion of the theory of wages and a number of then
current ideas were discussed.

The course in general could be characterized as "middle of
the road" or "traditional" for its time, but it was not a mere
parroting of John Stuart Mill, as was Roosevelt's course at
Groton. The basic outlook was typified by Andrew's statement that

The competitive system is more advantageous than any other.
If prices were fixed by law the price would not be raised by increasing demand, and hence supply would not be increased to meet the
demand of the community. Competitive forces adjust prices and
demand much better than could a government.[17]

The theoretical description of the functioning of a market
economy was supplemented in the second half-year by a discussion of four major problem areas: international trade and
tariffs, banking, the trust problem, and labor and social
insurance.[18]

In discussing these problems Professor Andrew showed a critical, reforming bent within the framework of his traditional economic theory. He vigorously demolished the arguments in favor of tariffs, and presented the tariff history of the United States as a succession of special interest enactments detrimental to the consumer and benefiting only relatively small groups. His discussion of banking was devoted to a description of the National Banking System and the contrast with foreign central banks; the failings of the American system were clearly delineated. The growth of trusts in America was strongly criticized. Although Andrew pointed out the advantages of large-scale production, he insisted that "the main aim of promoters of combination is to secure such a control over a particular article as to allow the fixing of a monopoly price" and that "the attempt to prohibit combination has proved futile and has simply driven the competing concerns into closer consolidation." [19]

Although convinced of the evils of monopoly, Andrew advocated no drastic remedies, relying on such proposals as publication of corporation accounts, a federal incorporation law, reduction of tariffs, and changes in the patent law. He was optimistic: "the development of the Trust does not mean we are leaving behind the era of competition." [20]

The course closed with a discussion of the labor problem, with Andrew taking a middle-of-the-road position: unions have a definite place, but also some faults. Unions were necessary to protect the worker, whose bargaining position was poorer than the employer's, and recognition of the right to organize resulted in changes for the better in trade union policy: namely, elimination of political goals and reduction in socialistic tendencies. But restrictive practices like the closed shop and the union shop were bad aspects of trade union policy. As for strikes, Andrew deplored them, but considered them necessary preludes to the development of collective bargaining. He criticized the settling of strikes by injunction instead of by bargaining. He favored the laws to promote welfare of the worker that were then being debated: the eight-

hour day, restrictions on child and female labor, old age pensions, social insurance. The final lecture in the course was on
socialism: Owen, St. Simon, Fourier, Blanc, Proudhon, Las-
salle, and Marx were all covered in one hour.

Roosevelt did not follow up his introductory economics
course immediately. In the next school year he completed
the undergraduate requirements, concentrating heavily in history, government, and English. Nevertheless, Roosevelt
stayed at Harvard for a fourth year, in part because he had
been elected editor of the *Crimson,* Harvard's undergraduate
newspaper, and took graduate courses in history and economics. The courses Roosevelt took in this year, 1903–4, that
are relevant to the tracing of his economic thought were:

History 10B.   American History: The Development of the
West. Professor Frederick J. Turner

Economics 5.   Economics of Transportation. Professor William Z. Ripley

Economics 9B.   Economics of Corporations. Professor Ripley

Economics 8B.   Banking and the History of the Leading Banking Systems. Professor Oliver M. W. Sprague

Economics 8A.   Money: A General Survey of Currency Legislation, Experience, and Theory in Recent Times.
Professor Andrew

Roosevelt's course in "The Development of the West" was
taught by Frederick Jackson Turner, whose "frontier theory"
not only reshaped the writing of American history but also
was a forerunner of the "mature economy" economics of the
1930's. Turner at this time (1904) was at the height of his
analytical powers: his path-breaking essay, "The Significance
of the Frontier in American History," had been published
eleven years earlier, and had been followed by a series of
articles which discussed the economic and political effects of
the passing of the frontier.

Turner's basic thesis was that "American institutions . . .
have been compelled to adapt themselves . . . to the changes
involved in crossing a continent, in winning a wilderness, and
in developing at each area of this progress out of the primitive

economic and political conditions of the frontier into the complexity of city life." [21]   The influence of the frontier was a dual one: it promoted unity and it helped develop ideals of democracy and individualism.   Furthermore, American development was the history of a series of frontiers, with a perennial rebirth of the influence of frontier life on the larger society as America moved westward.

But what was to happen now that the frontier was gone? Turner noted two developments.   The first was imperialism: the impulse toward expansion that characterized the frontier period continued in demands for a vigorous foreign policy, for an interoceanic canal, and for the extension of American influence to outlying islands and adjoining countries.   The second development was the extension of government activity to alleviate discontent that formerly was alleviated by moving to the West: now that the free lands were gone "western discontent" was allying itself with the depressed farmer and the workingman of the East in demands for extension of government activity.   At the same time, the rise of big business raised the question of whether popular government could be reconciled with the great industrial society of modern America, particularly since lines of cleavage were appearing because of a large proportion of foreign-born in the working class.[22]   It was clear to Turner that a mature economy and a maturing society faced a set of severe adjustments—one feature of which was an increased economic role for government.

Turner's course at Harvard was a course in history and not current politics.[23]   As a consequence, the history of the development of the West was covered in detail, along with much discussion of the effect of the westward movement on political and economic currents.   The emphasis was placed upon the interrelationships between economic, political, and social changes in the frontier regions and upon the continuation of change after the West was occupied.   Turner presented his analysis of current trends in his last lecture: the free lands are gone, economic concentration is growing, and the West is turning toward Federal control and away from individualism.

While Turner was presenting his economic interpretation of American development, William Z. Ripley was documenting with a vast array of facts the abuses of monopoly and big business.

Ripley was a man of many pursuits. His earliest interest was in ethnology, and his book *The Races of Europe,* published in 1899, has remained a classic in its field since its appearance. But a strong reforming bent took him into economics and he took up the study of the "trust problem," the "railroad problem," and public utilities. When Roosevelt was at Harvard, Ripley taught statistics, problems of labor, economics of corporations, and economics of transportation. F.D.R. studied the latter two subjects under Ripley in the school year of 1903-4.

"Big business" and the "trust" were major economic and political issues in the early twentieth century. The Sherman Act had been passed in 1890 in response to a great public demand for some kind of hindrance to the development of monopoly, but lack of enforcement and emasculation of the law by adverse court decisions had opened the way for the formation of such giant combinations as United States Steel Corporation, International Harvester Corporation, and many others. This great merger movement, which determined the structure of many basic industries for decades to come, remained a major political issue up to World War I.

Ripley's attitude toward the "trust problem" was expressed in the introduction to his book of readings, *Trusts, Pools and Corporations,* published a year after Roosevelt took his course. After tracing the development of the corporation, pools, trusts, and holding companies, Ripley pointed out two types of evils: first, "evils in corporate finance" that included "extravagant" promotions, payment of unearned dividends, speculative management, and overcapitalization; and second, monopolistic control that kept prices "much higher than the price level under competition." All of this called for action by the Federal government. The possible means of reform were Federal incorporation, Federal licenses for participation in interstate commerce, and, most important of all, "reasonable publicity and administrative supervision for railroads and great industrial monopolies akin to that now applied to National Banks." [24]

Underlying Ripley's attitude was a conviction that the competitive economy was the most desirable, but he recognized that large corporations and giant combinations were a feature of the modern economy that had to be regulated rather than eliminated:

The ultimate remedy, as applied to all classes of corporations, must come from the courts and the legislatures. But in either case the continued necessity of a strong and steady administrative control through some permanent board or commission, supplementing and giving due effect to the law is apparent.[25]

Ripley's course in the economics of corporations was a detailed exposition of these views.[26] He began with the development of the corporation and big business, the pools of the 1880's, and trusts. But the heart of the course was a discussion of financing of corporate mergers or combinations. The first step is for a promoter interested in financial profits to organize a company and, as secretly as possible, buy up the properties to be combined, disregarding high prices or over-capitalization. After options to acquire properties are obtained the parent company is formed, preferably with dummy directors subservient to the promoters or bankers. Then, after sale of properties to the parent company, securities are sold to the public, often with exaggerated or false prospectuses and with "wash sales" to keep the sale price of the securities at a high level. In most cases the capitalization of the new company is too large and reorganization often is the result. Throughout this whole process speculation by insiders is rife and sometimes is featured by stock market "raids" by outsiders to wrest control from the "ins." Of course, in addition to the profits of the promoters and financiers (20 percent was "moderate") are the advantages derived from control of prices, of suppliers, and of labor.

All of this was related with much detail and documentation. It was scholarly muckraking of the highest order. The students must have loved it.

Ripley closed with a brief discussion of cartels in Germany and the favorite prescription, in those days, for relief from business abuses: the enforcement of full publicity, both to the public and to the stockholders, of corporate actions.

One of the most important phases of the problem of big business in the early years of the twentieth century was the "railroad problem." Those were the days of Harriman and Hill, of the Northern Securities Company, of the attempt by George Gould to develop a coast-to-coast system, of the "secret agreement" between the Pennsylvania and New York Central to eliminate competition in the "trunk line" area, of J. P. Morgan's development of the southern railroads. It was also the period of the Elkins Amendments (1903) to the Interstate Commerce Commission Act, the Hepburn Act (1906), and the Mann-Elkins Act (1910), all of which dealt with this pressing economic and political problem.

It was in the field of railway economics that Ripley achieved his greatest competence and renown. His two books on the subject [27] were standard works for many years.

Ripley's course on the economics of transportation [28] dealt with the problems of railroad rates, finance, consolidation, and regulation in much the same terms as his course on the corporation. A short historical treatment emphasized developments peculiar to the American scene: cheap construction, speculation, and public aid. Then followed a discussion of the major railroad problems from the viewpoint of protection of the public and the investor, with a great deal of detailed documentation of abuses in rate-making, finance, and consolidation. For example: the American railroads were built through the device of construction companies, by and large, which were manipulated by promoters for high, quick profits; the results were overcapitalization, "irresponsible or possibly fraudulent" management, and premature or excessive building of lines. Railroad finance as a whole was characterized by speculation, financial manipulation by insiders, stock-watering, and so forth. As far as railroad rates were concerned, the major problem was discrimination resulting from localized and imperfect competition—charging more for a shorter than for a longer haul, for example. The problem of obtaining "reasonable" rates in the face of the companies' attempts to charge as much as the traffic will bear received secondary emphasis. Consolidation and combinations were treated as part of over-all railroad strategy designed to control traffic flows, to reduce competition and rate-cutting, and to obtain profits for the promoters.

Government regulation was the main remedy for the railroad evils. Reliance on a *laissez-faire* attitude was impractical in the face of high fixed charges [29] and the activities of promoters, speculators, and financiers. Since competition could not be expected to survive, government regulation was needed to protect consumer and investor. But Ripley was not opposed to voluntary agreements between railroad companies if they would lead to improvement of service and if they were properly supervised.[30]

Economics 8A and 8B, Money and Banking, were the last two economics courses taken by Roosevelt at Harvard. By 1904 the free silver controversy that had dominated the 1896 presidential campaign and had been an important issue in 1900 had died down. But the echoes remained, along with a growing dissatisfaction with the banking system and awareness of business fluctuations. Concern with these latter issues led to the great research project of the National Monetary Commission from 1908 to 1912 and the passage of the Federal Reserve Act in 1914. Harvard's courses on money and banking thus had a dual aspect—they looked backward at the older controversies and forward to the unsolved problems.

Professor Andrew taught the course on Money, although a more appropriate title might have been "The Quantity Theory of Money." [31] The students were given a long reading list on the quantity theory,[32] and were to write a thesis evaluating it.

"Read and think," said Andrew, "write your own ideas on the subject." While the students were thinking, Andrew lectured on monetary history—the use of gold and silver, origins of paper money, early coinage and its debasement, the monetary history of England, the Bullion report and the banking vs. currency schools in England, inflation in France, and the monetary systems of Russia, Japan, India, and Mexico. The thread running through the discussion was the general validity of the quantity theory. In this connection Andrew discussed the relationship between the price of gold and the general price level, concluding that "in the long run Ricardo and the Bullion Committee were right in saying that the gold premium and the price level will follow each other. They were wrong, however, in saying that the two movements were simultaneous." Andrew was careful to point out that the connection was indirect: a rise in the price of gold relative to the general price level will increase exports and reduce imports, thereby increasing total demand and tending to raise prices.[33]

After this long historical analysis came a discussion of price levels: should prices rise, remain stable, or fall for best economic results? Andrew presented the arguments for and against all three, pointed out that rising or falling prices each had special advantages which were balanced by disadvantages, and ended by endorsing a stable price level.

The next question taken up was the effect of bimetallism on the price level. Andrew presented the more sophisticated arguments of the bimetallists that prices would tend to be stabilized at higher levels if free coinage of silver were adopted, but then he pointed out the failure of the government's silver purchase program since the passage of the Bland-Allison Act of 1873. He described with approval the final adoption of a gold standard in 1900.

Andrew summarized his views in the last lecture. A definite relationship exists between the quantity of money and the quantity of credit, and between those two and the price level. "The quantity theory holds." Andrew's position was that of sound money, stable prices, and the gold standard.

Banking and the History of the Leading Banking Systems, the full title of Economics 8B, was taught by Assistant Professor Oliver M. W. Sprague. Sprague was very much interested in monetary and banking reform and the relationship between monetary factors and business activity. This interest was to lead to the publication, a few years later, of two books that helped set the stage for the passage of the Federal Reserve Act in 1914.[34] In conformity with most orthodox economists at this time, Sprague looked upon the business cycle problem primarily in terms of financial "crises" and attributed their causes to malfunctioning of the monetary or banking systems. This led him to the belief that a strong central bank, well managed and using the devices of credit control developed by the Bank of England, could do a great deal to eliminate or mitigate the effects of "crises." A strong note of reform along these lines ran through his teachings and writings.

In later years Sprague was to become a leading expert on monetary and banking problems. He was economic and statistical adviser to the Bank of England from 1930 to 1933, and in 1933 Roosevelt appointed his old teacher as Assistant to the Secretary of the Treasury.

The emphasis in Sprague's course was on the relationship between commercial bank loans, central bank policy, and the quantity of money on the one hand, and price levels and business conditions on the other.[35] The course began with an historical treatment of the development of banking, with emphasis on the policies used by the Bank of England at times of financial crisis. Sprague's attitude was that speculative crises normally occurred from time to time and that proper action by a central bank could avoid them:

Crises occur in times of speculation. A tendency of them is to bring about an unfavorable trade balance—specie flows out, credit falls. If speculation is checked trouble may be averted. But if contraction [of commercial loans] comes too late and [the central] bank is weakened by withdrawal of specie, disaster may arise. Contraction may be caused by successive failures [rather than by central bank policy]; this condition makes people fearful of credit. The moment for contraction [by central bank policy] has now gone by and contraction will be dangerous.[36]

But in the American economy, with no central bank, there was nothing to stop a financial crisis. At such times

All banks must combine their powers.... The big banks must help, for a general derangement of credit affects all institutions. Sudden contraction of loans blocks transferrence of commodities, deranges payments and raises hell generally.[37]

On top of this, the American currency was inelastic: its quantity did not change as business needs changed. Clearly, reform was needed: some form of central bank and a more elastic currency.

It is not possible to determine what or how much Roosevelt learned from Harvard's economics courses. Any comments he may have made about them at the time have not been preserved, for the most part because his mother had taken a house in Boston to be near her son and there were no letters home. Although in later life Roosevelt made a few comments about Harvard, he seldom mentioned the courses he had.

Nevertheless, it is significant that Roosevelt chose a major in economics for his last year and that the courses he took were oriented toward economic problems. He was obviously interested in the problem of big business (Ripley's courses) and in monetary issues (courses given by Andrew and Sprague).[38]

Of equal significance is the fact that his teachers—Ripley, Andrew, and Sprague—were advocates of economic reform, a characteristic they shared with many of their contemporaries. They were not men who believed in a *laissez-faire* state, in which the government provides merely the minimum legal framework within which the economy operates freely. Nor, on the other hand, did they believe that government should take an active role in directing economic activities; they were not advocates of planning. The method of reform advocated was government regulation to avoid abuses when and where those abuses existed. Whether it was a problem involving corporate financing, monopolistic pricing, railroad rates, or monetary instability, Roosevelt's teachers advocated an increased role for government in order to meet the problem, and the role they advocated was for the most part one of regulation. If we can distinguish between a *"laissez-faire* state," a "regulatory state," and a "welfare state," Roosevelt's teachers would fall in the second category.

After graduating from Harvard, Roosevelt entered the law school of Columbia University. He did not distinguish himself as a student and showed no great interest in the law. His grades varied considerably; in courses in which he was interested he did well, while in courses he did not like he did poorly.[39] F.D.R. was married during the spring of his first year in law school, and, probably because of the distractions involved in the early months of married life, failed two courses, Contracts and Pleading and Practice. He took make-up examinations after he returned from his honeymoon, however, passed them, and entered the second year with full credit.[40] He never did graduate from law school or obtain the LL.B. degree: he took the bar examinations in the spring of his final year, passed, and then dropped out of school.[41]

Roosevelt's law school courses were, for the most part, the usual ones taken by any law student. Only a few of them are important to a study of his economic thought.

In his first year Roosevelt took Professor John W. Burgess's course in American Constitutional Law.[42] Burgess was a famous teacher and a leading expert on his subject; his basic preconceptions were conservative and nationalistic.[43] He treated the subject historically, beginning with the constitutional history of the American colonies and bringing it up to the Civil War by the end of the semester. Burgess's basic theme was taken down by F.D.R. in his notebook: "the purpose of const. law is to bring the political system into accord with the social. This the one great aim of political development." [44] Throughout the course Burgess sought to demon-

strate that constitutional law reflected social and political
conditions and that changes inevitably came when the social
and political environment changed. He pointed out that one
of the great advantages of the American Constitution was its
flexibility, although he felt that the process of amendment
was too difficult "and has thrown a strain on judicial
power." [45] Roosevelt attended the course quite regularly, and
his interest in it is shown by the fact that he borrowed other
students' notes for the classes he missed—and sometimes did
not return them.

In his second year Roosevelt took Burgess's course in Comparative Constitutional Law, and, although no textbook was
required, bought Burgess's two-volume *Political Science and
Comparative Constitutional Law.* This course was a detailed
comparison of the American, British, French, and German
constitutions.

He also had Professor Jackson E. Reynolds's course in
Bailments and Carriers, or public utility law.[46] In this course
F.D.R. studied the growing body of law developing around
government regulation of public utilities and common carriers. The textbook, Beale and Wyman's *Cases on Public
Service Companies,* was vigorously underlined by F.D.R. and
numerous marginal comments were made.[47] When Roosevelt
took the course the modern development of public utility
regulation under the rules laid down by *Smyth vs. Ames*
(1898) had hardly begun, but earlier cases were well covered.
Roosevelt's marginal notes in his book indicate that Professor
Reynolds believed in strong regulatory commissions and did
not approve of court decisions that weakened the commissions.
The case of *Munn vs. Illinois* (1876), which laid the basis for
public utility regulation by state commissions, was carefully
annotated as a result of class discussions, and at one point in
the margin of *People vs. Budd* (1889) is the remark, "knocks
out Field's dissenting opinion in the Munn case." [48] Reynold's
belief in strong regulation is illustrated by notations made by

F.D.R. on two cases involving the Interstate Commerce Commission:

The court held the business of carting had nothing to do with the business of the R.R. ——— but Reynolds says this is a rather extraordinary decision, for in this case there was a clear case of rebate. The Commission have bitterly complained of the attitude of the Sup. Court in attempting to limit as much as possible their powers. The case is clearly wrong to my mind, but has never been overruled.[49]

It was another great shock to the I.C.C. that U.S. courts could go back of their findings as to fact and decide the case on its merits. But it is largely the fault of the RR's in not submitting all their facts to the Commission.[50]

Roosevelt got one of his better grades in this course, a "B," [51] and these early studies in public utility law gave him some familiarity with one of the major economic problems he encountered as Governor of New York.

In his third year at Columbia School of Law, which was not completed, Roosevelt had Professor George F. Canfield's course on Corporations and Professor Frank J. Goodnow's course on Municipal Corporations.[52] The former took up the law of corporations—their nature, powers, and obligations and the rights and duties of stockholders and directors—while the latter covered the powers of town and city governments, with special emphasis on the police power as the foundation of government regulations affecting private property and business enterprise. The growth of government regulations under the impact of the problems of growing cities was chronicled in case after case.

Roosevelt's courses in law school continued his education in economics. In particular, they took up a broad economic problem that has lain at the center of most of the economic controversies of the twentieth century: the relationship between government and the economy. Burgess's courses in Constitutional Law, Reynolds's course in Bailments and Carriers, and Goodnow's course in Municipal Corporations all bore upon that problem. These courses in law school looked upon the relationship between government and business from the legal point of view—just as Roosevelt's economics courses at Harvard had looked upon it from the economic point of view. Bailments and Carriers and Corporations in the Columbia law school supplemented Economics of Corporations and Economics of Transportation at Harvard, for example.

In the world of the twentieth century, when the growth of big business and giant corporations was raising a most important issue, and when the relationship of government to the economy was a persistent problem, Roosevelt had gotten a good background at Harvard and Columbia upon which to build. Later in life when he became a great figure in public affairs these two areas in his economic philosophy were to be the most strongly developed.

On the other hand, F.D.R. learned little at Harvard or Columbia that might fit him to meet the problems of the great depression of the thirties, in particular, or the problem of economic instability, in general. His formal education gave him little basis for development in that area, and it was there that his economic philosophy was weakest.

CHAPTER III

Franklin D. Roosevelt, Progressive

FRANCES PERKINS has told of the first time she met Franklin D. Roosevelt. At a tea dance in 1910 she heard that "tall, thin young man with the high collar and pince-nez" vigorously defending the progressive ideas of Theodore Roosevelt.[1]

F.D.R. was indeed a progressive. It was as a progressive that he first entered political life, and he was always considered by his contemporaries to be part of the progressive wing of the Democratic party. F.D.R. always felt that the progressives Theodore Roosevelt and Woodrow Wilson were his political preceptors.[2]

America, in the first two decades of the twentieth century, was undergoing some dramatic changes. The diminishing supply of free land on the frontier, a new wave of immigration, and growing urbanization were creating some of the basic problems of modern America and forcing governments at all levels to increase their intervention in economic affairs. The American ideal was moving away from the philosophy of individualism and *laissez-faire* toward government action and intervention in the everyday life of the individual.

To contemporaries the growth of big business and concentration of economic power was one of the most important economic issues raised by the growing maturity of the American economy. That issue became the great theme which the "muckrakers" publicized and on which the progressive movement was built: the concentration of economic power endangered the ideal of democracy in America. Not only was it an economic problem, but it was largely the cause of political corruption: the "vested interests" supported corrupt political machines that created and protected special privileges for the business or financial titan. Such was the view of contemporary reformers, and the result was a two-pronged attack on "bossism" and the "vested interests." Thus, stronger anti-trust laws were a natural supplement to the referendum, attacks on the "money trust" a supplement to the movement for civic reform.

The growth of the labor movement and the rise of labor unions were another cause of ferment. The growing acceptance of the union movement was typified by the first intervention on the side of a union in a labor dispute by the Federal government in 1902, when President Theodore Roosevelt threatened to seize the nation's anthracite mines unless the owners agreed to arbitrate their dispute with the United Mine Workers.[3] By 1913 union membership had grown to over 2,700,000,[4] but not without a good deal of employer opposition and violence.

A changing and maturing America, beset with important economic problems, was the stage on which appeared the progressive movement. Its reform emphasis dominated the political scene in the years immediately preceding the First World War and was the environment in which F.D.R. first entered politics.

Of the important progressives in both major parties, Theodore Roosevelt and Woodrow Wilson were the ones who most influenced Franklin D. Roosevelt. The midwesterners, Bryan and LaFollette, influenced him least.

Theodore Roosevelt and Franklin D. Roosevelt were distantly related. Fourth cousins, they had a common ancestor in the eighteenth century. Their social backgrounds were similar: both came from wealthy families and both had good educations. Both started in politics in the same fashion: as members of the state legislature each led a fight against political corruption and bossism and incurred the displeasure of those in control of the party. Their ideals showed a similar development: both were greatly concerned about social justice and their earliest emphasis was on political reform, but both moved toward a broader program of economic reform that became their main appeal as mature political figures.

Early in his political career Theodore Roosevelt was known for his opposition to corruption in government and to the influence of "special interests" through the political boss. As a member of the New York State Legislature in the early 1880's he won a name for independence and honesty, and in the Republican national convention he was one of the "progressive elements" in the party that opposed the nomination of Blaine for the presidency. Appointed by President Harrison to the Civil Service Commission, he dramatized the fight to place more jobs under the civil service classification, and later as police commissioner of New York City he instituted a merit system for promotions and introduced other reforms that were opposed by both major parties. But the developing social struggles of the nineties and the rising agitation for reform caused Theodore Roosevelt to shift his emphasis to economic problems, although he never lost his interest in honest government. As Governor of New York from 1898 to 1900 he had to fight not only the opposition of the Democrats, but also the leaders in his own party; nevertheless, he did manage to push some reforms through the legislature: reenactment of civil service legislation, the beginnings of wild life and forest conservation, a pure food law, the taxation of public utility franchises, and a series of labor laws designed to improve working conditions. His attitude at this time was middle-of-the-road: he rejected "Bryanism," but also felt that "improper corporate influence" was just as bad.[5]

When Theodore Roosevelt became President in September, 1901, he moved further along the road toward economic reform. His domestic policies as President featured increased government intervention in and regulation of the affairs of big business: intervention in the coal strike of 1902; the case against the Northern Securities Company (1902-4) and the introduction of anti-trust suits against United States Steel

Corporation, Standard Oil Company, and American Sugar Refining Corporation; the Elkins Act (1903) that forbade railroad rebates and the Hepburn Act (1906) that gave power to regulate railroad rates to the Interstate Commerce Commission; creation of a Department of Commerce and Labor, including a Bureau of Corporations (1903); a pure food act (1906); and an act providing for inspection of slaughter houses (1906). His administration was also notable for great advances in conservation: a rapid increase in the area of national forests, the reclamation program of the Newlands Act (1902), creation of the Inland Waterways Commission (1907), and a Governors' Conference on Conservation (1908).

But while Roosevelt caused the Federal government to intervene increasingly in economic affairs, he accepted the large corporation as an inevitable development of modern industrialism. Distinguishing between good trusts and bad trusts, he concluded that the mere size and power of a combination did not necessarily mean that it was inconsistent with the public welfare.

It was with Theodore Roosevelt's return from his African and European trips in 1910 that his reforming views reached maturity. Advocating a "new nationalism" that was to be a struggle for "social justice and popular rule," Roosevelt spoke in favor of recall of elective officers by popular vote, the referendum, the direct primary, and recall of judicial decisions, and continued his opposition to the alliance between professional politicians and financial and business interests. To this was added a program for economic reform. In a speech at Osawatomie, Kansas, on August 31, he outlined his "square deal." [6] He wanted a more substantial equality of opportunity and reward, and this meant that "government ... must be freed from the sinister influence or control of special interests." He advocated government supervision of the capitalization of all corporations doing an interstate business, and regulation of the public utility type over "combinations which control necessaries of life." He believed in a graduated income tax and an inheritance tax to reduce unearned incomes and inequalities of income. He advocated numerous labor laws to regulate the terms and conditions of work: workmen's compensation, regulation of child labor and work for women, and factory laws to improve sanitation and safety. Above all, "whenever the alternative must be faced, I am for men and not for property":

We are face to face with new conceptions of the relations of property to human welfare.... The man who wrongly holds that every human right is secondary to his profit must now give way to the advocate of human welfare, who rightly maintains that every man holds his property subject to the general right of the community to regulate its use to whatever degree the public welfare may require it.[7]

It was Theodore Roosevelt who was the model F.D.R. adopted when he began his political career. Indeed, it was Theodore Roosevelt's fight against the Republican party leaders in New York State in 1910 that split that party and enabled F.D.R. to be elected in a normally Republican district.[8] In the campaign F.D.R. attacked the same Republican bosses who were attacked by Theodore Roosevelt and sought to identify himself with the insurgent Republicans.[9] His tactics were a living example of the philosophy of direct responsibility of the legislator to the electorate: F.D.R. visited almost every town and village in the district—the first time any candidate had done such a thing. The theme of his campaign was opposition to "bossism" and "legislation for special interests"[10]—an issue on which the Republican as well as the Democratic party was extremely vulnerable. To further this end he advocated direct state-wide primaries to nominate candidates for office.[11] The progressive tone of his campaign, the Roosevelt name, the grass roots method of vote-getting, and the Republican split all combined to send F.D.R. to the State Senate at the age of 28.

Franklin Roosevelt then lived up to his campaign attacks on bossism in a dramatic fight to prevent the election of William Sheehan to the United States Senate. This was be-

fore the days of direct election of senators and the first job
of the new legislature was to elect a man to the Senate. The
man proposed by the party leaders was a Tammany stalwart,
William Sheehan, a man whom Roosevelt and other upstate
Democrats could not accept. Not only were they opposed to
his affiliation with the notoriously corrupt New York City
machine, but they recognized that the party could not remain
the choice of the upstate voters and still retain the dominance
of Tammany in its affairs.[12] Thus, it was a fight for the
allegiance of the voters in the home districts as well as a fight
against bossism.

F.D.R. took the leadership of the small group of Democrats
who abstained from voting so that "Blue Eyed Billy" Sheehan
could not obtain the majority necessary for his election, and
for three months the business of the legislature was halted
while the deadlock continued. Roosevelt maintained that the
party caucus which nominated Sheehan had been "fixed in
advance" and that the insurgents were fighting against the
"boss rule system" and for the basic principle of representation of the desires of their constituents.[13] "Business must get
out of politics," said F.D.R., "the Murphys who represent
business must be cleaned out." [14] In the end Roosevelt and
his cohorts won and a compromise candidate was elected.

The remainder of F.D.R.'s career in the legislature was less
spectacular. He continued his advocacy of political reforms
designed to promote more democratic procedures, even though
these measures were more talked about than acted upon in
the legislature. Among the reforms F.D.R. favored were
direct nomination of candidates through primary elections
instead of the then customary procedure of nomination by
party caucus; [15] the short ballot, which would provide fewer
candidates to be voted on and more subordinate administrators to be appointed by the governor; [16] and direct election
of United States Senators.[17] Roosevelt thought that the
direct primaries bill was particularly important, offering the
voter a weapon with which the bossism of both parties could
be defeated.[18] He took an equivocal stand on woman suffrage,

however: although he favored it, he wanted the proposal submitted to a referendum.[19]

One of the major targets of all progressives was special privilege for big business and F.D.R. entered this fight also. Years before, the legislature had granted a very valuable power site on the St. Lawrence River to the Aluminum Company of America, and in 1913 a bill was introduced to annul this action. F.D.R. denounced the original grant as a "steal" and helped lead the fight for annulment. In this effort he co-operated with a not too enthusiastic Tammany.[20]

Coming from a constituency that was largely argricultural, and being a gentleman farmer himself, F.D.R. took a strong interest in conservation and agricultural legislation. In the 1911-12 sessions he was a member of the Agriculture Committee and chairman of the Forest, Fish and Game Committee. In the 1913 session he was chairman of the Agriculture Committee and a member of the Conservation Committee, the latter replacing the Forest, Fish and Game Committee of the previous session.[21]

The major project of the Forest, Fish and Game Committee in 1911-12 was a codification of the existing conservation laws, and along with it, a few advances. Among the proposals made by F.D.R. was the creation of a fish and game board as a permanent part of the state government and restrictions on the cutting of private forests,[22] both of which were killed by the committee. The latter proposal, which was designed especially to protect the great forests of the Adirondack Mountains, was vigorously opposed by lumbering interests, and F.D.R. wrote that

The opposition, while aimed at every detail of the bill, was really based on the assumption that the State has no right to tell a private individual how he shall cut trees on his own land. Personally, of course, I think the state has a right to preserve all its forests and water sheds, but it is going to take a good many years before this can be effectually brought about.[23]

Roosevelt had been interested in conservation for years. The country estate at Hyde Park had always been well

managed, and a program of forest management was begun
there. In the twenties F.D.R. was to propose a cooperative
forest management program with his neighbors, utilizing professional help. This early interest in conservation was to
broaden into a belief in land-use planning that culminated in
the TVA and Resettlement Acts of the New Deal. The germs
of these later beliefs are to be found in the earlier years.
Speaking before the Business Men's Luncheon Club of
Poughkeepsie, Roosevelt spoke of "the necessity of developing the country, hand in hand with the city."

I believe it would pay the business men of this city, and pay them
well, if they would study the question of development of the surrounding country—its development along lines that will consider
the problem of providing homes and small farms in the country;
the problem of increasing and making more available the produce
of the country and the problem of securing better transportation.
This is no real estate scheme. . . . It should be handled by intelligent cooperation among the citizens of the city.[24]

It was about this time that F.D.R.'s uncle Frederic Delano,
got the young State Senator interested in the "larger aspects
of planning" when the two talked with Charles D. Norton
about the city plan of Chicago.[25]

Interest in conservation supplemented his interest in agriculture. When at Hyde Park, F.D.R. frequently spent hours
talking with farmers about crops and the farmers' situation
and the history of the locality. In this way he got to know
not only people but also their viewpoints, hopes, and aspira-
tions.[26] Management of the estate at Hyde Park also contributed to F.D.R.'s interest in and knowledge of the problems
of the farmer. Thus, as chairman of the Agriculture Committee in 1913 he was in a position to apply his progressivism
to another area in which he was interested.

A major project was a bill to regulate and supervise commission merchants: they were to be bonded and licensed, with
the object of securing honesty in their dealings with farmers.[27]
Interested in finding out exactly what happens in the middle-
man's job, F.D.R. took an early morning train from Hyde

Park to arrive before dawn at the New York docks and follow a crate of spinach from the ship to the retail grocer. This trip and his studies in connection with the commission merchants' bill left F.D.R. convinced that measures must be taken to eliminate some of the expenses of distribution. The bill was passed. Other projects to aid the farmer supported by Roosevelt were bills to promote the organization of cooperative agricultural credit banks and agricultural cooperatives.[28]

Aid to the farmer was to be balanced by a program of labor legislation. The Democrats in the state legislature advocated a workmen's compensation law, limitation of hours of work for women, strengthening of the existing labor laws and the State Labor Department, and, after the disastrous "Triangle Fire" in 1911, provision for a factory investigating committee. Roosevelt supported this program fully.

Arrayed against us on the other side was the silent, powerful pressure of the old school of thought, which held the theory that when an employer hired a working man or a working woman, that employer became the master of the fate of his employee; that when a worker entered his factory door it was nobody's business as to how he worked, how long he worked, or how much he was paid.[29]

F.D.R. himself introduced two important labor bills: one provided for a six-day work week in factories, which was referred to the Labor and Industries Committee and pigeonholed there; the other provided for an eight-hour day for mechanics employed in state institutions, and was passed. F.D.R. had tried to make his six-day week bill more inclusive, but limited it only to factories in a futile attempt to obtain passage. He also offered to introduce the workmen's compensation bill proposed by the American Federation of Labor, supported a bill to bring canneries under the jurisdiction of the state factory laws that was designed to eliminate child labor in those enterprises, and favored a bill for fire protection in factories.[30] To indicate his support for labor legislation F.D.R. became a member of the American Association for Labor Legislation.[31]

Much of this legislation was bitterly fought, and one of the greatest fights involved a bill to limit the work week for women to 54 hours. Supported by numerous legislators from the cities and by the labor unions, it was opposed by business interests and farmers. The farmers opposed the measure because most of the canneries were employers of large groups of women: reducing the work week for women would, it was felt, hinder the operation of canneries and reduce this large market for agricultural products. F.D.R., a member of the Democratic majority that was pushing the bill, also represented a predominantly rural constituency. His loyalties were divided. To further complicate matters, one of the organizations most active in support of the bill was the Consumers' League of New York, of which Mrs. Roosevelt was an active member: the League's chief lobbyist for the measure was Frances Perkins, who was later to be one of Roosevelt's chief advisers on labor matters. At first F.D.R. was noncommittal on the "54-hour bill," [32] but voted for it after an amendment to exempt canneries was added. At no time did he give the bill his active support.[33]

The Democratic program of labor legislation in New York State was greatly promoted by the public reaction to the fire in the Triangle shirtwaist factory on March 11, 1911, in which 145 workers, mostly young girls, lost their lives. The heavy loss of life resulted from inadequate fire escape facilities that should have been provided if the company had complied with existing laws. The outcry for remedial action was tremendous, and the legislature appointed a Factory Investigating Commision to study safety, health, hours, and other aspects of factory work. Among the members of the Commission were Alfred E. Smith, later Governor and political preceptor of F.D.R., and Robert F. Wagner, later United States Senator and staunch New Dealer; one of the committee's investigators was Frances Perkins. As a result of the work of the Commission the labor laws of New York State were largely rewritten and extended: 36 laws pertaining to labor were passed by the

legislature between 1912 and 1914.[34] Although F.D.R. was a
member of the legislature at the time, he took little active interest in the work of the Commission; he did, however, introduce several of the labor bills that were passed and voted for
the others, and he spoke in favor of the bills at a legislative
hearing.[35]

Roosevelt did take an active part in another labor controversy, however, this one concerning the upstate area. Wither-
bee, Sherman and Company operated iron mines at Mineville,
N.Y., just west of Port Henry on Lake Champlain. The employees were largely immigrants, many of whom could not
read or speak English. A union organizer charged the company with extortion—workers paying kickbacks to supervisors
to obtain and keep their jobs—and with an extremely high
accident rate caused by inadequate safety provisions. An investigation by the State Department of Labor found these
charges to be substantially true. F.D.R. was among the legislators who prodded the Department of Labor into action to
remedy the situation. He felt this would be more effective
than the appointment of an investigating committee, but said
that "if the department does not act with speed and determination I will do what I can to have the conditions at Mineville remedied by other means." [36]

Although Roosevelt supported the legislative program of
labor unions to a great extent, he was opposed to boycotts by
unions and to legislation that would legalize them.[37]

Among the progressive measures favored by F.D.R. at this
time were a national parcel post system to replace private express companies and the establishment of mutual insurance
companies.[38] He was opposed to a bill to increase mandatory
reserves for savings banks in order to set up a guarantee fund,
and to a bill that would prohibit intermarriage and cohabita-
tion of races.[39] His liberal sentiments in these and other respects brought forth a few words of advice from his uncle,
Frederic A. Delano:

Don't let your reform friends induce you to undertake too many
things which may *look* all right but which are untried.... They

are also impatient in trying to undertake too much and too many things instead of making *slow but steady* progress—I would rather be called conservative and reactionary than impractical and visionary; and I think you can accomplish more real reform in that way.[40]

Only once during his years as State Senator did Roosevelt make a comprehensive statement of his political-economic philosophy. Speaking before the People's Forum of Troy, N.Y., on March 3, 1912,[41] he presented what was to develop into the philosophy of the New Deal.

Roosevelt began by pointing out the existence of considerable unrest and demand for reform. This unrest was present in spite of the fact that the struggles of the people of Europe and America to achieve "individual freedom" had been largely successful. Then came the heart of his argument:

Conditions of civilization that come with individual freedom are inevitably bound to bring up many questions that mere individual liberty cannot solve. This is to my mind exactly what has happened in the past century. We have acquired new sets of conditions of life that require new theories for their solution.... I have called this new theory [sic] the struggle for the liberty of the community rather than liberty of the individual.... Every new star that people have hitched their wagon to for the past half century, whether it be anti-rebating, or anti-trusts, or new-fashioned education, or conservation of our natural resources, or state regulation of common carriers, or commission government, or any of the thousand and one other things that we have run after of late, almost without any exception come under the same heading. They are all steps in the evolution of the new theory of the liberty of the community.

The right of any one individual to work or not as he sees fit, to live to a great extent where and how he sees fit is not sufficient. ... To put it another way, competition has been shown to be useful up to a certain point and no further. Cooperation must begin where competition leaves off and cooperation is as good a word for the new theory as any other.

As an example of this idea Roosevelt presented the case of the conservation movement:

One hundred and fifty years ago in Germany the individual was not restricted from denuding his lands of the growing trees. Today he must cut only in a manner scientifically worked out, which is calculated to serve the ends of the community and not his ends. They passed beyond the liberty of the individual to do as he pleased with his own property and found it was necessary to check this liberty for the benefit of the freedom of the whole people.

But if the state could compel the individual to use his forest properties only in certain prescribed ways, could it not do the same for other productive resources? Roosevelt recognized that his ideal led to acceptance of over-all planning of production, at least in agriculture:

As it is with conservation of natural resources so also is it bound to become with the production of food supply. The two go hand in hand, so much so that if we can prophesy today that the state (in other words, the people as a whole) will shortly tell a man how many trees he must cut, then why can we not, without being called radical, predict that the state will compel every farmer to till his land or raise beef or horses. After all, if I own a farm of a hundred acres and let it lie waste and overgrown, I am just as much a destroyer of the liberty of the community—and by liberty we mean happiness and prosperity—as is the strong man who stands idle on the corner, refusing to work, a destroyer of his neighbor's happiness, prosperity and liberty.

In addition to his endorsement of planning, Roosevelt also presented his views on labor and big business in his Troy speech. A favorite theme of his was that there was no permanent basis for conflict between labor and capital:

There is no such thing as a struggle between labor and capital. Not only is there no struggle, but there is and has always been the heartiest cooperation for neither can capital exist without the cooperation of labor, nor labor without the cooperation of capital. Therefore, I say there is no struggle between the two, not even a dividing line.

Roosevelt's picture of basic harmony in economic affairs was marred by the presence of big business, but the disharmonies could be removed by government regulation:

The mere size of a trust is not of necessity its evil. A trust is evil if it monopolized for the benefit of a few and contrary to the interests of the community. Just as long as trusts do this it is necessary for the community to change this feature of them.

So, too, with common carriers—as long as they fail to fulfill the needs of the community they must be, and are being regulated.

These views of F.D.R.'s were clearly derived from those of Theodore Roosevelt. His "liberty of the community" that might limit the "liberty of the individual" is in direct line of descent from Theodore Roosevelt's championing of human welfare as opposed to the rights of property. But it also goes well beyond T.R.'s humanitarian idea of "people before property." F.D.R.'s view could embrace a paternalistic state that orders everyone to do what the state feels is for the community's good; F.D.R. did not suggest any limits on the power of the state or any reserved areas of personal liberty, and his "liberty of the community" was potentially totalitarian. Other speeches and actions of F.D.R.'s indicate his emphasis on democratic decision-making in government and on responsibility of the legislature to the electorate. But his failure in the Troy speech to include limitations on the kind of community ends to be obtained and the kinds of dictation over individuals that should be used indicates that his ideas were not carefully worked out. The Troy speech shows that F.D.R. was willing to accept a greatly extended role for government in the direction of the economy—but it represents only a first, and somewhat superficial, step toward the New Deal philosophy.[42]

As Roosevelt's first term in the legislature approached its end the national election of 1912 grew near. This was the year in which the progressives vs. conservatives split in the Republican party resulted in the nomination of Taft on the Republican ticket and Theodore Roosevelt by the new Progressive party, and in the election of the Democratic candidate, Woodrow Wilson. The same sort of split existed in the Democratic party. It was typified in New York by the fight in the legislature over the election of a United States Senator in 1910. In 1912 Franklin D. Roosevelt, leader of the progressive forces in that earlier battle, again entered the fight against the old guard, which was led by Tammany and supported by Thomas F. Ryan, the utilities magnate. It was

clear that the leading candidates for the Democratic nomination were the conservative Champ Clark of Missouri, Speaker
of the House of Representatives, and Woodrow Wilson,
progressive Governor of New Jersey. It was equally clear
which side Tammany would support.

The State Democratic party met on April 11 to take up the
question of the presidential nomination, and F.D.R. invited
to a dinner held the night before all those who might help
support Wilson: the purpose was to map out a strategy. Most
of those invited declined. The next day the Tammany-
dominated convention voted to send an uncommitted delegation to the national convention. But the conservative bias
of the Tammany bosses would put them on the side of Clark
and with the so-called unit rule in effect the whole Tammany-
dominated New York delegation would vote for Clark or
some other conservative.

Against these forces F.D.R. helped rally the New York
progressives in support of Wilson. With others who held
similar views, he helped organize the New York State Wilson
Conference and was chairman of its executive committee. The
goals were candidly stated:

New York has a large "Progressive" vote. Unless you give us a
candidate that will get his vote, we shall lose the State.[43]

The opposition to Tammany was based on more than just
political self-interest, however. The group wanted

the nomination of that Presidential candidate who can most certainly lead the party to victory because he best typifies in himself
the great Democratic issue of the time: the struggle to secure the
Rights of the People waged against the politicians who make themselves the agents of Special Privilege.[44]

The Wilson Conference was superseded by an organization
called Empire State Democracy, of which F.D.R. was temporary chairman. Active in July and August, 1912, it supported Wilson for the presidency, but its major object was the
nomination and support of anti-Tammany candidates for
Congress and for state and local offices in the coming elections.

It supported persons "pledged to represent the people only and to support the cause of genuine and progressive democracy." [45]

Roosevelt was neither a delegate to the national convention nor an alternate, but he was, nevertheless, present in Baltimore and worked hard for Wilson. On the fourteenth ballot the New York delegation swung to Clark, but William Jennings Bryan, who was determined that no Tammany-supported candidate should win, declared for Wilson, and the New Jersey Governor finally won two-thirds of the votes on the forty-sixth ballot. The progressives of the party were in the saddle.

F.D.R. explained his support of Wilson in good progressive terms. Wilson was "keenly alive to the social and industrial welfare of the great body of workers" and had worked for "better conditions of life for people of all kinds," while "his knowledge of great economic questions such as the tariff, monopolies, and the conservation of resources, should appeal to all who wish to see these matters taken up." In addition to being noted for "honest and clean political methods," he was a successful leader in the drive "to remedy conditions which the American people will no longer tolerate." [46]

Woodrow Wilson had emerged as an important political figure only a few years prior to his nomination for the presidency. In 1910 he had moved from the presidency of Princeton University to the governorship of New Jersey, and pushed through a series of important reforms that immediately made him a leader of the progressive wing of the Democratic party. A direct primaries law was passed, along with a corrupt practices act to supplement it; provision was made for commission government for municipalities; a Public Utilities Commission was created; an employers' liability act was passed. Most important, the corporation law of New Jersey was reformed with the passage of the "Seven Sisters" acts, designed to prevent the abuses of the former extremely liberal incorporation laws that permitted large-scale speculative promotion of corporations.

Wilson's views at the time he received Roosevelt's vigorous support were expressed in his campaign speeches of 1912, the most important of which have been published in the book *The New Freedom*. This volume sums up the progressivism of Wilson, which became a major element in the political education of Franklin D. Roosevelt. Many of the ideas which appear in Wilson's writings recur in Roosevelt's utterances in the decades to come.

At the heart of Wilson's political-economic philosophy was the belief that economic changes, especially the development of the large corporation, required changes in our laws to meet the new situation. The individual generally had become the employee of a large corporation, submerged in the organization, while a few individuals at the top "are exalted to a power which as individuals they could never have wielded." [47] This new relationship has made the old laws regarding employers and employees "wholly antiquated." [48] One important task of reform was to define accurately the responsibility of corporate executives to their stockholders, their workers, and the public.[49]

A second major theme of Wilson's was the belief that the growth of big business and monopoly had made it difficult, if not impossible, for the small businessman to succeed:

American industry is not free, as it once was free; American enterprise is not free; the man with only a little capital is finding it harder to get into the field, more and more impossible to compete with the big fellow.... Because the strong have crushed the weak the strong dominate the industry and economic life of this country.[50]

Brains and efficiency no longer determined success, argued Wilson, but economic power and monopoly. Ruthless competition in the form of local price cutting drove out the small businessman, raw materials had fallen into the hands of monopolists, big firms demanded exclusive buying from them only, and the giant corporations were interlaced with the great shipping interests and railroads.[51] Most significant of all, however, was the development of a "money trust" that had created a closely-knit community of interest among the great corporations:

The dominating danger in this land is ... the combination of combinations—of the railways, the manufacturing enterprises, the great mining projects, the great enterprises for the development of the natural water-powers of the country, threaded together in the personnel of a series of boards of directors into a "community of interest" more formidable than any conceivable single combination that dare appear in the open.[52]

Wilson did not condemn all big business. Businesses that grew large because of superior efficiency were, of course, desirable. What Wilson wanted was to get rid of monopoly and giant firms that grew because of unfair competition or control over capital or patents or raw materials:

A trust is an arrangement to get rid of competition, and a big business is a business that has survived competition by conquering in the field of intelligence and economy. A trust does not bring efficiency to the aid of business; it buys efficiency out of business. I am for big business, and I am against the trusts.[53]

A third major theme of Wilson's was his belief that concentrated economic power had come to dominate government, and that a small group of business leaders were using government to obtain special favors by which they had been able to extend their control over the nation's economy.[54] Wilson played many variations on this theme of business domination of government: it was the source of "bossism" and corruption; it had resulted in high tariffs that enabled the monopolist to exploit the public; and so on.

Several political reforms were necessary in order to put government back into the hands of the people, Wilson felt. He advocated a number of measures popular at the time, including the direct primary, direct election of Senators, the initiative, the referendum, and the recall of elected officials. Wilson did not go as far as some, however: he did not advocate recall of the judiciary.[55]

The major themes of Wilson's progressivism are to be found also in the statements and letters of Franklin D. Roosevelt in the years to come: the need to meet new problems with new solutions, the development of a concentration of economic power in the hands of a few, and the necessity to replace those few by the many in determination of government policy. Indeed, one of the most interesting developments in Franklin D. Roosevelt's economic thought is his shift away from emphasis on political corruption and bossism to economic problems as the major issues of the day. His experience in the Wilson administration, which brought him into direct contact with business and labor, was a major factor in that shift of emphasis.

To these influences from Wilson should be added the theme of "men before property," so strongly expressed by Theodore Roosevelt, that was to grow into the welfare legislation of later years. The conservation movement, also greatly promoted by Theodore Roosevelt, was another aspect of progressivism that was to appear in F.D.R.'s thinking in the years ahead, developing into advocacy of regional planning for New York State, and later for the great river valleys of the nation.

F.D.R. also derived his attitude toward big business from Wilson and Theodore Roosevelt, although those two had somewhat different views about the problem of the large corporation in American society. Theodore Roosevelt, while not ignoring the monopolistic aspects of big business and its influence on government, emphasized more than did Wilson the inevitable growth of big business under modern conditions. Wilson, on the other hand, tended to emphasize the predatory, unfair competitive aspects of big business and the obstacles those practices raised in the path of small business, as well as the evil influence of big business on government. While Wilson agreed that big business that grew big because of superior efficiency was desirable, his emphasis lay on the monopolistic aspects of the modern large corporation. The attitude of Theodore Roosevelt toward big business appeared in revised form in the trade association movement of the twenties—in which F.D.R. participated—and in the N.R.A. legislation of the early New Deal, while Wilson's approach underlay F.D.R.'s attitude toward the power company mergers in New York in the twenties and reappeared in the T.N.E.C. investigation of the late thirties.

CHAPTER IV

The Navy Department

As a reward for his support of Wilson, Roosevelt was appointed Assistant Secretary of the Navy. He brought Louis Howe, who had managed his campaign for reelection to the State Senate in 1912, with him to Washington as his assistant. The Secretary was Josephus Daniels, North Carolina editor and strong supporter of Bryan and Wilson. Daniels's main job in the new administration was that of liaison man between Wilson and Congress, and the job of running the department rested with the secondary administrators. Under Roosevelt's immediate direction were the Department's civilian personnel, the navy yards and docks, and purchasing of supplies.

In this job Roosevelt for the first time had direct dealings with monopolistic big business and with organized labor, and when he left the job in 1920 he was much more aware of economic problems. When he had entered the State Senate in 1910 his reforming bent centered on political problems: bossism and government for special interests; when he left the Navy Department in 1920 he recognized more clearly the importance of economic issues: monopoly, the conflict between capital and labor, income inequality, and others. Even though his work in Washington was largely taken up with administrative functions and the problems of defense and war, these years showed the same development in F.D.R.'s thinking that Theodore Roosevelt and Woodrow Wilson had experienced. He came to realize that economic reform was a prerequisite to political democracy.

One of the first problems to arise concerned armor plate for the new battleships then being built. Only three steel companies had facilities for the production of armor plate: Carnegie (United States Steel), Bethlehem, and Midvale, and they were in the habit of submitting identical bids on armor plate contracts. The Navy Department was partly responsible for this: whenever the bids had differed the Department divided the contract among the three companies at the lowest bid price.[1] One of the objects of this procedure was to insure that the three companies all maintained their facilities so that in time of war there would be adequate production. But one of the results was that the companies had every incentive to conspire with each other to keep bid prices high. For example, when the bids for armor for battleship 39 were opened they were found to be identical: $454 for Class A armor, $518 for turret armor, and $496 for Class B armor.[2] Asked why the bids were identical, two of the companies replied that since the contract would be divided anyway "the only effect of competitive bids would be to reduce the profits made by all three firms."[3] Daniels remarked that "the three companies make affidavits that they are in no combination and have no agreement affecting prices, as they are required by law to do. This does not, however, prevent their availing themselves of a mental telepathy which works against the government and denies real competition in the bidding."[4] The situation was not unknown to the public. The American Anti-Trust League had charged that there had been collusion between the manufacturers and the Department, and these charges had been repeated by Representative William J. Cary of Wisconsin early in March, 1913. Daniels found there was no evidence of collusion, but wrote to the President that the only way the government could compel competition was to establish "its own facilities for the manufacture of armor plate, gun forgings and other steel products."[5]

Daniels rejected the first bids on armor plate for battleship 39 and asked for new ones, emphasizing that they had to be competitive. Midvale made the lowest bids this time, re-

ducing its prices to $440 for Class A, $504 for turret, and
$482 for Class B armor,[6] but reserving the right to sublet parts
of the contract, which it did when the award was made and
Bethlehem and Carnegie each got its customary share.
Daniels called this type of competition, which had resulted
in a saving for the Department of only $14 per ton, "purely
nominal": the same companies were selling similar armor to
the Japanese government for $406.35 per ton for Class A
armor, or about 10 percent less than they charged their own
government.[7]   Daniels also charged that the American companies had divided the world market with European firms:
the American armor plate manufacturers did not bid for
European contracts and the European companies did not bid
for U.S. government contracts.[8]

The Department was faced with a difficult situation.   It
had been, in effect, subsidizing a close-knit group of monopolists under the guise of maintaining competitive bidding.
Roosevelt's office recommended that

If we are going to subsidize the ... companies ... then let us do so
honestly and man-fashion by statute. . . .   But if our object is to
get armor as cheaply as possible ... I shall certainly be disposed
to recommend the establishment of an armor plate factory by the
Government ... or an offer to all existing steel companies to equip
for the one offering the best terms an armor plate department which
would be exclusively under government control.[9]

A study was made of the cost of production of armor plate,
and it was estimated that a government plant of 20,000 tons
annual capacity could produce at a cost of $279 per ton, as
compared with $318 in a private plant.[10]   Daniels then recom-
mended that the government build its own armor plate factory, estimating that the government could save over $3
million annually.[11]

The effect of this action was immediate.   The price for
Class A armor was gradually reduced by the companies from
$440 to $420 per ton,[12] and Bethlehem offered to sell armor
plate to the government "at any price the Federal Trade Commission might fix" that would be fair both to the government

and to the manufacturers.[13] But with the war in Europe going full blast by this time, Congress appropriated funds in
1916 for the purchase or erection of an armor plant by the
Navy Department. The companies did not even reply when
the Department queried them in regard to sale of an armor
factory [14] and the government proceeded to build a plant at
Charleston, West Virginia. One of the arguments that helped
convince Congress was the greater secrecy with respect to
improvements that could be maintained in a government
plant as compared with a private one.[15]

The reaction of Daniels and Roosevelt, and the policy of
the administration, when faced by monopolistic collusion in
this instance, was not to take action under the anti-trust laws.
Indeed, this possibility seems not to have been considered.
Nor was the proposal made by Bethlehem that the new
Federal Trade Commission set a fair price—in a sense, arbitrate the dispute—seriously considered as an alternative solution. It was necessary to "compel actual competition" in the
pricing of armor, and a government plant was the "only
method." [16] Nor was the "yardstick" nature of such a plant
ignored: the Department would be able to determine "by
actual experience the prices the Navy should pay for such
products when secured from private contractors." [17]

The fight for a government armor plate plant was carried
on largely by Secretary Daniels, and F.D.R. did not agree with
him on one basic point: How much should the Navy manufacture? Daniels wanted the Navy to be able to make everything it needed in the way of ships and munitions, and wanted
plants constructed that could manufacture one-third of the
Navy's needs in one eight-hour shift a day. Production could
be expanded readily "if the prices are higher than the government can manufacture for" or "if the private contractors make
prices that are exorbitant." [18]

Roosevelt, on the other hand, did not think the government should manufacture everything it needed. He thought
it was "a very difficult thing" for the government to offer in-

centives to its own employees comparable to incentives in private business.[19] When Congress appropriated funds for the armor plate plant in 1917 Roosevelt did not approve of a plant of the size contemplated—he wanted only a "yardstick" plant, and wrote to his uncle:

Confidentially, I agree with you about the asininity of the project as it went through Congress. I did my best to have the eleven millions cut to five, with the idea of building only a small plant for three purposes:

(a) To determine actual cost of manufacture.
(b) To experiment in the improvement of armor.
(c) To use as a nucleus for great expansion in time of war.

All of these objects were entirely legitimate and would not have ruined anybody's legitimate business. I hope now to have the plant combined into an armor plate, projectile and heavy forging plant. If these other items can be added for the original amount of eleven millions it will cut down the total production of armor plate and at the same time give us testing and cost-keeping facilities which are entirely legitimate.[20]

The armor plate affair was not Roosevelt's only brush with monopoly in the steel industry. The same three companies produced turbine casings for the Navy and they submitted identical bids. This time the Department went abroad: the Cyclops Steel and Iron Works of Sheffield, England, provided the casings at about one-third the lowest American bid.[21]

At the same time that the Navy Department was fighting monopolistic practices in the steel industry it was seeking to develop competitive bidding on Navy coal contracts.

The Bureau of Supplies and Accounts of the Department had developed a list of approved mines from which the highest grade of steaming coal could be obtained, but its tests were so rigid that practically the only mines on the list were in a small area of the West Virginia coal fields. The Bureau did not advertise publicly for bids on coal contracts, but sent out requests for bids to the firms on its "accepted list." The bids "were practically always identical." [22] As F.D.R. put it, "a system of purchase had gradually grown up which automatically barred competition and permitted a few dealers practically to name their own price for the coal they were furnishing the Navy." [23]

Roosevelt and Howe did not take kindly to this situation, but "hoped that the attitude of this administration in regard to noncompetitive bids had been made so clear in the matter of armor plate that the dealers supplying coal would read the handwriting on the wall and would engage in real competition." [24] This hope was forlorn, however, for early in 1914 nineteen bids for coal to be delivered at Hampton Roads were practically identical.[25] All of these bids were rejected and new specifications were drawn up. Tests were made of coal from Pennsylvania mines, more firms were added to the accepted list, and the Department advertised publicly for bids.[26]

When the new bids came in there were ten more companies seeking the contracts and there was some variation in the bids: for Hampton Roads coal the low bid was $2.80 per ton, while for Philadelphia coal the low bid was $2.57. Nevertheless, of the eighteen bidders on Hampton Roads coal, thirteen submitted identical bids at the old price of $2.90 per ton.[27]

Roosevelt was satisfied that the Department had obtained competition among the coal dealers. At the 1915 hearings of the House Naval Affairs Committee the following colloquy took place:

Mr. Roberts [Representative Ernest W. Roberts]: ... You think you got real genuine competition?
Mr. Roosevelt: I am sure we did, from reports received subsequently. In fact, I might say that we created consternation.[28]

While coal was the chief fuel for the Navy at this time, the Department was beginning to shift increasingly to fuel oil, and sought to insure adequate supplies for the future. This brought up the issue of government oil reserves versus private development of petroleum resources, with Daniels and Roosevelt advocating creation of Navy-owned reserves. Daniels recommended that the Department own its own oil wells and refine its own oil "to relieve itself of the necessity of purchasing what seems fair to become the principal fuel of the Navy in the future at exorbitant and ever-increasing prices from the private companies that now completely control the supply." [29]

The Navy began acquiring reserve oil lands to protect the fuel supply of the fleet, with some especially valuable properties being set aside in California for Navy use. The question of these reserves came up several years later. In 1916 Senator Phelan of California introduced an amendment to the General Development Bill that would have permitted oil land claimants to drill for oil on those lands. The Department fought to retain its reserves, and Roosevelt wrote a speech which was read before the American Mining Congress in the "opening attack" in the battle to retain government control.[30]

Granting that the government should not take property without compensation, but insisting that the government must set aside reserve oil lands, he said:

What is needed now is not a fight by those who see the possibility of personal exploitation and possibly large gains; what is needed is the cooperation for the sake of the nation as a whole on the part of the hundreds of patriotic Americans who have today interests in the production of oil.[31]

In this instance the Department was successful in protecting its reserves; it was less successful eight years later during the Harding administration, when these same reserves and others in Wyoming were transferred to the Department of the Interior and then leased to private oil companies in the great Teapot Dome affair.

Disposal of the Navy's wartime-acquired radio stations after the close of World War I raised again the issue of government vs. private ownership and operation. During the war the Navy had taken over all American overseas radio facilities. To the 54 Navy-owned and operated stations prior to the war were added 53 bought from private interests, 67 built by the Navy, and 59 privately owned but Navy-operated.

The stations were located at numerous coastal cities and in foreign locations all over the world, and comprised a world-wide communications network.[32]   In addition, the Navy had developed a great number of improvements that would be invaluable in any postwar development of radio.

In the spring of 1919 representatives of General Electric Corporation, headed by Owen D. Young, approached the Department with a proposal to buy the Navy's stations and patents.   With Secretary Daniels in Europe at the time, Roosevelt turned down the offer on the grounds that the company that was to be set up to own and operate the properties would not be wholly controlled by American capital. When Daniels returned the whole matter was discussed and it was agreed within the Department that the Navy should retain a monopoly of all overseas radio.   The plan was agreed to by President Wilson and presented to Congress, where it was pigeon-holed in the furor of demobilization and the return to normalcy.[33]   Daniels presented a strong case for government ownership as a "practical common-sense matter, having no relation to any abstract considerations of government ownership," in letters to the President of the Senate and the Speaker of the House of Representatives.   The Navy had to have its own radio stations, he argued, and during peacetime they would not be fully utilized and would be available for commercial use.   A parallel private network would mean duplication of facilities.   Furthermore, "efficient radio communication requires effective control; effective control requires a monopoly and the government should exercise that monopoly."   Daniels proposed a government monopoly of ship-to-shore, transocean, and international radio, with the government stations carrying on a commercial business, but with government encouragement of American radio enterprises abroad.[34]   Daniels's advocacy of monopoly is interesting: he was afraid of "divided authority" in case of war and thought that a monopoly "guarantees the greatest success in peace." [35]

With Congressional disapproval of the plan for government ownership, the Department accepted a second offer by Owen D. Young and his associates to set up a radio corporation which would be wholly owned by American capital, and "a reluctant consent was given to the transfer of the Navy patents and stations to the radio corporation." [36] As far as Roosevelt's views on this affair were concerned, he wrote some ten years later that

I personally and flatly turned down the first proposition of Owen Young because of the un-American ownership of the scheme. And I am equally certain that I was in hearty accord with the proposal for permanent government control until such time as it was clearly impossible to get it from Congress.[37]

If relations with big business raised some basic issues and helped Roosevelt clarify his attitude on the relationship between government and the economy, problems concerning labor were of equal importance in broadening his experience and viewpoint in this field. Roosevelt's labor policies were characterized by a full recognition of labor unions and their right to bargain with management, and a willingness not only to listen to grievances but also to bring representatives of labor into the job of decision-making where those decisions affected labor. In part, these policies were dictated by political considerations: the administration wanted no blots on its record as a friend of labor. But the policies were also heartily believed in by Roosevelt; he did not merely carry out administration policies in a halfhearted fashion, but was in large measure responsible for the Department's labor policy. Roosevelt's policies were stated to the unions in the Washington Navy Yard shortly after he joined the Department:

We want cooperation. We want to get down and talk across the table with you and to right your wrongs.... If I had my way we would create a board composed of the heads of departments and some of the men and would send them to Europe to look into shop conditions there, with the idea of benefiting men here.[38]

I hope that any of the men of the Navy Department will come to the office of the Secretary of the Navy or Assistant Secretary

and talk things over concerning the department any time they
want. . . . We want you to talk to us as human beings.[39]

These sentiments were certainly not those of the average
business-minded person of that time, and represent a sharp
contrast to the open-shop policies dominant in business
thinking.

It was fortunate that Roosevelt held such cooperative
views, for there was substantial labor unrest in some of the
large Navy Yards. In particular, the Yards were plagued by
seasonal patterns of work, and workers were generally employed at wages somewhat lower than prevailing wages in
private industry. These conditions were complicated by
efforts of some of the Navy engineers to introduce some aspects of scientific management.[40] The net result was a time
of labor troubles in 1913 and 1914 that put to the test Roosevelt's cooperative attitude toward labor.

A typical dispute was that at the Charlestown, Massachusetts Navy Yard in the spring of 1913. Unrest among the
workers centered on a rumored installation of the "Taylor
system" of scientific management, but even when the com-
mandant of the Yard was directed to inform the workers that
the Department had no such intentions, the unrest continued.
Roosevelt made a special trip to Charlestown and, in line with
his policy of direct presentation of grievances, met with a
committee representing the workmen. The workers wanted
assurances that scientific management would not be adopted,
a promise that the system of piecework payment of wages
would not be introduced, representation on the wage board
that determined rates of pay in the Yard, and a promise of
more permanent employment. Roosevelt's method of handling the dispute was to grant the demands of the workers,
subject to approval by Secretary Daniels. Upon returning to
Washington he said further that he planned to grant concessions asked by the Charlestown Yard employees as far as
possible in the near future, remarking that he was "favorably
impressed" by their grievances. All of the demands of the

workers were met, except that membership of workers on the wage boards was prohibited by law, a detail that Roosevelt was not aware of when he visited the Yard.[41]

The question of scientific management had not been settled, however. Felix Frankfurter, then an attorney in the War Department, visited Roosevelt and described the success of the War Department in installing the Taylor system of scientific management at the Watertown Arsenal. He persuaded F.D.R. to allow an expert to make a study of the Charlestown Navy Yard, but when the expert reported favorably on the Taylor system F.D.R. disagreed. Roosevelt did not think any such drastic move toward efficiency "should be imposed from above on an unwilling working force." [42]

Once the Department had established good relations with the unions by granting their reasonable demands, its major labor troubles were over. The only strikes in Navy Yards during World War I were wildcat strikes, primarily of unskilled workers who had no unions to represent them. Typical was the strike at the Norfolk Navy Yard in 1917, which was quickly settled by increasing the wages paid the dissatisfied men.[43]

During the war the administration's basic labor policy was laid down by the War Labor Board.[44] That policy was very favorable to labor unions: the American Federation of Labor gave a no-strike pledge, but in return it obtained the right to organize and to bargain collectively, as well as recognition of two of its major goals, the eight-hour day and higher wages.

These policies did not solve all of the administration's labor problems. The scarcity of labor during the war led to attempts by both business firms and by government departments, especially War and Navy, to obtain adequate supplies of labor by raising wages and offering other inducements. A high rate of labor turnover resulted, with workers moving from job to job to take advantage of increasingly better offers. Output and efficiency suffered. It was felt that standardization of wages and working conditions, and improvement of working conditions where they were poor, would help to solve this problem, and to this end the War Labor Policies Board was set up in May, 1918.[45] The purpose of the Board was to harmonize the policies of the numerous government agencies dealing with labor matters and "to eliminate all those factors which at the time were reducing the productivity of the workers." [46]

Roosevelt represented the Navy Department on the Board, but he attended only three meetings. His alternate, Louis Howe, attended most of the other meetings. Nevertheless, Roosevelt was in accord with the efforts of the Board to standardize labor conditions at a much improved level. The Board advocated a basic eight-hour day with time and a half for overtime and double time for Sundays at a time when the steel industry, for instance, was operating on a ten- to twelve-hour day. Roosevelt thought that Sunday work should be permitted only in emergencies, and that "a desire to complete generally the work under contract more speedily or to bring up one branch of the work to a condition of completion parallel with other branches will not be considered an emergency." The Board agreed that Sunday work was undesirable and should be reduced to a minimum.[47]

With the wartime shortage of workers growing in importance, more and more women were being employed, and the question of labor standards for women assumed greater importance. The Board advocated numerous safeguards for employed women, including a basic eight-hour day and forty-eight-hour week, no more than a ten-hour day and fifty-five-hour week in emergencies, one day of rest in seven, no night work, and equal pay with men. The resolution embodying that policy was introduced by Howe at one of the few Board meetings attended by Roosevelt, who spoke at that meeting on the labor situation in England and France.[48]

The wartime labor policies of the Wilson administration were closely parallel to the labor policies of the New Deal, at least in essentials if not in detail. The right to organize, protection against firing of workers for union activity, the eight-hour day, and improvements in wages and working conditions may have been policies adopted in an emergency situation under Wilson; they were everyday policies during the New Deal period. The wartime policies represented acceptance of the program of the American Federation of Labor by the government, and Roosevelt's participation in the development and administration of these policies cannot be overlooked in seeking the genesis of the labor policies of the New Deal.[49]

But Roosevelt did not accept fully the trade union position. Immediately after the war the problem of nation-wide strikes in essential industries arose, as labor sought to consolidate and expand its wartime gains and as business largely returned to its prewar anti-union activity. A short wildcat strike of railway shopmen in the summer of 1919 was followed by a strike of steel workers in September and of soft coal miners in November. The press devoted itself to considerable anti-union propaganda, and the National Association of Manufacturers launched its open-shop movement under the slogan of the "American Plan"; at the same time the "anti-Red" campaign of Attorney General Palmer was gathering strength. In this supercharged atmosphere Roosevelt spoke in opposition to strikes in essential industries and advocated a system of labor courts to eliminate labor strife. At Syracuse he said:

We wish to give labor a larger share of the profits, successes and improved condition of the country, but we can't stand for any small group in a community holding up the whole community.[50]

After the coal strike began Roosevelt spoke again on the subject in Philadelphia. He wanted the government to set up a court to arbitrate disagreements between capital and labor and with power to enforce its decrees. He declared that employees in public service and essential industries were not free agents: they owed a duty of service to the people and could not "throw up their jobs whenever the fancy strikes them." [51]

Roosevelt's years in the Navy Department were of great importance in broadening his knowledge of both economic and governmental problems. He had dealt with big business and had firsthand experience with monopolistic practices in the steel and coal industries. He had taken a stand on the issue of government versus private enterprise in the case of the armor plate plant and in the case of the Navy's radio facilities. He had dealt with labor and had proved himself friendly to the working man. Although he had been at least aware of economic problems since his college days, he felt by 1919 that the major problems facing the nation were economic and not political.

Speaking on "The National Emergency of Peace Times" at Worcester, Massachusetts, in June, 1919, he spelled out the dangers that faced the nation in the postwar world:

Think for a moment of what you and I have to lay hold of and wrestle with and solve even today—the disposition of the railroads, of the telegraphs, in fact of all so-called public utilities; the extension of our commerce in American ships upon the seas; matters of combinations among great industries; relations of capital, labor and the national interests; the development of natural resources above and below the surface; the distribution of population so as to prevent unhealthy congestion; the control of wealth through taxation.[52]

Almost as an afterthought he added the problem of "the actual conduct of government itself." And he closed with a plea for an active interest in government and public affairs, along with "some form of universal training for the youth of the country."

In contrast to his first campaign for the State Senate in 1912, when he opposed bossism and corruption, Roosevelt in 1919 placed economic problems in a more important position than political problems.

CHAPTER V

The Campaign of 1920

THE YEARS FOLLOWING World War I were bad ones for the reform movements that had culminated in the Wilson administration, with its high idealism for better conditions at home and a world made safe for democracy. Replacing it was an emotional conservatism that has never been better expressed than by Herbert Hoover:

I returned in 1919 from several years abroad ... steeped with two ideas: first, that through three hundred years America had developed something new in a way of life of a people, which transcended all others of history; and second, that out of the boiling social and economic caldron of Europe, with its hates and fears, rose miasmic infections which might greatly harm or even destroy what seemed to me to be the hope of the world.[1]

The keynote of the era was truck by Senator Warren G. Harding of Ohio, who spoke in Boston in May, 1920, saying that

America's present need is not heroics but healing; not nostrums but normalcy; not revolution but restoration; ... not surgery but serenity.[2]

The idea of normalcy was taken up by those who wanted to go back to the pre-progressive ideals of McKinley and, fundamentally, to the Hamiltonian ideal of republicanism. As the election of 1920 showed—and the ensuing elections of the twenties, too—this view was shared by a large majority of the voters.

The movement toward the conservatism of Harding was aided by the state of the Wilson regime. Amid the confusion of rapid demobilization and elimination of wartime controls, Wilson no longer had a program of liberal reform: as early as 1914 he had pushed through all of the major measures he advocated. To complicate matters, the President himself was stricken by illness and the administration lost all effective leadership after September, 1919. Attorney General Palmer, seeking the presidency himself, sought publicity by a campaign against "Reds," using methods that were condemned then and later, and succeeded in alienating from support of the administration many persons who resented his prosecutions. The lack of leadership in Washington allowed a postwar inflation of substantial proportions to run its course free of any strong hindrance, while the price of the Liberty Bonds in which much wartime saving had been patriotically invested was allowed to fall as the price level rose. Reactivation of the War Finance Corporation was not effective in meeting the problem of large surpluses of farm crops as the wartime demand slackened and European production recovered. But overriding all other issues was the League of Nations and the peace treaties, the former attacked by nationalists as a means of entangling the nation in European affairs, the latter by internationalists as a surrender to the imperialism of Britain and France. It was clear to almost everyone that the progressive movement had collapsed into ineffectuality, that the idea of collective action through government to solve national problems was in eclipse.

Many of the supporters of Wilson and reform stuck to their beliefs, however. Among them was Franklin D. Roosevelt.

While still in his Navy Department job, Roosevelt began preparing for the nominating convention of 1920 by drafting platform resolutions that would continue the tradition of progressivism. Taking up the immediate problem of the high cost of living, Roosevelt attributed it to "the unnecessary number of middlemen" instead of to the wartime and postwar spending. He advocated positive government action to remedy the situation rather than reliance on the equilibrating forces of a market economy:

The existing system of bringing the necessaries of life to the user is in itself at fault. We, therefore, advocate the control of the intermediate steps so as to prevent transportation delays and overstocking of supplies in storage, and to insure the minimum number of dealers through whose hands the goods pass.

The role of the states was to provide adequate local markets, while the Federal government "must bear its share of the responsibility when interstate transportation is involved or where great private business enterprises control in part or in whole the commodities of life in more than one state." [3]

The responsibility of government for a solution to this problem was restated in more finished form:

We believe that recent investigations clearly show that one of the largest factors in the abnormally high cost of the necessities of life to the consumer is due to the increasing number of speculative middlemen, who, standing between the producer and the consumer, takes constantly increasing toll from both for his own pockets, without having served any useful part whatever in the necessary machinery of purchase and sale. We believe it to be a proper governmental function to exercise the full powers of the National Government, for the elimination of this parasite upon American business. [4]

It was also a proper function of government to solve the problem of scarcity of farm labor, with the Department of Labor acting as a recruiting agency for urban workers to work in the country. [5]

A long list of "platform recommendations" was drawn up by Roosevelt and Louis Howe, including the following proposals concerning economic affairs:

Energetic and intensive development of the Farm Loan policy and extension of the same principle to urban home builders.

Complete reorganization of the railroad system, more Federal aid for highways, and encouragement of consumers' cooperatives. All of this was designed to reduce the high cost of living by reducing the cost of marketing.

Assurance of labor's right to organize and a fair share in the rewards of industry: "We believe the best results in quieting present unrest to be from active participation by labor with employers in the management and profits of all industry."

Revision of tax laws, especially to differentiate between

earned and unearned income, to reach "the profiteers," and
to impose heavy inheritance taxes.

A government market for Liberty Bonds at par.

Government deficit spending in times of depression to com-
pensate for inadequate private spending.

The last recommendation is startling enough to quote in full:

We also favor the authorization of "Prosperity Bonds," or short
term notes, to be issued at the discretion of the President whenever
he declares a state of acute industrial depression to exist. The
proceeds of such bonds shall be spent on an authorized program
of economic-defensive works, such as intercoastal canals, roads,
reclamation and land-settlement projects, and administered by the
army. We believe such policy to be the constructive preventative
for acute depression otherwise almost certain to come, providing
a way of "taking up slack" and probably forestalling the hysteria
and manipulation which leads to panic and untold public suffering.[6]

It was a queer collection of proposals. The high cost of living, essentially a short-range problem resulting from excessive
wartime and postwar spending, was to be attacked by long-
range solutions designed to reduce the cost of distribution.
This was clearly inconsistent and represented an attempt on
Roosevelt's part to push one of his pet proposals. His letters
at the time of the ensuing campaign indicate that he was well
aware of the basic causes of inflation. Most of the other proposals were well within the framework of progressivism, but
the last, involving "Prosperity Bonds," clearly anticipated the
pump-priming and deficit spending of the thirties. Roosevelt's program was a combination of weak economics, orthodox liberal proposals, and rare insight into economic realities;
the basic framework was a predilection for government action
and intervention in economic affairs whenever a problem arose
that could be tackled that way.

Meanwhile, Roosevelt's friends were booming him for the
Democratic nomination for United States Senator from New
York, and Roosevelt himself was working for a campaign for
progressivism:

I would not run this autumn for dog-catcher if the Democrats
nominate a party hack or a reactionary or a Bryan at San Fran-

cisco. If the party shows vision, puts up a Progressive Democrat who can make a strong appeal to the country, and in general shows signs of common sense in working out the great problems of the day, I shall be entirely willing to do what I can to help the party.[7]

The leading candidates for the Democratic nomination were William G. McAdoo, Wilson's son-in-law and former Secretary of the Treasury, A. Mitchell Palmer, the Red-baiting Attorney General, and James A. Cox, former Governor of Ohio. The pro-Wilson forces centered their support on McAdoo while the anti-Wilson groups supported Cox. The nomination of Cox was a victory for those in the party who were opposed to Wilson's policies, especially the city machines which had not fared too well under the idealistic Wilson. As a sop, the vice-presidential nomination was given to Roosevelt, Wilson supporter, easterner, bearing a well-known name.

To Roosevelt the campaign was a clear conflict between progressivism and conservatism. Harding was "McKinley-minded" and the Republican party offered a "conservatism so deep as to prevent any progress towards meeting the new conditions which have arisen in our national life" and "a return to the days of McKinley." Cox, on the other hand, was a "true Liberal" whose record as Governor of Ohio included "all of the progressive legislation." [8]

But the main issue of the campaign was no longer the progressives' movement for reform. The issues now were the League of Nations, the World War I peace treaties, and the general subject of America's relations with other countries. Harding adopted an equivocal position that enabled his supporters to argue against the League when necessary and for the League when necessary: the candidate did not approve the League, but he did speak favorably of an "association of nations." Cox, on the other hand, as the heir of Wilson's policies, had to support the League in general if not in all particulars. The Democrats found this issue to be an albatross around their necks, given the prevailing mood of the country.

There were other issues that the Democrats found hard to

handle: the high cost of living, high taxes and high government spending that were the aftermath of war, and the falling
prices of Liberty Bonds. But these were secondary issues,
with the high cost of living being the only one that assumed
importance during the campaign. The propaganda, the
editorials, the major orations were all concerned with foreign
affairs.

In his speeches Roosevelt devoted much of his attention to
the issues of foreign policy, but as a good progressive he also
spoke at considerable length on economic affairs. In defer-
ence to the prevailing political climate, the word "reform"
was replaced by "progress," and as in all of Roosevelt's campaigns the emphasis was on general principles rather than on
specific proposals. In his speech accepting the nomination
for vice-president, F.D.R. listed the "most pressing" national
needs, including the "improvement of working conditions,
especially in the congested centers, the extension of communications to make rural life more attractive, the further
protection of child life and women in industry" and "the
further development of our natural resources" by means of
"a well-considered coordinated plan of development." The
proposal for planned development of natural resources was
little more than a systematic approach to public improvements, as contrasted with "pork barrel" methods: "Every
dollar of our expenditures for port facilities, for inland waterways, for flood control, for reclamation of swamp and arid
lands, for highways, for public buildings, shall be expended
only by trained men in accordance with a continuing plan." [9]
It was more of an attack on special-interest legislation than
advocacy of the principles of economic planning.

Starting on a campaign through the West, Roosevelt criticized Harding's "return to normalcy" as a repudiation of the
progressivism of Theodore Roosevelt and his Republican supporters. Harding was characterized as a man "who had not
discovered that the world was moving on," as a man "who
supported the Ancient Regime." [10] Continuing through the

Midwest, F.D.R. took up the problems of the farmer. Speaking at Minneapolis, he gave a typical Rooseveltian explanation of why farm problems required positive action by the Federal government: first, changing conditions had pushed into national importance a problem that was at one time a local or regional affair, and second, "vast improvement can be made in the existing situation." Then followed the long-range program of action to increase farm incomes and reduce selling prices to the ultimate consumer that Roosevelt had advocated for some years: reduction of distribution costs through better transportation and marketing facilities and "reduction of the present number of hands through which an article must go before it reaches the ... consumer." [11] But what made the greatest impression on his audience was Roosevelt's statement that "we must assure the farmer who raises the big wheat crop that he can market it when he wants to market it, and we must help him get a fair price for it." [12] These sentiments were repeated at other stops in the farm belt, along with the warning that the Democratic party was the farmer's friend while, by inference, the Republicans were "friends of the packers, ... big bankers, ... and the Eastern middlemen." [13]

That Roosevelt desired a long-range plan of government action to aid the farmer is borne out by a statement solicited from him by a farm magazine:

It is undeniable that the conditions surrounding the life on farms in this country have not kept sufficient pace with the progress of our civilization. This is shown by the difficulty throughout the country in keeping the young men and an adequate supply of labor on the farms. Progress must come through better organization of farm life; through a more intelligent interest on the part of the dwellers in cities; through further development of the farm credit system; through a definite and constructive policy on the part of the Government looking towards the creation of improved communications; and through the development of heat, power and the establishment of better markets. So far we have only scratched the surface. A great constructive program must be carried out in every portion of the country.[14]

Continuing into the mountain states of the Northwest, Roosevelt's subject changed from farm problems in general to conservation and reclamation. In Montana he repeated that a continuous development program was necessary, and in Washington he advocated expansion of reclamation work "to provide additional lands and a greater food production" and he approved Federal aid for the Columbia Basin project. He promised annual expenditures for reclamation of at least forty million dollars,[15] which would represent a $32,500,000 increase over expenditures for that purpose in the year 1920. Pausing at Centralia, the scene of a pitched battle between the American Legion and the I.W.W. some years earlier, he attacked "the alien anarchist, the criminal syndicalist, and all similar anti-Americans" and pledged that the nation "shall be made unsafe for those who seek by violence to destroy the Constitution and Institutions of America." [16] The return trip to the East was featured by short talks at numerous stops emphasizing that the election was a contest between progressive and reactionary ideas. Roosevelt stated that "I am a progressive Democrat and I think that the emphasis is on the 'progressive.' " [17]

Returning to his home state, Roosevelt spoke at the Brooklyn Navy Yard on Labor Day, where he was presented with a loving cup from the employees. Frankness, justice, and square dealing, he said, were all that was needed for perfect harmony between capital and labor:

I have no patience with the phrase "the labor question" or "the labor problem," as if it were some unsolved riddle of the Sphinx, hopeless of solution. My first experience as an employer of labor came when I entered the "Navy" Department. . . . I found nothing terrifying in the task, because I believed the men in the navy yards at the bench and the men in charge at Washington at their desks were, after all, the same kind of American citizen, and that all that was needed was frankness and justice and square dealing on both sides to insure perfect harmony and cooperation between them. The employer who insists on having his own way, right or wrong, . . . who tries only to get the most service for the least money will always find a "labor problem" on his hands, but the man who tries to be fair can look, as I look, with considerable amazement upon those who hold that employer and employee must necessarily stand in a state of constant conflict and perpetual misunderstanding.[18]

The policies stated at Brooklyn were worked out in some detail in Roosevelt's proposals for Federal employees. He was in favor of joint administrator-employee boards to consider wages, employment conditions, discipline, and dismissal.[19]

The candidate could not ignore the high cost of living. He recognized in his letters that high prices were basically due to "inflation of currency for war purposes as well as to a relative scarcity of goods," while high rents were the result of wartime restrictions on private building that caused the post-war housing shortage.[20]

But as his projected platform recommendations forecast, he advocated, in a speech at Albany, a long-range program designed to attack other factors in the problem of the high cost of living, including reclamation projects, better transportation facilities, measures to make farm life more attractive, elimination of excessive middlemen, strict laws against profiteering, and "such regulations of commodities like coal that the average citizen may be assured that the supply will be adequate and the price reasonable." [21] Roosevelt's failure to state publicly his views on the causes of the inflation was a clear example of political disingenuousness. If the Democrats publicly acknowledged that wartime government spending was the major cause of high prices, they would be admitting their own responsibility for inflation, but this does not alter the fact that Roosevelt expressed views that were contrary to his actual beliefs.

Roosevelt continued his campaign with a speech at Charleston, West Virginia, site of the Navy's armor plate factory. In the old muckraking tradition he attacked the monopolist, the influence of big business in politics, and the opposition of vested interests to reform legislation. After describing the Navy Department's troubles with the armor plate trust, and pointing out that Harding voted against setting up the government factory, he went on to explain the essence of progressivism:

For twenty years and more the American people have conducted a fight to take their government . . . out of the control of an element in the community which was in politics for its selfish interest. . . . We know in many cases where Senators of the United States have been recognized by the public as representing this group or that group among the great trusts. But it has been rather in a negative way that the old guard in the Senate have helped their privileged friends. It has been through opposition to any legislation of a progressive character, any legislation that would tend to cut down the enormous profits of the selected few, . . . that would give a squarer deal to the working men of the nation, . . . that would prevent child labor, . . . that furthered the cause of social justice. It was this group which stood out against the income tax and against the direct election of United States Senators.[22]

Harding defeated Cox by the largest majority in American history up to that time. Roosevelt felt that the nation had "taken a step backward" and that "the only thing we can hope for is that they [the Republicans] will not be so tremendously reactionary as to fan the flames of Radicalism too far." But "the fight for progressive principles has only just begun," and the Democratic party, "by remaining the progressive party of the nation, is bound to succeed." "Very few real fights," he wrote to a young supporter, "are won at the very beginning, and I think this is going to be a fight of that kind, because I know we are right."[23]

CHAPTER VI

Roosevelt Emerges as a Party Leader

IT HAS BEEN SAID many times that Roosevelt's attack of infantile paralysis and slow recovery marked a turning point in his thinking, that prior to August, 1921, his approach to economic and political problems was superficial, if not frivolous, while afterwards he was more penetrating in his thinking.[1]

Those writers who have called attention to Roosevelt's development after his illness were only partially correct. His basic philosophy deepened and broadened, and it was in this period that Roosevelt the political philosopher appeared. But it was a development and continuation of ideas already present, not the appearance of something new that characterized Roosevelt after 1921. The Jeffersonian ideals of his heritage, the progressivism of Theodore Roosevelt and Woodrow Wilson, and the idea of the positive state taking action to better the world—these ideas were present before 1921 and were developed after 1921. There was no clear break in his thinking; no basic ideas appeared after Roosevelt's illness that were not present before it.

In one respect Roosevelt's illness influenced his development greatly. Immobilized in part, he was unable to participate in the hurly-burly of politics and devoted himself to reading. History, the sea and the navy, and biography were his favorites, along with mystery stories, but he also found time to read the agricultural journals extensively.[2] Mrs. Roosevelt became active in politics, both to keep her husband interested and to keep his name in the public eye.[3] She also brought to talk to her husband two friends of hers active in the Women's Trade Union League, Rose Schneidermann and Maude Schwartz. In long talks with them F.D.R. heard much about the history and theory of the trade union movement, about sweatshops and occupational disease, about wages and hours, about the cooperative movement.[4] Other persons interested in social problems and reform were brought to the house by Mrs. Roosevelt and Louis Howe as they sought to keep him abreast of current events. Discussion of current affairs as well as reading enabled F.D.R. to grow intellectually as he convalesced.

Prior to 1921 Roosevelt could be best described as a progressive. He embraced the ideas of progressivism, he followed the progressive leaders. After his illness he began to develop the foundations of his political philosophy more than he had done previously. He went back to Thomas Jefferson and Jeffersonian political philosophy. Roosevelt was familiar with Jefferson's ideas from extensive reading. He had always been interested in American naval history, and that meant, among other things, the first forty or fifty years of general American history, when the new nation was in large part a seaboard country of sailors. His collection of books and prints was centered on early American history and naval history. This emphasis in his reading and collecting of books was to be found as early as 1904,[5] and continued through the governorship [6] and the presidential years.

Roosevelt came to look upon himself as a modern follower of Jefferson. He did not try to follow the Jeffersonian philosophy blindly, but recognized that conditions had vastly changed since the early nineteenth century. The task was one of fitting the Jeffersonian views to the requirements of a modern machine age:

We have today side by side an old political order fashioned by a pastoral civilization and a new social order fashioned by a technical civilization. The two are maladjusted. Their creative interrelation is one of the big tasks ahead of American leadership.[7]

Roosevelt's Jeffersonianism, then, was not what Jefferson would have conceived it to be, but a Rooseveltian version, much simplified and reduced to a few basic concepts. Roosevelt shared two basic attitudes with Jefferson—a belief that country life was, somehow, better than that of the city and that the nation's strength lay in the countryside; and a distrust of speculators and middlemen. To this was added Roosevelt's belief that in the 1920's the Republican party represented wealth and privilege and that the Democratic party had to represent the true interests of the common man; he interpreted Jefferson's political battles with the Federalists in the same light. In this respect, Roosevelt's rediscovery of Jefferson added nothing really new to his political-economic philosophy, but it did serve to strengthen his beliefs and offered him a weapon to use against his opponents.

Like Jefferson, Roosevelt had a bias in favor of rural and small-town life. Bettering of conditions on the farm, not just economically, but socially, was a major element in his political program in the State Senate, when he campaigned for the vice-presidency, and as governor. In 1921 he made a typical statement of this position. Speaking at Lenox, Massachusetts, he decried the fact shown by the 1920 census that more than 50 percent of the American population lived in cities. This trend must be stopped, he said, "for the growth of cities while the country population stands still will eventually bring disaster to the United States." A "nice balance" must be maintained between industry and agriculture. Roosevelt advocated a program to aid agriculture and a back-to-land movement undertaken by local communities—put families back on idle farms, build better roads and schools, and provide an improved marketing system to reduce middlemen's profits. "Legislation will not do it," he said, "paternalism by Washington or Boston or Albany will give no panacea. We have more than enough laws—what we need is action." [8]

The most important element in Roosevelt's interpretation of the Jeffersonian philosophy—an element that was also a major foundation of progressivism—was opposition to a privileged position for the wealthy and support of a government dominated by the ordinary man. It was this viewpoint that Roosevelt developed at great length in the twenties. Just as Jefferson had fought Hamilton on this issue, so Roosevelt conceived the struggle between Democrats and Republicans in the twenties. The Democratic party must be made into a party of the people, opposed to the Republicans, who represented the wealthy vested interests who were using control of the government for their own enrichment. In Roosevelt's eyes it was the old conflict of "wealth versus commonwealth," with the whole future of American democracy at stake.

In 1925 he reviewed Claude Bowers's book *Jefferson and Hamilton* for the New York *World*. Roosevelt argued that the differences between Hamilton and Jefferson could be applied to the "present day policies of our two great parties" and criticized those "smug writers" who denied that "the forces hostile to control of government by the people which existed in the crisis of 1790-1800 could still be a threat to our present day and land." Hamilton he described as a supporter of an aristocracy of land and wealth, Jefferson as the supporter of the small farmer and the poorer groups in the nation. "Jefferson's faith in mankind was vindicated; his appeal to the intelligence of the average voter bore fruit; his conception of a democratic republic came true." Roosevelt closed on a prophetic note:

I have a breathless feeling as I lay down this book—a picture of escape after escape which this nation passed through in these first ten years; a picture of what might have been if the Republic had been finally organized as Alexander Hamilton sought. But I have a breathless feeling, too, as I wonder if, a century and a quarter later, the same contending forces are not again mobilizing. Hamiltons we have today. Is a Jefferson on the horizon? [9]

Bowers thought very highly of Roosevelt's review, which applied "the lessons of the Jeffersonian period to the problems of today.... I wish I could tell you how delighted I am at the revelations of yourself that appear in the review.... I wrote the book really to recall the party of Jefferson to the real

meaning of Jeffersonian Democracy, and you have brought
it out." [10]

Roosevelt's conviction that the Democrats must oppose the
new attempt to impose an aristocracy of wealth on America
became a recurring theme in his political-economic thinking.
Shortly after his review appeared he wrote:

We are approaching a period similar to that from 1790-1800 when
Alexander Hamilton ran the Federal government for the primary
good of the chambers of commerce, the speculators and the inside
ring of the national government. He was a fundamental believer
in an aristocracy of wealth and power—Jefferson brought the government back to the hands of the average voter, through insistence
on fundamental principles, and the education of the average voter.
We need a similar campaign of education today, and perhaps we
shall find another Jefferson. [11]

Franklin D. Roosevelt, with his modernized Jeffersonianism, had begun to emerge as an important political leader in
the campaign of 1924, a year before his review of Bowers's
book. He was Alfred E. Smith's campaign manager and
made the nominating speech for Smith in the 1924 convention. It was one of the few bright spots of the convention,
and F.D.R. was one of the few Democrats who emerged with
enhanced reputation from that strife-torn gathering, split by
wet-dry, Klan and anti-Klan, South-North, Catholic and
anti-Catholic differences. William Jennings Bryan, afraid of
domination of the party by the big-city political machines,
supported McAdoo once more, while Smith was pushed by
Tammany as the only candidate who could carry the eastern
states. The southern delegates, dominated by the resurgent
Ku Klux Klan, refused Smith because he was a Catholic and
because he was opposed to prohibition. [12] The final compromise candidate, after 103 ballots, was John W. Davis, a
conservative corporation lawyer, about whom no one was
enthusiastic. The Republicans swept into office once more,
electing Coolidge, in spite of the Teapot Dome and other
corruption exposures, by a very wide margin. LaFollette,
heading a third-party Progressive ticket, polled more than

half the total popular vote obtained by Davis. The Demo-crats were a badly split, badly demoralized, badly beaten party. Roosevelt set out to revitalize them with a strong dose of his developing Jeffersonianism.

The goal of the revitalized Democratic party was to be reform within the framework of already existing institutions. Radicalism was abjured, but new schemes were not:

The Democratic Party is *the* Progressive Party of the country, but it is not the ultra-radical party of the county, which is a very different thing. We cannot surely progress unless each advancing footstep is placed on firm and tried ground. To rush blindly along the paths proclaimed as highways to Utopia by some of our friends would be to find ourselves hopelessly mired in the quicksand of untried political theories of government.

I believe there is a place for the most optimistic dreamer in our party, because our party in its very foundation principles is com-mitted to the doctrine of adopting every new thing that makes for the comfort and happiness and well being of all the people of our country just as soon as it is certain that such new ideas are sound and will have that effect.[13]

The first step was a letter to party leaders throughout the nation a month after the defeat. The party needed a better national organization, he pointed out, but more than that it needed unification around a program of progress and liberal thought. The party should devote itself to "organizing for party principles, for the taking advantage of our opponents' errors and omissions, and for presenting our own logical and progressive program." [14]

With a large number of favorable replies, the second step was an open letter to Senator Walsh, setting forth the basic principles necessary for party unity:

First, as to what may be called fundamental principles which the Democratic Party advocates, my correspondents are over-whelm-ingly agreed that the Democracy must be unqualifiedly the party representative of progress and liberal thought. In other words, the clear line of demarcation which differentiated the political thought of Jefferson on the one side and of Hamilton on the other must be restored. The Democracy must make it clear that it seeks primarily the good of the average citizen through the free rule of the whole electorate, as opposed to the Republican Party, which seeks a mere moneyed prosperity of the nation through the control of government by a self-appointed aristocracy of wealth and social and economic power.

The party must concentrate on basic issues and not be distracted by "matters of momentary or temporary nature which are principally of local interest," it must adhere to "principles rather than personalities." There followed a half-dozen practical suggestions that would make the party a more closely knit and effective organization.[15] In effect Roosevelt was saying that the Democrats must stop quibbling over divisive issues and candidates and express principles that would appeal to the average voter, that the party must base itself on the economic issues of the privileged versus the poor.

The reaction of the party leaders was not favorable. Senator Walsh approved, and so did Senator Robinson of Arkansas. But most party leaders were not favorably impressed, including the chairman of the national committee and the ageing Bryan. The New York *Times* noted how thoroughly the Democratic party itself had become "Hamiltonized." [16]

One of Roosevelt's correspondents suggested that party finances should be based on a large number of small contributions. F.D.R. agreed:

Just as the idea of the professional Republican politicians is an endless chain of obtaining public office so as to grant favors to wealthy corporations so that wealthy corporations will give them large sums to enable them to elect their candidates so as to grant them more favors and so on indefinitely, the fundamental Democratic idea that a political party is a piece of machinery by which the ideals of its principles can be put in actual practice in government should be carried into the financial side by refusing to permit large contributions and make instead almost every Democratic voter an equal partner through his subscription in our enterprise.[17]

In spite of his rebuff from the older leaders of the party, Roosevelt continued in his efforts to give his party a solidly

progressive basis.   A lengthy correspondence with Democrats
of similar views occupied much of his attention for the next
several years.   Cordell Hull bombarded Roosevelt with four
drafts of a "confidential memorandum" that restated the
issues that Roosevelt had raised:

The dominant leaders of the political party in charge of the
federal government have viewed with careless indifference the
gradual collapse of agriculture.... A continued redistribution of
property as between industry and agriculture is inevitable under
existing inequitable economic policies....

The directing forces of our government are confined to a relatively few persons of large pecuniary interests ... who are naturally
shaping legislation and government so as most to favor those interests.... This narrow, vicious and dangerous philosophy teaches
that ... the most exclusive governmental favors to them are equally
beneficial to the entire people; and that they naturally and always
should constitute the governing class....

Equality, justice and fairness alike to all afford a far broader and
sounder base for permanent prosperity than the narrow and artificial
base offered by ultra high tariffs and other handouts by the government to a small cross-section of business.... There was never
such a glaring instance of rule by a minority in the history of free
government.[18]

Louis Howe, continuing as Roosevelt's private secretary, added
fuel to the fire:

Prosperity from the Republican standpoint means the prosperity
of a few great corporations and such crumbs of prosperity as drop
from their table for the benefit of the country at large.   On the first
page of today's *Tribune* you will find a little two-column story ...
which, it seems to me, would make a wonderful illustration of this
point.   The story tells in a rather nasty way how the head of
Burns Bros., who are the leading coal robbers of the City of New
York, left for Europe in the most expensive suite that could be
bought on any steamer, and tossed out through the porthole to his
clerks and heads of departments who came to see him off, five
dollar gold pieces, for which they scrambled like so many starving
children.   Is not this, in parable form, the whole theory of Republican prosperity? [19]

If the major issue was "wealth versus commonwealth,"
what were the specific economic measures advocated by

Roosevelt at this time in his new role of interpreter of Jefferson for the twentieth century? They were "a scientific tariff, not written by and for a favored few, a general setttlement of all debts between all nations, and the rejuvenation of the agricultural population." [20] None of these measures could be considered revolutionary.

The Democrats had favored a "scientific" tariff for many years. Roosevelt explained that the party did not favor free trade, but a tariff for revenue and to protect American industry from "dumping." The tariff was to be "scientific" in that it would be based on the difference in manufacturing costs between American and foreign producers plus the cost of transportation. Such a tariff would protect American manufacturers by equalizing production costs. The tariff schedules would be determined by an impartial commission. Such a system would result in lower tariffs, and would not permit manufacturers to overcharge the public. These were the ideas behind the tariff act of 1914 passed during the Wilson administration, but a new tariff act passed under Harding's administration abolished the commission and raised the general tariff level over the 1914 level. This latest act, said Roosevelt, "was drafted with the aid of and for the purpose of enriching many special interests." [21]

As for the problem of war debts and reparations, Roosevelt advocated a sympathetic and tactful settlement or compromise, rather than insistence on full and immediate payment— or at least he so implied.[22]

The rejuvenation of agriculture required some form of "agricultural relief" and F.D.R. thought highly of the so-called Lowden plan. Former Governor Frank O. Lowden of Illinois was a leader in seeking a solution of the farm relief problem. The plan Roosevelt referred to was a variation of the McNary-Haugen plan that had recently failed of passage in Congress; its object was to raise prices of staple farm products through the so-called equalization fee procedure.[23]

Roosevelt was well aware in 1925 that his efforts toward

party unity required that he soft-pedal all issues that might be creating disunion; indeed, he ignored the very existence of the issues that split the 1924 convention. This tactic is clearly indicated by a series of newspaper columns written by F.D.R. for the Macon (Georgia) *Daily Telegraph* in the months of April and May, 1925.[24] Almost all controversial material was eliminated from the columns, especially the Klan and prohibition problems; and F.D.R. was lavish in his praise of Georgia and the South.

The column for April 18, however, discussed conservation, a subject dear to Roosevelt's heart. He decried the waste of lumber lost through fire, but criticized even more the failure of many owners to treat their forests as a crop. This great waste, resulting from the shortsighted view of landowners, would ultimately force the government into the lumber business:

Many of the nations of Europe found themselves, about 150 years ago, practically stripped of their forests. They learned that individuals are, as individuals, essentially selfish—that if it was left to the sweet will of the individual landowner he would not bother his head to plant new trees or protect young seedlings where he had cut off his original piece of lumber. Over in Europe, the timber shortage become so acute that the governments had to step in and create state forests.

Like most Democrats, I am pretty thoroughly opposed to having the Federal, or even the state governments, embark in new enterprises which should be handled by individuals, but unless we, in the United States, take immediate steps to compel the growing of new timber by individuals I prophesy that it will become a government enterprise in the next generation.

The owner of land owes it to the community, and to the state, and to the nation, to use that land in the best possible way for humanity.[25]

Roosevelt had not forgotten the basic criticism of private property he had first expressed as a State Senator in his speech at Troy, New York, in 1913.

Other columns dealt with problems of immigration—Roosevelt advocated restricted, selective imigration—efficiency in government administration, American-Japanese relations, and defense. His last column took up tax problems. F.D.R. pointed out that many of our taxes overlapped and there was considerable double taxation. Especially, he inveighed against personal property taxes that were evaded or did not have honest and complete enforcement:

If all taxes, especially those on property, were enforced 100 percent, the average man's taxes could be cut from a third to a half.[26]

There was little in Roosevelt's 1925 columns to indicate that he had any opinion on the major issues of the mid-twenties. He gave every indication of being merely a pleasant politician who did not have any ideas of consequence. As a good politician he was letting sleeping dogs lie.

This evasion of issues was only a temporary phenomenon, however, and stood in sharp contrast to his support of Alfred E. Smith and Smith's program in New York State. In fact, Smith's "little welfare state" in New York must be considered an important forerunner of the New Deal and a direct connecting link between the pre-World War I progressive movement and the Roosevelt administration of the thirties. Although Smith's program may seem rather mild when viewed from the perspective of a quarter of a century later, in his day it was highly controversial. And although his accomplishments fell short of his goals, it must be remembered that Smith, a Democrat, had to work with a Republican-dominated legislature that was noted for its obstructionist tactics.

Smith's basic goal was the welfare of the people, and he felt it to be the duty of government to promote that welfare in every possible way. He asserted that

The Democratic party believes that law in a democracy is the expression of that particular thing which does the most good for the greatest number and goes the furthest to relieve and to protect and care for the great mass of the people, who, after all, make up the country.[27]

In brief, welfare legislation was the major function of government.

Smith's whole career as governor was devoted to expressing that philosophy in legislation. In the field of education he increased state aid to municipalities from about $9 million in 1919 to $82.5 million in 1927. In 1925 New York began its great state park system with the approval by the electorate of a $15 million bond issue for that purpose. A friend of labor, Smith pushed minimum wage legislation and the 48-hour week for women and children in industry. The first failed of passage, and in place of the second Smith had to be satisfied with a compromise 49½-hour bill. In 1925 he urged a referendum on the child labor amendment to the Federal Constitution, but did not press the issue in the face of concerted business opposition. He successfully resisted efforts to weaken the state's workmen's compensation law.

Another area that felt Smith's welfare emphasis was health: a large-scale program of reconstruction of hospitals and mental institutions was begun, and state aid for county public health services was greatly increased. Prison reform was also undertaken. Laws to prevent rent-gouging were passed, and other laws were designed to promote construction of housing and slum clearance.

A second major accomplishment of the Smith regime at Albany was reorganization of the state government. Government efficiency had been a favorite theme of Smith's ever since he participated in the New York Constitutional Convention of 1915. When he became governor this became a pet project, and over several years he effected a consolidation of the state bureaus and departments and the adoption of an executive-controlled budget in place of the former legislature-controlled general appropriation bill.

Reorganization of the government permitted Smith to reduce both income and property taxes by 25 percent, in spite of the large welfare expenditures. A major innovation in state financing contributed greatly to the tax reduction: capital improvements such as hospitals and parks were paid for by bond issues instead of by the pay-as-you-go plan formerly used for such projects. This policy, closely akin to the "deficit spending" of the thirties (although it had no anti-depression goals in Smith's day), was strongly defended by the Governor as the application of business principles to government.

With the accomplishment of the major elements in his program for governmental reorganization Smith turned to the problem of water power. Here he met with no success whatsoever beyond the acceptance of the basic principles he advocated. Smith felt that water resources owned by the state —and these included much of the Niagara and St. Lawrence power potential as well as important sites in the Adirondacks —should be developed by the state itself. He would have set up a State Water Power Authority with power to issue bonds, build power plants, and generate electricity; the power was to be distributed by private companies under contracts that would prescribe the rates to be charged. This policy was opposed by the Republicans: they wanted the power sites leased to private companies for periods up to 50 years, with annual rentals to be paid to the state; at the expiration of the lease the properties were to revert to the state, subject to payment to the private company for improvements. The issue was clear: public vs. private enterprise.

Because the fight over water power policy was taken up by Roosevelt when he became governor and his statements on the problem represent an important element in his economic thought, it is worth while to chronicle some of the major events that took place in Smith's terms as governor in the development of the State's water power policy. A State Water Power Commission had been created by the Republican administration of 1921-22, empowered to grant 50-year leases to private companies for the development of power sites, but with Smith's return to the governorship in 1923 no action was taken. Then in 1926 Smith pushed through the legislature a bill creating a new Water Power and Control Commission, with two of the three members to be appointed by the Governor and with authority to issue licenses only with his approval. This new legislation was to become effective on the first of January, 1927.

In the meantime two things happened. Smith made the development of water power by a state authority the major issue of the 1926 gubernatorial campaign and was elected by a large majority. And two private companies applied for licenses to develop the vast power resources of the St. Lawrence River—just before the powers of the Republican-dominated Water Power Commission to grant those licenses were to expire. The final hearing on the applications was to be held less than a month before the new legislation was to take effect.

Smith looked upon this as a deliberate flouting of the will of the electorate, and telegraphed the chairman of the Water Power Commission to use his influence to prevent issuance of the licenses. Upon the chairman's refusal, Smith engaged Samuel Untermeyer as special counsel—the State Attorney General was a Republican member of the Commission—and on the day of the hearing Smith informed the commissioners that, in Untermeyer's opinion, the licenses were illegal. This was probably true, because various obscure clauses in the applications made them, in effect, 50-year options, and the Commission was empowered to grant leases only. At the last moment the applications were withdrawn and the whole matter was dropped.[28] This was the situation that Roosevelt inherited when he was elected Governor in 1928.

Roosevelt had been a strong supporter of Smith and his program for many years. In 1918, when Smith needed support from upstate Democrats to obtain the gubernatorial nomination, F.D.R. came out strongly for him and expressed confidence that Smith would bring a "liberal and progressive" administration to the state.[29] Then, in 1920 F.D.R. was one of the seconding speakers for Smith's presidential nomination, with the nominations eventually going to Cox and Roosevelt. In 1922 he supported Smith for the governorship of New

York as a man with a truly democratic attitude and a "true understanding of the needs and desires of the average American" who had consistently supported laws "aimed to meet new conditions and a higher standard of living."[30] In 1924 Roosevelt was floor manager of Smith's unsuccessful bid for the Democratic presidential nomination and made the nominating speech in which he characterized Smith as the "happy warrior." He wrote with the highest praise of Smith's "comprehensive program for social and human welfare" and his progressivism.[31] In 1928 he refused to permit his own nomination for the presidency[32] and again acted as Smith's floor manager and nominated him again. As Mrs. Roosevelt pointed out:

Franklin and I had long supported Governor Smith politically because of his social program; we believed that he wanted the welfare of the average man and woman.[33]

Not only was Roosevelt one of Smith's leading supporters, but the two men were close friends. The break between them did not come until Roosevelt was Governor, although as early as 1928 F.D.R. disapproved of the appointment of John J. Raskob as Chairman of the Democratic National Committee. This attempt on the part of Smith to placate business interests was a mistake in Roosevelt's eyes, and represented the first serious disagreement between them.[34] But in spite of his feelings that Smith had made serious mistakes in his campaign, F.D.R. consented to run for the governorship of New York on Smith's personal plea that it was necessary if Smith was to carry the state in the election.

Roosevelt's support of Smith and of the growing use of governmental power in New York to promote public welfare was expressed in a series of newspaper columns written for the Beacon (N.Y.) *Standard* following Smith's nomination for the presidency in 1928. They fully supported the welfare legislation of New York and Smith's stand on the power issue. On August 23 he wrote about the development of state parks and parkways. Roosevelt, who was chairman of the

Taconic State Park Commission, defended the development of state parks against property owners whose land was taken:

Most of us can recognize the disturbed feelings of the owners of costly estates who are horrified at the invasion of their privacy by the multitudes who will use a new parkway cutting directly through their lands, but in the final analysis there seems to be no question that the fight will be won by the multitudes, because more and more we are, as a nation, working for the greatest good of the greatest number.

It is all very well to talk of the sanctity of private property, yet since the earliest days our institutions have recognized the right of eminent domain "on behalf of citizens where the taking of privately owned property will benefit the body of citizens." [35]

Turning next to the tariff, F.D.R. pointed out that the Democrats did not advocate any substantial change in tariff policy, but would revive the Tariff Commission and eliminate favoritism for special interests.[36]

Two columns were devoted to agricultural problems. Roosevelt called attention to the serious problems that had been afflicting the farmer in the postwar period, especially the problem of surplus crops. He pointed out that President Coolidge had vetoed the two McNary-Haugen Bills, which were the first comprehensive attempts to solve the problem of surpluses that had passed Congress, and that candidate Smith had promised to take some kind of action to meet the problem on the basis of recommendations by a body of experts. F.D.R. said that Hoover's promise of higher tariffs on agricultural imports would hardly touch the problem, since the tariff is ineffective on commodities for which there is an exportable surplus. He supported the basic demand of all the farm lobbies—the demand for complete economic equality of agriculture that was behind farm legislation both under Hoover and under Roosevelt as president.[37] These columns showed Roosevelt to be well acquainted with the agitation for farm relief and the major possibilities for legislation that had received substantial support up to that time.

The column devoted to water power development supported

fully the position of Alfred E. Smith. The government should, through a government-owned corporation or authority, construct power plants and generate electricity, selling the power to private companies for distribution. This plan was proposed for government-owned power sites at Muscle Shoals and Boulder Canyon, and was contrasted with the Republican belief in private power development with public utility regulation to protect the public.[38] Roosevelt expressed the basic issue in broad terms:

In the final analysis the same difference between two schools of thought applies to the problem of the development of our natural resources. These resources both above and below ground are the common heritage of the people of the United States. They need to be developed and at the same time we must prevent them from being wasted. Many of the resources, such as our timber supply, are being exhausted. It is certainly a very necessary part of the function of our government to see that the use of these resources shall be allowed only for the best interests of the population as a whole and that no private individuals should be allowed to make huge profits at the expense of the great mass of ultimate consumers.[39]

Roosevelt's support of Smith indicates that he had accepted, in his own thinking, a positive role for the Federal government in promoting the general welfare. This view contrasted with the ideas of Thomas Jefferson, whom Roosevelt professed to follow. Jefferson was opposed to extension of the powers of the Federal government and believed strongly that the proper locus of political power was local government. Both Roosevelt and Jefferson may have believed in control of government by a broad electorate and no special privileges for the wealthy, but Roosevelt was willing to use "Hamiltonian" means to achieve the "Jeffersonian" ends he believed in.

Use of Federal powers on behalf of the common man—a viewpoint characteristic of progressivism and the Wilson administration—was a response to the complexities of the modern urban-industrial world. Roosevelt stated as much when he keynoted the New York State Democratic Convention in 1926, pointing out that "the march of modern civilization

brings forward new problems for solution and new possibilities
for the greater happiness of human beings." He continued:

If we accept the phrase "the best government is the least government" we must understand that it applies to the simplification of
governmental machinery, and to the prevention of improper inter-
ference with the legitimate private acts of the citizens, but a nation
or a state which is unwilling by governmental action to tackle the
new problems, caused by immense increase of population and by
the astounding strides of modern science, is headed for decline and
ultimate death from inaction.[40]

As an illustration of Roosevelt's view of the proper role of
the Federal government—and the contrast with the views of
Coolidge and Hoover—the case of the Mississippi River floods
of 1927 is illuminating. The floods of that year were especially bad and a great deal of relief work was necessary. President Coolidge was satisfied that Federal responsibility ended
with Army rebuilding of broken dikes, that Red Cross relief
and local and state governments could take care of the victims,
and that local banks could provide capital for rebuilding.
Secretary of Commerce Hoover took charge of the relief work,
which was privately financed. Roosevelt, on the other hand,
thought that stronger measures were needed. He demanded
a special session of Congress to pass flood relief legislation:
he wanted special relief funds to be appropriated by Congress,
loan funds for reconstruction, a debt moratorium in the affected areas, and an easy lending program by the Federal
Farm Loan Banks.[41]

Roosevelt's view of the proper role of government was made
fully clear when he became Governor of New York. Government was "something more than a necessary evil," it was "an
agency first to protect society and then to promote and guide
all the people into better ways of living." [42] The great achievement of the Democratic party in New York, he said, was

the realization of the greatly changed relationship between government and the people; the understanding of the real duties of the
government to be the servant and not the master of its citizens;
to pension its aged, to provide compensation for its injured toilers;

to construct great hospitals for its sick; to modernize its unspeakable prisons; to adopt the modern penal theory of parole and probation whenever possible; to develop its vast water power as a State resource for the primary benefit of the citizens of the State.[43]

New York's welfare program was, in Roosevelt's eyes, the modern embodiment of the Jeffersonian tradition. When as Governor he was faced with a Republican majority in the legislature, which, because of the election district set-up, actually represented a minority of the voters and continually obstructed the program on which he had been elected, he said:

It is the same old conflict which Thomas Jefferson faced. Jefferson believed in human rights above property rights, the rights of men above the rights of possessions. Today we have selfish groups which have been able to block much important and human legislation because some employer's pocketbook would be affected if he had to pay a living wage in every instance, or if he had to pay a workman who became ill from some cause associated with the kind of work he was doing.[44]

CHAPTER VII

Interlude: Business Affairs

ROOSEVELT'S BUSINESS AFFAIRS during the twenties are significant for two reasons. First, he took an active part in the trade association movement that was to develop into the N.R.A. of the early New Deal. Second, his attitude toward business was a curious mixture: on the one hand, he insisted that mere profits were not a full justification for business activity, that the businessman must also have the motive of public service; on the other hand, he himself participated in a number of outright speculative and promotional ventures that had little to do with serving the public.

The most significant of F.D.R.'s business affiliations during the twenties was his connection with the American Construction Council.

In 1920 the construction industry in New York City was in very bad odor. Prices were soaring to peaks never before reached, labor unrest was endemic, and there were rumors of graft, monopoly, and racketeering. In particular, high prices of building materials were causing much agitation. The State legislature authorized an investigation headed by Senator Charles C. Lockwood, while in Washington Senator Calder called for a Federal investigation into price-fixing. Attorney General Palmer ordered an inquiry into the subject, as did New York State Attorney General Newton.[1]

The Lockwood Commission blew the lid off, under the direction of anti-trust lawyer Samuel Untermeyer. It showed that builders paid graft to the head of the Building Trades Council, that uncooperative contractors were driven out of business, and that those who remained in business were subject to extortion. Much evidence of price-fixing, combinations of sellers, and excessive profits was found and many indictments under the State and Federal anti-trust laws were handed down. Testimony before the Commission showed that Bethlehem Steel Corporation and United States Steel Corporation forced contractors to deal exclusively through the Iron League Erectors Association, and to erect steel only under open-shop conditions.[2] The investigation continued on into 1921, each week turning up some new fact of graft or corruption.

Aggravating the disclosure of graft and corruption was the great instability in the construction industry that appeared in the immediate postwar period. A sharp decline in building activity occurred concurrently with the Lockwood Commission investigation, a decline that was one of the major factors in the depression of 1920–21. The industry was also troubled by great seasonal instability—little construction work was done during the winter—and local instability—large construction projects in one area with little activity in another. It seemed to Herbert Hoover, then Secretary of Commerce, and his friend from wartime Washington, Franklin D. Roosevelt, that something should be done about this huge but disorganized industry. Together they decided to form the American Construction Council,[3] an organization within the industry designed "to place the construction industry on a high plane of integrity and efficiency and to correlate the efforts toward betterment made by existing agencies through an association dedicated to the improvement of the service which the construction industry renders."[4] The other major objective was:

to stabilize the entire construction industry by eliminating the "peak and valley" conditions, to the advantage of capital, labor, and the public in general.[5]

But above all, the Council had to repair the damage done to the industry by the disclosures of the Lockwood investigation. As F.D.R. put it, "building public confidence in the construction industry is primarily the aim of the American Construction Council," adding that, "if the members of the construction industry are unable to keep their own house in order, an exasperated public will some day regulate their house for them." [6]

The Council was fundamentally an association of trade associations within the building industry, with financial support coming from some 250 trade associations. In the spirit of self-government of industry that was to appear in the N.R.A. legislation of 1933, the construction industry was to remedy its own defects by voluntary action. Although Secretary Hoover was one of the organizers, he felt that the Council should be completely independent of government, and that its policies should originate wholly within the industry, while F.D.R. stated that "it is my desire and the desire of those responsible for the organization of this movement that the construction industry work out its own salvation." [7]

The salvation of the industry was to be found in stabilization to avoid seasonal unemployment and labor migration, a code of ethics for the industry, and a national study of building codes with a view toward standard practice, as well as "promotion of vocational guidance of youth into the trades . . . and gathering of helpful statistics." [8]

F.D.R. put more strongly the job of the Council, at least as he, president of the organization to 1928, saw it:

Muddling through has been the characteristic method employed by the construction industry for the last few years. There has been no system, no cooperation, *no intensive, national planning.*[9]

But what kind of planning did F.D.R. have in mind? Obviously, it was not centrally directed planning by the Federal government, for the whole purpose of the Council was to enable the industry to regulate itself. The planning was to be voluntary cooperation through the Council, which would seek to determine national policy on problems facing the entire industry, with the policies to be voluntarily carried out by the various members of the industry.

For this type of "planning" a certain amount of harmony and agreement on basic principles among the various elements of the industry would be necessary. That a fundamental harmony of interests prevailed was one of the basic assumptions of those who organized the Council, F.D.R. stating that

We represent a get-together movement in the three great divisions of the Construction Industry: those who plan and design; those who transform the paper drawings into actual structures; and those who furnish the materials.... A closer relationship between these elements would result in a better understanding and a cooperation which would eventually benefit the public by reducing building costs in many indirect ways.[10]

That the cooperation necessary for voluntary "planning" of the type contemplated by F.D.R. was difficult to achieve in the construction industry should have been evident from the results of the Lockwood investigation. In 1925 F.D.R. was still trying to convince certain parts of the industry of the need for cooperation. Writing to the executive director of the American Institute of Steel Construction, he said:

I am more and more convinced of the need for cooperation in the whole construction industry.... In the old days there was too much tendency to feel, for instance, that those interested in steel construction were necessarily antagonistic to those interested in wood construction; that brick manufacturers are merely rivals of the cement makers. Today, however, we know that in construction as in so many other human activities, what makes for the good of one is apt to make, also for the good of others.

The American Construction Council seeks to bring together these component parts of a great whole..., and to bring about cooperation towards ends which will serve the industry as a whole.[11]

F.D.R. believed strongly that there was a harmony of interests among individuals, especially when their vital interests were concerned. In spite of "jealousies" and "points of friction" he expected that in the construction industry "we would all become, as far as possible, one happy family." [12]

The type of "planning" actually engaged in by the Council is exemplified by the recommendations made by it in May, 1923. Feeling that speculative building was reaching a dangerous level, it recommended that "banking interests curtail the financing of speculative building until after the close of the summer," that governments should "delay their [construction] work as much as possible until September or October," and that publicity be given to rising construction costs.[13]

This action came a week after Secretary of Commerce Hoover had written President Harding suggesting that the Federal government should not expand its construction activity at that time: the industry was fully employed and Federal construction would displace resources used by private enterprise rather than add to employment and production.[14]

The attempt to publicize the proper action to be taken by the industry as a whole did not meet with unanimous support. The *Manufacturer's Record* attacked the Council's recommendations editorially and its editor wrote to F.D.R. that "organizations should not undertake to direct action of individual members" and that "for an organization such as yours to urge that no new work should be begun for 90 days is merely a strike of capital against labor and materials."[15] Roosevelt answered with a diatribe against one of his favorite targets, the philosophy of rugged individualism:

I fear that you deliberately insist that no organization of individuals, whether of capital or labor or both combined, should ever suggest a course of action to its individual members.   Yours is a creed of "every man for himself and the devil take the hindmost ...."   It is perfectly clear that some self-seeking interests have deliberately and maliciously distorted the recommendations of the Council in order to serve their own immediate purpose—in other words, to make the biggest possible profits while the going is good—another case of "the devil take the hindmost," of "after me the deluge."

F.D.R. went on to say that inflation and depression can be eliminated "only by collective action and by the education of the public" and that "correct public information will, by and large, bring about a more continued prosperity than the old system of infectious buying followed by infectious panics."[16]

In spite of the objections raised by *Manufacturer's Record*, F.D.R. felt that the policy of publicity was successful:

As a result of our widely publicized statements the public "took stock," eliminated speculative building to a large extent, put off unnecessary building, and as a result the raw materials and labor situation have been improved.[17]

Whether or not the statements of the Council were instrumental in reducing speculative building is doubtful, but the use of publicity was the essential tool in the system of voluntary "planning" envisaged by the group.

In addition to publicity emanating from the Council's board of governors, annual meetings were held, at which a number of speakers discoursed on some of the industry's major problems. Some of the major subjects of discussion at the meetings during the years of F.D.R.'s presidency of the council were "Better Building," "Elimination of Construction Peaks and Depressions," "Apprenticeship in the Building Trades," and "Fundamental Relationships Pertaining to Building Construction." It was hoped that industry-wide policy could develop from these discussions plus committee reports, but nothing of the sort developed.[18]

The American Construction Council was an intermediate stage in the development of the trade association idea that culminated in the N.R.A. legislation of 1933. With the publication in 1912 of J. A. Eddy's *The New Competition*, which advocated "open prices" known to all sellers as well as buyers, trade associations began providing all kinds of information to their members, looking toward a reduction of price competition. This developed into a program for trade-practice agreements in each industry drawn up by the trade associations, which were to be autonomous and self-regulating and led by public-spirited business leaders. This policy, backed by Secretary of Commerce Hoover,[19] was greatly weakened by an adverse opinion by the Attorney General, who felt that the codes violated the anti-trust laws. But the Chamber of Commerce of the United States took up the idea during the early thirties, advocating them as a means of reducing cutthroat competition and as an aid to recovery. This proposal, with modifications, became one of the elements that went into the N.R.A.

The American Construction Council represents a middle

stage in this development, seeking to obtain concerted action on a voluntary basis to meet problems of the industry. It may be regarded as a forerunner of the N.R.A. and the philosophy expressed by F.D.R. in his speech at San Francisco in the 1932 presidential campaign, in which he called upon "the responsible heads of finance and industry" to "work together to achieve the common end," while at the same time reserving to the government the right "to apply restraint" to "protect the public interest." [20]

The basic idea behind the American Construction Council was that there was a large area within which business firms could cooperate without injuring the public or violating the anti-trust laws. It paid little attention to prices charged by individual sellers, and did not take steps to reduce competition. It represented the less dangerous type of trade association than those which sought to achieve collusive action. It concerned itself with the cyclical behavior of the industry, building codes, apprenticeship, public confidence, better building, and so forth. "Our aim is solely to further the Public Good," said F.D.R.[21] This type of "self-government" has little in common with the restriction of competition usually associated with trade associations and codes of fair practice. That it might develop into the restrictionism typified by the N.R.A. codes was not anticipated by Roosevelt.

Roosevelt was aware that his trade association activities toward "self-government in industry" might fall afoul of the anti-trust laws. After pointing out the desirability of creating "one happy family" in the industry, he said:

There are, of course, a good many difficulties in the way, including the United States Government and the Department of Justice.[22]

Nevertheless, F.D.R.'s belief that industry's basic responsibility to the public could be discharged by development of trade associations led by public-spirited citizens was part of the orthodox economic thought of the twenties. His position was supported, for instance, by one of the most popular textbooks on the problem of monopoly then in use. Seager and Gulick had this to say about trade associations:

Trade associations ... are contributing in many branches of industry to efficiency, economy, and improved relations and standards among the groups affected. The demonstration they have afforded of the extent to which cooperation among competing business men may be carried on to their advantage and without disadvantage to the public has contributed more than anything else to a better understanding of the combination and monopoly problem.[23]

Seager and Gulick echo Roosevelt's attitude. If it was subject to perversions inconsistent with the public welfare it was certainly consistent with F.D.R.'s belief that business enterprise must have a goal beyond profits, the goal of social responsibility. Public service and public welfare were as important as, if not more important than, profits. F.D.R. had little sympathy with those businessmen who thought that the seeking for wealth was the only justification necessary for business activity.

Roosevelt could afford to hold the belief that public service was important in business. He had inherited properties worth about $100,000 upon his father's death, the annual income from which was about $5,000. Eleanor Roosevelt had inherited a similar amount when she was a child, and prudent management of her estate brought the annual income up to about $7,500. Then, in 1927 F.D.R. inherited $100,000 from his half-brother, James, who had married the sister of John Jacob Astor. We can reasonably suppose that this inheritance also brought in about $5,000 annually. All of this wealth was invested in bonds.[24] Thus, the Roosevelts had an annual income from inheritances of about $12,500 until 1927, and about $17,500 after 1927.

During the twenties F.D.R. turned his attention toward business affairs more than at any other period of his life. He held no public office from 1921 through 1928, and, in spite of infantile paralysis and the political affairs that were his major concern, he attempted to add what he could to the family wealth.

Law practice did not bring in much income. After he left the Navy Department in 1921, F.D.R. formed with two friends the firm of Emmet, Marvin and Roosevelt. His illness prevented his doing much law work, and he left the firm in 1925 to form Roosevelt and O'Connor, another law partnership. His annual income from the new firm was about $1,500. F.D.R. managed to make that much, also, as referee in a suit between the Village of Larchmont, N.Y., and the New York, New Haven and Hartford Railroad in 1925.

At the same time he was dabbling in law practice, F.D.R. took a job with the Fidelity and Deposit Company of Baltimore, a surety bonding company, as vice-president in charge of its New York office. His salary was $25,000 a year. Van Lear Black, president of the company and a friend of Roosevelt's, was a prominent Maryland Democrat; he wanted to offer F.D.R. a haven during the lean years out of office and preserve him for future political campaigns. At the same time the company would obtain the advantages of the Roosevelt name and F.D.R.'s New York connections. F.D.R. took an active part in the operation of the New York office until his attack of infantile paralysis in the fall of 1921. He continued in this position until 1928, with Louis Howe taking care of most of the essential business of the office after Roosevelt's illness. In February, 1928, Roosevelt became General Vice-President, a title that was largely honorary: both he and Howe were relieved of responsibility for the New York office and could devote themselves to Al Smith's campaign for the presidency.[25] Whether it was because of F.D.R.'s business ability, or his contacts, or the Roosevelt name, or because of the great boom of the twenties, the business of the New York office was greatly increased under his management. He made one important contribution to the company, at least. In 1925-26 the directors were considering entering the business of writing surety bonds to guarantee the interest and principal on loans for new building construction. At the time this seemed almost a no-risk proposition, but Roosevelt opposed it: it would violate the true function of a surety company by, in effect, making it an endorser of notes and mortgages. The directors accepted Roosevelt's judgment, which the depression only five years later proved to be sound when principal and interest on loans on even first-class buildings began to be defaulted.[26]

Because Roosevelt had an income from his inheritance he was not particularly interested in a moderate but steady return from the new investments he made during the twenties. Instead, he invested in new companies that sought to exploit new products or new devices—and this type of company could produce large returns, or none. Essentially speculative, this aspect of F.D.R.'s business affairs was in harmony with that same element in his nature that enabled him to look with favor on "experimentation" in the political sphere. It was also in harmony with the speculative boom of the twenties.

A number of outright speculations were made by F.D.R. For example, in May, 1923, he invested in the Montacal Oil Company, a wildcat operation described as "the best gamble you could ever take." It owned a small oil well in Montana that paid the expenses of speculative drilling in California and Wyoming fields; the California wells turned out to be unproductive, while the one in Wyoming produced only natural gas, to the great disappointment of all concerned. Nor did the stock and land speculations of the twenties leave F.D.R. untouched. At times he speculated in stocks, and at one time considered a speculative venture into Louisiana rice lands.[27]

More characteristic of F.D.R.'s business ventures were firms that sought to market new services and devices, in which he could invest when the company was young and prospects for rapid growth were good. Typical of such enterprises was the American Investigation Corporation, formed in 1922 to investigate the feasibility of air transport by dirigible. F.D.R. was vice-president and a member of the board of directors, as well as a stockholder. He felt then that commercial dirigible lines, rather than the airplane, were the type of air transport that would succeed, and at the same time he wanted to develop aeronautics for national defense.[28] The company had good prospects: its financial backing was of the best, for Owen D. Young (President of General Electric and R.C.A.) and Arthur V. Davis (President of Aluminum Company of America) were behind it, and its stockholders included Marshall Field, Philip N. Wrigley, R. B. Mellon, W. L. Mellon, L. C. Hanna, Jr., W. E. Boeing, and Cecil B. DeMille; it acquired American rights to the basic patents for rigid airships; and F.D.R., as former Assistant Secretary of the Navy, was just the man to help it obtain government aid in the form of use of hangars and landing fields, experts and technical knowledge, and supplies of helium from the government monopoly. The whole plan, however, depended on aid from the government, which was not forthcoming, and the company sold out in 1924 to Airways Corporation of America. The latter company proposed a grandiose scheme of transcontinental and trans-Atlantic dirigible lines which came to nothing.[29]

A more successful venture was Photomaton, Incorporated. This company manufactured and rented automatic photographic slot machines that took eight pictures and delivered the developed strip in eight minutes; it also operated a number of stores of its own. The Morgenthaus were interested in the company and F.D.R. joined them early in 1927 and was elected a director. The new machines proved very popular and in a year were installed in eighty locations throughout the country. The Morgenthaus and F.D.R. sold out late in 1928, and F.D.R. received $17 per share for the stock he had purchased at $3.00.[30] This was one of F.D.R.'s few successful ventures.

A similar company was Sanitary Postage Service Corporation, which owned and rented stamp vending machines. F.D.R. was a stockholder and a member of the board of directors beginning in January, 1927. The company at this time was much interested in expanding into the general field of automatic vending machines, and merged in June, 1928, with several other companies in that field to form Consolidated Automatic Merchandising Corporation, of which F.D.R. was briefly a director until he became Governor of New York. Automatic vending machines were something of a novelty in the late twenties and the company was widely heralded as inaugurating the "automatic age in merchandising" when United Cigar Stores opened a completely automatic outlet on Times Square in New York City. This spectacular promotional scheme was typical of Consolidated Automatic Merchandising, which was one of the many holding companies of the twenties that were based largely on prospects for the future and were developed primarily for financeering profits. Its promises of vast profits remained only promises and it failed in the thirties.[31]

One of Roosevelt's ventures led him into the field of international finance. Many Americans invested in German marks in the early twenties, expecting the currency to rise in value as Germany recovered from World War I. Instead came the drastic inflation of 1920-23 and the speculators saw the value of this investment dwindling away to nothing. To prevent further losses it was planned to form a company to invest German marks in real assets in Germany—real estate, mortgages, stock in business and commercial enterprises and in financing of goods in transit. United European Investors, Ltd., was formed, with F.D.R. as president with a salary of $10,000 and William Schall, of the investment house of William Schall and Company, as vice-president. The capital stock of the company was purchased with German marks held by Americans and Canadians, and the marks were then invested primarily in common stocks of German manufacturing concerns. The policy of the company was successful and the value of the purchased stocks appreciated slightly more than the mark depreciated. After the new mark was stabilized F.D.R. withdrew from the enterprise, selling his interest to Schall in May, 1926.[32]

The ties with German enterprise led F.D.R. to take part in the organization in 1927 of International Germanic Trust Company, a New York bank designed to facilitate commercial and financial relationships between the United States and Central Europe. Its subsidiary, International Germanic Company, engaged in a banking business in Europe. Although F.D.R. did not take part in the details of organization, he did own shares in the company and was a member of the board of directors. Basil O'Connor, law partner of F.D.R., felt that his connection with the banking concern was a political liability, and F.D.R. agreed: he resigned as a director in February, 1928.[33]

One of F.D.R.'s most interesting ventures in international finance never materialized. Together with Georges St. Jean he attempted to organize the Federal International Investment Trust, which was to sell stock to banks and invest the funds in stocks of foreign banks. These investment relationships would be used to facilitate American foreign trade by making it possible for foreign firms buying American goods to pay for them by selling securities in the United States. The process would have worked somewhat as follows:

An American exporter would sell goods to a European buyer. The buyer would then issue long-term securities equal in amount to the value of the goods he purchased. The securities were to be guaranteed by a European bank in which Federal International Investment Trust had a stock interest, and then sold to the Trust, which would pay the American exporter. The Trust would then issue its own bonds, backed by the securities of the European firm, and sell them to the public. The net result would be that the European firm would have its goods, the American exporter would be paid, and the American public would have financed the deal by purchasing bonds of the Trust, backed by long-term securities of European business firms. This ingenious idea, broached in 1928, was designed to avoid the decline in United States foreign trade that F.D.R. felt would result from high tariffs and the inability of foreign firms to obtain dollars by selling

here. Instead of selling goods they would sell securities.[34]
Fundamentally the same mechanism, but substituting governments for banks, is the foundation of the International Bank
for Reconstruction and Development.

Although there was a speculative and experimental basis
for these business ventures of F.D.R.'s, there was also another aspect: Roosevelt usually kept in mind the usefulness of
the venture to the public at large. He did not lose sight of
the goal of public service that he so often spoke about in connection with his political career.

With some of Roosevelt's business interests the public service aspects were primary. For example, in 1926 he bought a
farm of 1,750 acres three miles south of Warm Springs,
Georgia. There, in order to show the local farmers that cotton
was not the only cash crop they could grow, he raised cattle
for market, refusing to allow his foreman to grow cotton.[35]

The Compo Thrift Bond Corporation was one of Roosevelt's
business ventures that had a social purpose. Organized in
1922, it was to furnish Thrift Bonds to banks. The bonds,
bearing 3½ percent compound interest, were to be sold to
savers and were to be redeemable upon sixty days notice.
Maturing after 20 years, they would be worth double the
purchase price. The purpose was to encourage thrift. Compo
Clubs were organized, mainly in the offices of business firms,
with the members making weekly deposits toward the purchase of Thrift Bonds. The broader social purpose of the
company, along with its profit possibilities, is illustrated by a
statement by F.D.R.:

I feel very strongly that this company is on the right track and
that it will not only prove a stimulus to saving on the part of the
public in general, but that it is a mighty good proposition for the
banks which handle it.[36]

F.D.R. was a director of the company from its beginning
until April, 1923, when he resigned because he thought its
business might conflict with that of Fidelity and Deposit
Company, since the Compo Thrift Bond Company was enter-

ing the business of issuing bonds to guarantee corporate financing. This, F.D.R. felt, would conflict with the surety business of Fidelity and Deposit, and "it would be highly unethical for me to retain a connection as Director in another company which carried on even a remotely similar business." [37]

Roosevelt invested in several other financial enterprises that had purposes broader than profits. He became a member of the board of directors of American Bankers Corporation in 1922—the promoters wanted a big name on the board—and got 250 shares of common stock for his services. The company was designed as an investment organ for local banks throughout the country: it would finance large loans and the small banks would each take part of them. Democracy in banking was the appeal. F.D.R. did not take an active part in the affairs of the company; he resigned in 1923 and returned his stock when he felt the company was mismanaged. The firm went bankrupt shortly after.[38]

A similar enterprise, which did not get beyond the project stage, was the proposed General Trust Company. Its stock was to have been owned by local banks, while the company would operate in New York. It would give out-of-town banks an opportunity to take advantage of financial opportunities that might be known or available to New York banks only. Roosevelt was to have been a director, largely as window dressing. He thought highly of the idea.[39]

In addition to business enterprises of a speculative nature and those which combined profits with public service, Roosevelt made several investments that were simply for business purposes. In 1922 he bought control of Witham Brothers, Inc., a Maine lobster fishery on Penobscot Bay that supplied some of the leading hotels and restaurants in the East, including the Statler chain. The company was substantially expanded and placed temporarily on a paying basis under F.D.R.'s control, but mismanagement eventually cost the company heavily, and it went bankrupt in 1924, with F.D.R. a substantial loser.[40]

Then, in 1922-23, Roosevelt seriously considered establishing an intercoastal steamship line, notwithstanding a current rate war that was driving five of the lines then doing business to the wall. To F.D.R. the rate war meant not that there was too much shipping capacity in the trade, but

First, there is a lot of money to be made in the coast to coast shipping game, and secondly, there is a cut-throat crowd out to "hog" the whole business and eliminate competition.[41]

He considered buying into one of the existing lines in order to get good will and shipping contracts, but finally decided that "in spite of increasing freight there will be only room in the long run for four or five strong lines." [42]

Other enterprises that were discussed but not implemented were a chain of resort hotels in the South based on F.D.R.'s Warm Springs development, and a company to develop the resources of Haiti—cotton, coffee, and lumber.

F.D.R.'s experiences in the business world were partly stamped by his own personality, and partly a product of the major trends then current. Roosevelt saw business as another area in which the ideal of public service could be achieved. He tried to be a public-spirited businessman, one who obtained income from business enterprise, but who saw that profit was not an end in itself. At the same time he was a participant in the developing trade association movement and was affected by the speculative-promotional fever of business in the twenties. If he had any doubts that his speculative and trade association activities might be inimical to the public interest he gave no sign of them.

CHAPTER VIII

The Campaign of 1928

IN 1928 a reluctant Roosevelt was nominated for the governorship of New York by a Democratic party eager to carry the state for Smith in the presidential election.

The Republican nominee was Albert Ottinger, who had been State Attorney General since 1924 under Governor Smith. A popular vote-getter, Ottinger had a record of prosecutions of loan sharks, crooked stock brokers, profiteers, and unscrupulous businessmen. The Republicans claimed that he had aided labor by his administration of the workmen's compensation law, and helped veterans by his vigilant administration of the soldiers' bonus law. Ottinger promised that if elected the real property tax would be reduced and the state income tax would be abolished. He would end the policy of spending adopted by Smith and substitute a policy of saving, but he did accept the bond issue method of financing state improvements. He promised aid to the farmer and stated his friendliness toward labor. Ottinger's record on water power development was opposed to that of Smith. He had always stood for private development of power sites, and as Attorney General was an ex-officio member of the State Water Power Commission that had aroused Smith's ire in 1926 when it seemed as if the valuable St. Lawrence River power sites were to be leased to private companies. In the 1928 campaign he promised to appoint a board of experts to draw up a plan for water power development under which "the State's ownership of these great material resources shall remain inviolate." [1]

Ottinger's past record had been a conservative one, in opposition to progressivism and reform. He had denounced the progressivism of Theodore Roosevelt as leading to "bloodshed, revolution and destruction of government and the constitution itself." His career as State Senator (1916-18) was described by the Citizens' Union as that of a man who "had done much good work" but whose attitude on fundamentals firmly identified him with the "stand-pat group of the Senate." He had also served as Assistant Attorney General under Harding.[2]

Ottinger was handicapped by a state party platform filled with bitter and recriminatory invectives against Democratic "misrule" and "waste and inefficiency" under Smith, and which offered little in the way of a positive program.[3] Another handicap was the presence of Edmund Machold as state chairman of the Republican party. Machold was president of the Northeastern Power Company and author of the Machold Storage Law of 1915, which had provided for leases of power sites to private companies and was the basis of the Republican stand on water power development. It was obvious that water power would be a big issue in the campaign.

The Democratic party in the state adopted a platform that stressed Smith's achievements as governor: construction of hospitals, parks, grade separations and highways, tax reduction, and social and labor legislation. It criticized the Republicans for refusing to legislate a 48-hour week. A list of "pledges" were included, promising to develop and extend the welfare legislation initiated under Smith.[4]

In his acceptance speech Franklin Roosevelt stressed the issues he was to emphasize throughout the campaign: social welfare legislation, state development of water power sites, and aid to agriculture. He clearly stated the philosophy of government responsibility for welfare legislation:

In social legislation, in education, in health, in better housing, in care of the aged, we have gone far, but we must go farther. . . . The strides of science and invention, the shifting of economic balance, the growing feeling of responsibility toward those who need the protection of the State, call for ceaseless improvement to keep up to date those personal relationships of the individual to other individuals and to the whole body politic which we call Government.[5]

Roosevelt began his campaign with a swing through the southern tier of counties north of the Pennsylvania line. At Elmira on October 18 he pledged completion of Smith's "splendid program" and extension of it to meet new needs: "there is more to be done and each year we have got to accomplish a little more to keep up with the times because the times move." [6]

The next day at Salamanca he spoke of the "very critical situation" in agriculture in New York State and promised measures to strengthen the farmer and promote reforestation.[7] In Jamestown that same night Roosevelt explained his stand on the farm problem even further. He pointed out the decline in agriculture which followed World War I and that the major problem—surplus crops—was a national one. To bring the issue home to his listeners he said that farmers of the Middle West, unable to make a go of crop farming, had gone increasingly into dairying, taking markets away from New York dairy farmers, thereby "upsetting our balance." Roosevelt intended to go beyond the Democratic platform promises of a commission of experts to study distribution and adjustment of the farmer's taxes:

I want to see the farmer and his family receive at the end of each year as much for their labor ... as skilled workers under the best conditions in any one of our great industries.[8]

Following up this criticism of the market-price system as a means of allocating farm resources, he advocated a commission to study "the proper use of every acre within the borders of the state." [9]

On the 20th of October at Buffalo, Roosevelt gave his major speech of the campaign on labor legislation. He pledged completion of Smith's labor and welfare program, including an 8-hour day and 48-hour week for women and children in industry. He fully supported the many pledges of improve-

ments in labor and social legislation that were contained in
the party platform.[10]

Three days later Roosevelt spoke on water power at
Syracuse:

This is a history and a sermon on the subject of water power, and
I preach from the Old Testament—the text "thou shalt not steal."

He then detailed Smith's fight for state development of power
sites by a state power authority with distribution by private
companies, and the opposition to this program by the Republicans in the interests of the power companies. F.D.R. pledged
full support for a continuance of Smith's program:

The rights of the people are assailed in this election. Those who
would steal our heritage are within one day of success. I have been
placed by my party on duty as policeman to guard this heritage.[11]

The next night Roosevelt answered Herbert Hoover, who
had denounced Smith's policies as "socialism." Speaking at
Watertown, F.D.R. expressed opposition to any government
conducting any business function which could be better or
equally well handled by private enterprise, but argued that
this did not preclude government enterprise when private
organizations could not do the job as well. As examples he
gave the postal system, parcel post, local waterworks, the Port
of New York Authority, and the city-owned power system in
Watertown itself. The principle of the Port Authority, he
said, could well be applied to other public works.[12]

Returning to New York City, Roosevelt promised to continue Smith's program of state park development and felt
distrust of the Republican pledge to do the same. He spoke
in favor of a fair wages bill for women. Still fighting Hoover's
charge of socialism, he said:

If his [Smith's] program for the public park system is socialistic,
then we are all socialists; and if his program for the reduction of
hours of women and children is socialistic, we are all socialists. If
his program for public improvements for the hospitals of the state
and the prisons of the state is socialistic, we are all socialists. And
if his program for bettering public health in this state and for aid

to the educational program of this state are socialistic, we are socialists.[13]

On October 30 at a luncheon with the leaders of organized labor, Roosevelt spoke of his experiences with labor problems in the Navy Department. Collective bargaining was so successful, he pointed out, that there had been "no strike, no walkout, no serious trouble in all of the Navy Yards all over the United States during that whole period." He added that his policy of using the yards to manufacture products the Navy formerly purchased had stabilized employment. Roosevelt promised to continue Smith's program of labor and social legislation and to advocate further measures, which he did not specify.[14]

Then, on the first of November, speaking at Phillipsburg Hall in Yonkers, Roosevelt gave an explicit statement of his philosophy of politics. He began with a quotation from Herbert Hoover's book, *American Individualism:*

Acts and deeds leading to progress are born of the individual mind, not out of the mind of the crowd. The crowd only feels, it has no mind of its own which can plan. The crowd is credulous, it destroys, it hates and it dreams, but it never builds. It is one of the most profound of exact psychological truths that man in the mass does not think, but only feels.

With this Hamiltonian statement as a foil, Roosevelt went on to express his belief that the mass of humanity does think, that it can make up its mind on the pros and cons of all kinds of public questions, that it often originates, and that there is a definite relationship between the crowd and the continuation of progress. He used the state park system as an example: city dwellers came gradually to feel the need of open spaces in the country available to them, this spirit "was communicated to a man at the top who knew public opinion when he saw it, a man who, by the grace of God, was the Governor of this State," and gradually the program for state and county parks grew. Smith's water power policy and social welfare legislation stemmed from the same source, said Roosevelt.

I deny, and the Democratic Party denies, that the average man and woman in this State, who make up its electorate, are incapable of thought or constructive ability.   I know that the electorate does think, that it does originate, and that it does build, and it is on that fundamental belief that I base my campaign for the governorship.[15]

Roosevelt had made a great impression in the campaign. He was aided by the fine record of the Smith administration and the record of blind obstructionism of the Republicans in the State Legislature.   Although Smith failed to carry New York in the presidential race, Roosevelt squeaked into the governorship with a vote of 2,130,193 to Ottinger's 2,104,629.

CHAPTER IX

A Regional Plan for New York State

WHEN Roosevelt was Governor of New York from 1929 through 1932, he developed a program that emphasized especially the betterment of agriculture, reforestation, and development of electric power resources by the state. Although presented to the electorate separately, these major measures, along with a number of lesser ones, actually constituted a great scheme for a regional plan for the state. Roosevelt envisaged a "rural-industrial" society in which every acre was used for the purposes to which it was best suited, in which all areas of the state were served by electric power lines at cheap rates, and in which the State and local governments cooperated to achieve a better life for all through plans developed under the leadership of the state government. Although Roosevelt never publicly announced such goals, they were implicit in the measures he advocated.

Roosevelt looked upon the economic problems of agriculture within a broader framework of the whole rehabilitation of farm life and a reversal of the trend of population to the cities. Feeling that rural life was the real backbone of the nation, he wanted to reverse the decline, not just of farm prices, but of farm life as compared with city life. The means of accomplishing this was to be a comprehensive program of regional planning that involved a partnership of the state with farm cooperatives, farm organizations, and individual farmers.

This viewpoint was clearly stated shortly after Roosevelt took office. Speaking at Cornell University in February, 1930, he outlined his broad program for rural development. The causes of "the relative decline of agricultural prosperity" were several, he said.   First place was given to economic causes: cultivation of "many thousands of acres . . . which are not under modern conditions suitable for agriculture," use of lands "for growing crops unsuited to the particular soil," antiquated marketing procedures, and inequalities in the tax burden. But the social causes of agricultural decline could not be ignored: city life had been made more interesting as compared to that of the country, health care was expensive and medical facilities often inadequate in many rural communities, and the country church was faced with increasing financial difficulties.   Roosevelt felt that a change was coming, however, and he expected a swing back to the country in the near future because

Industrially the United States has made not only the greatest strides in history in this generation, but perhaps has come to the period when industrial expansion will slow up.   In other words, many economists are seriously questioning whether we have not for the time being reached the saturation point of industrial production calling for a period of digestion for a number of years to come.

His "great objective," Roosevelt said, was

the great fundamental of making country life in every way as desirable as city life, an objective which will from the economic side make possible the earning of an adequate compensation and on the social side the enjoyment of all of the necessary advantages which exist today in the cities.

To achieve this goal were needed "better roads, better markets, better schools, better health facilities, better churches, lower rates for electricity, lower rates for telephones."   And not to be forgotten was that "perhaps great betterment can be obtained through the development of the idea of regional planning," a principle which "has already been applied to the milk supply for New York City." [1]

Roosevelt's Cornell speech constituted a fuller explanation of his attitude toward agriculture than had been contained in either his inaugural address or his first message to the

legislature. Those speeches, however, did specify the first
steps to be taken toward the achievement of the broader goals.
In his inaugural address Roosevelt spoke of the "difficult
situation" in which the rural population found itself, saying:

It is time to take practical steps to relieve our farm population
of unequal tax burdens, to install economies in the methods of local
government, to devise sounder marketing to stabilize what has been
too much a speculative industry, and finally to encourage the use
of each acre of our State for the purpose to which it is by nature
most suited.[2]

These measures were spelled out in more detail in Roosevelt's first message to the legislature. He called for an agricultural commission representing the legislature, farmers, the
State College of Agriculture, farm organizations, and farm
cooperatives, which should investigate the use of marginal
land for reforestation projects, the readjustment of the farmer's tax burden, and means of reducing the "unnecessarily
high differential between what the farmer receives and what
the consumer pays." "The ultimate goal is that the farmer
and his family shall be put on the same level of earning
capacity as his fellow American who lives in the city," he
said.[3]

Roosevelt had already taken the first steps in this program
prior to his inauguration. In November, 1928, he had appointed a temporary commission of twenty-one experts to
offer recommendations in the agricultural field. Heading the
commission was Henry Morgenthau, Jr., and one of its members was Professor George F. Warren of the State College of
Agriculture. Designated by F.D.R. as his Agricultural Advisory Commission after he took office, the major recommendations of the group dealt with reductions in the farm tax
burden. It felt that counties should be relieved of paying
35 percent of the cost of constructing state highways and that
the state should assume the full cost of constructing grade
separations and of snow removal from highways. The state
should also make a larger contribution to the construction of

feeder "dirt roads." To provide necessary revenues for the state the commission recommended a tax on gasoline sales. The commission felt that relieving the counties of road expenditures would largely solve the rural school problem by releasing local tax funds for that purpose. Late in January, 1929, the Commission also recommended measures to remedy inequalities of taxation for schools.[4] The Governor transmitted all of these recommendations to the legislature, and since a large majority of the commission were Republicans and the bills would largely benefit the upstate constituents, most of the recommendations were successfully translated into law in 1929.[5] It was the most important series of enactments of farm legislation in decades.

Two more of the commission's recommendations were enacted the following year: a contribution by the state toward snow removal from highways, and a doubled contribution by the state toward the construction and maintenance of dirt roads.[6] The only important recommendation that did not become law was the proposal to establish a state-wide system of regional primary markets of a new type devised by the State Bureau of Markets that were to have facilities for marketing the entire supply of perishable products used by a city and its surrounding territory.[7]

The farm legislation passed in 1929-30 was, in effect, a major revision of the tax burden of the state. The cost of roads and schools, especially in rural areas, was shifted from the local to the state government and the latter obtained much of its revenues from city dwellers. At the same time the abolition of the state property tax shifted the tax burden to the income tax—from property or capital to income—and the gasoline sales tax. Since income taxes could be steeply graduated, the new tax system could more clearly be based on ability to pay. It also could be used to provide government services for general use, with the major costs being borne by persons with large incomes, and was a tool for redistribution of income in favor of the poorer groups in the state. Roosevelt was aware of these implications. Interviewed by a reporter from *The Country Gentleman* about his farm tax legislation, he said:

We should get a larger proportion of our tax revenue from those who can afford it. That may sound radical, but it is only common sense. Under the prevailing system of taxation real property is forced to bear an excessive share. It is actually being taxed out of private ownership on a large scale, as the thousands of tax sales over the country show. Our tax systems need to be brought into line with the facts and conditions of modern life. While real property once represented the chief source of income, today by far the largest percentage of it comes from salaries, commissions, profits, dividends and interest on accumulated wealth. We have come into a time when we shall have to rely less on the physical sources of wealth and more on the proceeds of wealth for our necessary tax revenue.[8]

The first step, then, in the rehabilitation of agriculture was tax revision that reduced the financial burdens of the farmer and made rural communities financially able to develop their governmental services to a greater extent. At the same time, by giving the state government greater responsibility for roads and schools, it made possible the inclusion of those elements of rural life in any system of regional planning that might be developed.

The second major step in Roosevelt's rehabilitation of agriculture was a survey of land usage in the state. This had been recommended by the Agricultural Advisory Commission and the legislature appropriated funds for that purpose. Roosevelt looked upon the soil survey as the first step in working out "a plan for using every acre for the purpose to which that particular acre is best suited."[9] Speaking on the problem at Silver Lake in September, 1929, Roosevelt said that "there are dozens of different kinds of land in the State, and it is not stretching the point to say that a very large percentage of agricultural land is now used for the production of the wrong kind of crop." The soil survey, he added, should go hand in hand with "a complete survey of the climatic conditions of the State" and "an inventory of all of the forest

resources of the State." Land should be classified for agriculture, forest, recreation, and residential purposes and
whether it should be used for orchards, vegetables, forests, or
pastures. A special study should be made of dairying. The
Governor was frank in his advocacy of regional planning:

I have long been interested in the general subject of city and of
regional planning. The present proposed survey of the whole State
is merely an intelligent broadening of the planning which heretofore has been localized. It is a study for a state-wide plan which
will include the use of every acre in the whole State. So far as I
know this is the first time in the United States that the city or
regional plan idea has been extended to take in a whole state.[10]

When a detailed survey of one county, including soil,
climate, land-use, and population had been completed, Roosevelt reported his views on regional planning to the State
Agricultural Society:

This study of Tompkins County includes a classification of the
land in the county into several groups with first-class land that
should always remain in farms at one end of the scale, and land
that clearly should be reforested at the other end of the scale.

A road system to serve the best interests of these areas is projected on a scientific basis. . . .

The plan also includes a location for electric power lines such
as will serve all people of an area and not leave some worthwhile
farms in pockets which can never be economically reached by
electricity. . . .

Hand in hand with this survey there should go a reforestation
program.[11]

Planned distribution of farm products was to supplement
land-use planning. Speaking at the annual farm dinner given
by Jerome D. Barnum, at Syracuse, only three days after his
Silver Lake speech, F.D.R. described the creation of the New
York "milkshed" by the New York City health authorities
and the efforts made by the Dairymen's League to keep milk
and cream production at the quality demanded by the City.
He argued that if all of the major eastern cities followed suit
"the dairy industry throughout the eastern states in a very

few years could automatically be stabilized." The same principle could be applied to vegetables and fruit:

What, for instance, is the economic use in the spectacle in [*sic*] huge dump scows being towed down New York Harbor and out to sea for the purpose of throwing overboard dozens of carloads of cabbages which have come to the New York City market from the eastern and middle western states and in many cases the far western states, all arriving the same day and in such quantities that they could only be consumed if the six million people in New York all decided to eat corned beef and cabbage three meals a day for a week.... The fault lies not with the commission merchants, but with the lack of planning by the communities and the growers as a whole.

This evil could be avoided, insisted Roosevelt, by putting the vegetable supply of the cities of the state "on a state-wide basis" similar to the milkshed arrangement through "cooperation between the city-dwelling public on the one side and the vegetable growing farmers on the other." The same system could be applied to fruit, but in either case there should be no attempt to keep out early or late fruits and vegetables from other parts of the country. The advantages of such a distribution scheme, he said, were numerous: "It will result, in the long run, in a more stabilized price, in the prevention of over-production, in the more permanent employment of labor, in the saving of transportation, duplication and waste, and in a better understanding between the city and farm populations." [12] Throughout this whole address ran the implication that government and cooperative farm associations must work together to achieve the goal, much as had been the case in the dairy industry.

Development of industry in rural areas was to complement efficient use of agricultural land and improved distribution systems. This point was emphasized in a speech made before the 1931 Governors' Conference. Roosevelt pointed out that "in times of booming industry we can overlook defects of organization and danger signals from industry and agriculture, but in times such as the present these symptoms attain a

new importance and show us the urgency of the new problems
we have to face." Among these problems he listed "dis-
location of a proper balance between urban and rural life,"
and proceeded to describe "land utilization and state planning"
in New York in terms of the development of a rural-industrial
type of society. The retirement of submarginal lands from
cultivation, which was part of the plan, was making a population group available for industrial employment:

> As a nation we have only begun to scratch the surface along
> these lines and the possibility of diversifying our industrial life by
> sending a fair proportion of it into the rural districts is one of the
> definite possibilities of the future. Cheap electric power, good
> roads and automobiles make such a rural industrial development
> possible. . . .
> It is for these reasons that I have spoken of a third and new
> type of American life. The rural industrial group. It is my thought
> that many of the problems of transportation, of overcrowded cities,
> of high cost of living, of a better balance of population as a whole
> can be solved by the states themselves during the coming generation.

Development of power resources, especially those of the St.
Lawrence River, he said, was an integral part of a system of
"state planning"—"a permanent program both social and
economic and statewide in its objectives." [13]

In Roosevelt's program for efficient land use a major element was retirement of marginal farm lands from production
and the use of such lands for reforestation projects. As he
had repeatedly pointed out, and as the soil survey indicated,
much of this land should not have been cultivated in the first
place. By taking it out of cultivation the production of in-
ferior crops would be reduced and they would no longer tend
to drag down farm prices; at the same time, a timber crop
could be developed and the problems of flood control and
water supply would be eased. When the argument was put in
this fashion there was not much that could be said against
such a proposal, and it was the logical place to begin the
planned use of land resources.

The reforestation program was pushed concurrently with

tax relief and the land survey. In the 1929 session of the legislature two bills to promote reforestation were passed. The first provided that the state could acquire through the Conservation Department tracts of 500 acres or more to be reforested by the state. The second enabled county boards of supervisors to acquire land in their county for reforestation purposes; if the acquisition were approved by the Conservation Department the state would match county funds, up to a maximum contribution of $5,000 in any one year in any one county.[14] To provide funds for reforestation a constitutional amendment authorizing a bond issue of $19 million was proposed, ratified by two successive legislatures and submitted to the electorate as a referendum in the 1931 general elections.

This so-called Hewitt amendment provided that the state acquire for reforestation about a million acres of abandoned farm lands. It made mandatory a schedule of appropriations beginning at $1 million in 1932, increasing $200,000 a year until $2 million was reached in 1937, and continuing at that rate for five additional years. The reason that the appropriation was put in the form of a constitutional amendment rather than legislative enactments was to insure a continuing program that would enable long-range plans to be made. The amendment provided that all lands acquired within the boundaries of the Adirondack and Catskill forest preserves would remain as untouched forest, while other lands would be developed as tree plantations and operated under a cropping system. Above all, it was to be a continuing, state-wide program of planned use of land that would utilize for a cash crop lands that were abandoned or about to be abandoned, protect the state's watersheds, and provide areas for hunting, fishing, and other recreational uses.[15]

The Hewitt amendment received support from both parties as well as from agricultural and sportsmen's organizations. Opposition came from *The Rural New Yorker*, chief rival of Henry Morgenthau's *American Agriculturist*, and, most surprisingly, from former Governor Alfred E. Smith. Smith argued that the amendment would put the state into the lumber business in competition with private enterprise, that it opened the way to future invasion of the Adirondack and Catskill forest preserves, and that it was a mistake to add things that were not fundamental to the State Constitution.[16] Smith was answered by Gifford Pinchot, Republican Governor of Pennsylvania, who pointed out that "putting the state into the lumber business" was an essential and inescapable part of forestry, that the forest preserves would be fully protected, and that a constitutional amendment was the only way purchase of the lands could be assured.[17] Roosevelt repeated these arguments in a radio address to the people of the state, in which he did not refer to Smith by name, but spoke on the issues. The amendment was carried by a large vote.[18]

With tax relief for the farmer an accomplished fact, and the soil survey and reforestation of marginal lands under way, Roosevelt next turned to problems of marketing. In a special message to the legislature in January, 1932, he urged diversion of a portion of the state highway funds for the immediate construction of farm-to-market roads. There were only 12,000 miles of concrete main highways in the state, he said, in contrast to 82,000 miles of secondary and tertiary roads, of which 70,000 miles were dirt roads. Many of the latter were almost impassable during the winter and in rainy weather, causing the cost of transportation of farm products to the markets to be unnecessarily high.

I believe that as the next logical step the State should proceed at its own expense and through its own Department of Public Works, to the construction of demonstration farm-to-market roads in each county of the State. In this way not only would many miles of improved roads be made available to the farmers of the State, but the State would furnish a practical example to follow.... [19]

With this, the road-building aspects of regional planning for New York were initiated.

Roosevelt's attempt to develop regional planning in New

York was not something that his agricultural experts had devised, but stemmed from a firm belief on his part that comprehensive regional planning could eliminate many wastes inherent in unplanned development, and at the same time readjust what he felt to be a serious imbalance between rural and urban life. The record shows that Roosevelt was a strong advocate of regional planning before he assumed the governorship.

As early as 1927 he had called attention to the "mushroom growth of many of the country's larger cities without definite and constructive planning" resulting in losses in "the health and convenience of the public as well as property values and economy of time."

This problem is not confined alone to larger centers, but affects every town and village, and intelligent planning on their behalf will prevent in the future for them the unfortunate conditions that are now causing untold waste in our larger cities either through the continuance of bad conditions or the cost of rebuilding. The undirected mushroom growth of our cities and towns must be controlled.[20]

When he became governor Roosevelt spoke glowingly of the possibilities of regional planning for the upper Hudson Valley region "so that in the succeeding generation we shall not regret the structures which we now build." [21]

Speaking before the Regional Plan Association late in 1931, the Governor called attention to the city plan of Chicago. Out of it developed

a new understanding of problems that affect not merely bricks and mortar, subways and streets; planning that affects also the economic and social life of a community, then of a county, then of a state; perhaps the day is not far distant when planning will become a part of the national policy of this country.

The New York milkshed was given as an example of planning, with farm organizations forecasting the demand for milk and helping the farmers adjust production to demand. The same thing, said the Governor, might be done for apples. Roosevelt expressed his advocacy of "total regional planning," not along any rigidly specified lines, but with each area experimenting in the type of planning best suited to it.[22]

Roosevelt's interest in regional planning had been fostered by his uncle, Frederic A. Delano, who had been chairman of the Committee on the Regional Plan for New York (City) and Its Environs. This group had carried out a path-breaking survey of the New York metropolitan area, the results of which were published in an eight-volume analysis.[23] It was through Delano that Roosevelt was asked to write the foreword to a book on planning of cities written by the Committee's general director of plans and surveys. The author suggested that Roosevelt stress the advantages of city planning in promoting health and general welfare, in promoting economy, and in developing a rapprochement between town and country. This the Governor, now President-elect, did, emphasizing that city planning was "among the most important needs of our modern civilization." [24]

It would be interesting to speculate on how Roosevelt's program of regional planning would have developed if he had remained longer in the governorship. The type of planning he envisioned was not centrally controlled, detailed planning. If we are to judge by his many statements, it was to entail cooperation between all levels of government led by the state government at Albany,[25] utilizing the scientific knowledge of the best scholars and practical men in the field. Above all, it was to be voluntary and required general agreement between all interested parties on both the problems to be tackled and solutions for them. Government was to lead, not direct. The planning was also to be comprehensive; that is, it would deal with all facets—social, economic, political, scientific, financial—of any problem tackled. It was to be, in short, the type of planning developed in the Tennessee Valley.

The program developed for New York was primarily land-use planning, but the most important part of it was provision of electric power at low rates, to be accomplished by construction by the state of power plants on the St. Lawrence River and by a revivified program of utility regulation.

In his first inaugural address as Governor, Roosevelt outlined the basis of his power policies:

I should like to state clearly the outstanding features of the problem itself. First, it is agreed, I think, that the water power of the State should belong to all the people.... The title to this power must vest forever in the people of this State.... The legislature in this matter is but the trustee of the people, and it is their solemn duty to administer such heritage so as most greatly to benefit the whole people.

It is also the duty of our legislative bodies to see that this power, which belongs to all the people, is transformed into usable electrical energy and distributed to them at the lowest possible cost. It is our power; and no inordinate profits must be allowed to those who act as the people's agents in bringing this power to their homes and workshops.

The Governor did not lay down any dicta as to the extent of state enterprise in the various parts of the power industry— construction and operation of powerhouses, long-distance transmission lines, and distribution to homes and factories:

How much of this shall be undertaken by the State, how much of this carried out by properly regulated private enterprises, how much of this by some combination of the two, is the practical question that we have before us. And in the consideration of the question I want to warn the people of this State against too hasty assumption that mere regulation by public service commissions is, in itself, a sure guarantee of protection of the interest of the consumer.[26]

The Governor presented his plans for power development in greater detail in a special message to the legislature in March, 1929. He stated that the state should operate power plants at state-owned power sites and again emphasized the problem of how to distribute it, adding that

The actual operation of a transmission or a distribution system in this field of activity should, if possible, with safety to the people, be undertaken by private enterprise, and ... the State should undertake it only if private enterprise proves that it cannot, or will not successfully carry out the task.

But this would raise the question of rate regulation, and Roosevelt did not feel that the Public Service Commission was adequate to the task of protecting the public, because of a "series of court decisions, especially in the Federal Courts" which, through valuation of properties at replacement cost, "have made legally possible investment returns as high as fifty percent or even one hundred percent annually on the original investment." In place of regulation Roosevelt wished to substitute contracts that would specify prices to be charged the consumer.[27]

The Governor then proposed a St. Lawrence Power Development Commission of five members to bring in a complete plan for development of the St. Lawrence River power sites by the state and for distribution by contract with private firms at "the lowest rates to consumers compatible with a fair and reasonable return on actual cash investment." [28] The commission was to report by January 15, 1930, and if the legislature approved, would then proceed to effect the plans.

The legislature, however, refused to pass the bills introduced by the Democrats to create the commission.

In the meantime the power companies were active. Three of the large power systems, encompassing most of the state, were planning to merge into the Niagara-Hudson Power Corporation. The Governor, of course, was concerned: if the state had to bargain with an effective monopoly for distribution of its electric power, what kind of prices would it be able to get for the consumer? Would not the monopoly be able to name its own terms under the fiction of "negotiating" a contract with the State Power Authority? The Governor questioned Attorney General Hamilton Ward on the legality of the merger, but Ward replied that there were no state laws under which it could be held to be illegal.[29]

Unable to take legal action, Roosevelt sought to arouse the public to the danger. Speaking extemporaneously at the dedication of the new Tammany headquarters at Union Square on July 4, 1929, he blasted big business in general and the power companies in particular.

Roosevelt warned that combinations of capital and the alliance between big business and government might make it necessary to proclaim a new Declaration of Independence if dangers to the liberty of the people were to be avoided. The New York *Times* reported parts of the speech as follows:

Governor Roosevelt declared that the vast economic changes through which the country was passing made it necessary to reconsider once more the whole problem of liberty. This problem, he said, assumes new aspects in the light of what has taken place in the economic structure of the nation, aspects which compel the people to see to it that "government and business are kept separate" if the nation's freedom is to be preserved.

The Governor painted the picture of the rise of a new economic feudalism dominating the life of the country. Citizens of the United States may have to don again the liberty caps of their Revolutionary forefathers and fight anew the struggle for independence, the Governor said. He took courage from the fact, however, that this time the struggle could be waged by the ballot instead of by sword and gun....

Governor Roosevelt declared that "it is perfectly possible we are headed for a new kind of rule by others."

"No period in history has been so rich in social and economic changes as those that have taken place in the last twenty-five years," the Governor said. "We may well ask: Are we in danger of a new caveman's club of a feudal system, of the creation in these United States of such a highly centralized industrial control that we may have to bring forth a new Declaration of Independence? "

"It is not that these great industrial and economic mergers are necessarily bad from the economic point of view," the Governor continued, "but the fact is that independence in business is a thing of the past. Can a man today run a drug store, a cigar store, a grocery store as an independent business? "

Roosevelt admitted that "the questions presented by the ever-growing aggregations of capital...may find a natural solution," but warned that this possibility does not eliminate the danger "from the development of a partnership between business and government." The "new tariff bill" was an example of this partnership, and the Governor added:

I want to preach a new doctrine: A complete separation of business and government.

He pointed out that the fight against business influence at
Albany had been made by "Al and me" for ten years and
promised to continue the battle.

Analyzing the process of concentration of capital in the United
States accompanied by a corresponding concentration of power in
the hands of a few persons, the Governor continued:

"This means something pretty serious. It is pretty serious for
any individual to go out against these big combinations. People
hesitate to do so. The intentions of the men working on these
consolidations may be the best. They doubtless think it is for the
best as far as they themselves are concerned. And it is, for them.
But they are becoming increasingly more powerful in the State
and nation, an influence that some day will have to be met. This
will have to be combated just as was the power of the old barons
and the earlier kings, all of whom believed they were conducting
things for the common good. How we shall successfully deal with
these problems will depend on two things: upon the attitude of the
people themselves and on retaining in office people who will look
after the retention of offices in the hands of the people." [30]

Reaction to the speech was immediate. The press services
carried only a meagre note that Roosevelt had spoken about
"industrial feudalism," but Will Rogers mentioned it favorably in his column, and F.D.R. received hundreds of requests
from all parts of the nation for copies of the speech.

The New York *Post* editorialized that Roosevelt "talked a
good deal of unreality" and accused him of "fighting an intellectual sham battle" by "digging up some dangers to our
democracy" which "seem to have singularly little substance
in the life of the nation today." Pointing out that the Governor had been vague in offering remedies for the evils he
presented, it said, "clearer phrases would come from a mind
that was more clear on the question at issue." [31]

The New York *World,* on the other hand, merely com-
mented that "Governor Roosevelt made an address applying
the orthodox principles of the Democratic Party to the new
era of super-trusts in which we are living." [32]

The *New Leader,* which continually criticized Roosevelt
for actions it thought ineffectual, published criticism by

socialist Norman Thomas. He called the speech "senti-
mental" and "muddle-headed," but granted that Roosevelt
was "right in thinking that his scheme of leasing state developed power to private distributing companies won't work
unless there is some competition between the distributing
companies." The only real solution, in Thomas's view, was
complete socialization of the electric power industry from
powerhouse to consumer.[33]

Spokesmen for the power companies were silent.

The furor in New York State over the question of water
power development had begun to attract nation-wide attention. When *The Nation* devoted a full issue to the electric
power problem Samuel I. Rosenman, counsel to the Governor,
was asked to contribute an article on Roosevelt's program.
He outlined it much as Roosevelt had done in his messages to
the legislature: the state was to build and operate power
plants through a board of trustees with power to issue and
sell bonds for that purpose; distribution was to be done by
private utilities under contract; the rates were to provide a
"fair and reasonable return on the actual cost." Rosenman
recognized that the recent merger raised the danger of monopoly in distribution which might hurt the bargaining power
of the state, and this, he said, might force the state into the
business of distribution.[34]

Roosevelt himself contributed an article on the subject to
Forum later in the year. He devoted most of his space to
the inadequacies of utility regulation in protecting the public,
but closed with the proposition that the power resources of
the St. Lawrence River, Muscle Shoals, and Boulder Dam be
developed by either the Federal or state governments "as a
yardstick with which to measure the cost of producing and
transmitting electricity." [35]

Roosevelt's article in *Forum* also indicated that he was
willing to have the state distribute power as well as generate
it. This might well have been necessary in the face of the

Niagara-Hudson merger. But F.D.R. wanted state transmission lines only if private enterprise would not do the job:

First the Power Authority would seek to interest other privately owned companies in providing transmission lines and distributing systems. If this did not succeed the Power Authority could bring in a plan for building its own transmission lines and getting municipalities or local lighting districts to take care of distribution. In any event, either of these alternatives would require legislative sanction.[36]

Governor Roosevelt returned to the battle for his water power program in the 1930 session of the legislature. He renewed his request for establishment of a commission to work up plans for building a dam and powerhouses on the St. Lawrence River by the state, and distribution of the electricity under contract. This time the Republican-dominated legislature was amenable to the Governor's plan: the utilities no longer objected.

This turnabout came as a result of negotiations between Roosevelt and representatives of the power companies. Immediately after the speech of July 4, 1929, Louis McHenry Howe began sounding out "the Morgan people." He discovered that they were perturbed about talk of an anti-trust prosecution under the state laws, and he sought their acquiescence to Roosevelt's program. These preliminaries led to discussions between F.D.R. and Floyd L. Carlisle, board chairman of Niagara-Hudson Power and an old acquaintance of F.D.R.'s, after which Carlisle withdrew his objections and expressed his willingness to cooperate.[37] The utility interests had little to fear: an international treaty would be necessary in order to develop the St. Lawrence, and with a Republican administration in Washington there was little chance for development by a state headed by the leading contender for the next Democratic presidential nomination.

However, the state legislature took prompt action. Bills embodying F.D.R.'s plans were introduced and passed. The St. Lawrence Power Development Commission was set up to report plans for state development of water power on the river, and to work out a contract for sale of the power. The report was to be made by January 15, 1931, and if approved by the legislature a permanent board of trustees would proceed to put the plan into effect. Significantly, the commission was given full latitude in drawing up plans for distribution by contract, through municipalities, or directly to the consumer.

The report of the commission was made to the 1931 session of the legislature. It planned a state power dam on the St. Lawrence with distribution by private firms under contract. If good terms could not be obtained from Niagara-Hudson, "other disposition" of the power was vaguely recommended by the majority, while the minority recommended state sponsorship of a private distribution outlet, or, as a last resort, building of transmission lines by the Power Authority. The legislature accepted these recommendations, but not without some astute political maneuvering by the Governor. A State Power Authority was set up, with power to issue bonds and build dams and powerhouses for the production of electricity. Rates were to be fixed by contract "with any corporation or corporations, whether now existing or to be formed in the future" for transmission and distribution. Finally, if advantageous contracts could not be signed with private firms, the Authority could draw up plans for building its own transmission and distribution systems; before actually building any lines of its own, however, the Authority's plan would have to be approved by the legislature and the Governor.[38]

In spite of all the effort, however, the utilities were the final victor. The Federal government, then negotiating the St. Lawrence treaty with Canada, refused first to reach an agreement with New York State on the ownership of the power resources and then asserted Federal authority over the power sites.[39]

Roosevelt's fight for public power development was based on a desire to provide electricity to rural areas that did not have it and to reduce rates paid by both urban and rural customers. In theory, both of these goals could be obtained by proper regulation of private companies, and Roosevelt predicated his power development program upon the belief that regulation was not adequate to achieve his basic goals. He felt that state enterprise was necessary because regulation of private utilities was inadequate or ineffective.

The Governor was not alone in this belief. Shortly after his inauguaration many complaints were made of the Public Service Commission, especially directed at the chairman, William A. Prendergast, and at George R. VanNamee, a member of the commission. The City Club of New York, the Public Committee on Power in New York, and the New York *World* were most vigorous in leading the criticism. They contended that rates for electricity paid by domestic users were inordinately high when compared with rates charged industrial users, that the Commission had permitted consolidations that gave excessive profits to the promoters, that the companies charged off propaganda to operating expenses, that recent cost-saving innovations had not been passed on to the public in lower rates, and that the Commission lacked aggressiveness in protecting the public. The *World* added a demand for an investigation of the holding companies that the Commission heretofore had ignored.[40]

Commissioner VanNamee, in answering these charges, contended that most of the difficulties in regulation were the fault of the Supreme Court, which had never laid down a sensible definition of the "fair value" on which rates were to be based. He also argued that the Commission was only a fact-finding body that had to be governed by the decisions of the courts.[41] Roosevelt was later to agree fully that much of the blame for inadequate regulation was to be laid upon the courts, but to disagree with the role of the Commission as a fact-finding body.

The charges against the Public Service Commission could not be ignored, and the Governor decided to ask the legislature for a commission to investigate revision of the public service laws of the state. In a special message he asked for a "non-partisan commission to make a thorough study of the whole subject of the public utility field," with special emphasis on the history of regulation in New York and elsewhere and on the "application of the principle of contract approval by a public body as distinguished from straight regulation." [42] On April 16, 1929, both houses of the legislature approved the establishment of a Commission on Revision of the Public Service Commissions Law; it was to have nine members, six from the legislature and three appointed by the Governor.

In a memorandum accompanying his approval of the bill, the Governor indicated what he thought was the proper basis for rate-making:

The theory of twenty years ago that the return to public service corporations should not exceed a fair profit on the money actually invested is constantly and flagrantly violated. Some method must be found to return to the original principle.[43]

Chairman Prendergast disagreed publicly with this view. Speaking at Schenectady less than a month later, he contended that the Supreme Court had decided that the return should be based on used and useful property reckoned at "present-day values." Prendergast supported the principle of reproduction cost of the plant as the proper valuation underlying the rates to be charged:

I do not believe that this question will ever be settled rightly until we find some fair means between the extremists who on one side favor ultra production cost and those who on the other side speak of book cost as if it were a divine command.... The purpose I have sought to achieve at this time is to offer proof that "money actually invested," as stated by Governor Roosevelt, has never been a theory underlying or existent in the Public Service Commission Law of the State of New York.[44]

The lines were clearly drawn for a battle between the adherents of the "reproduction cost" and the "original prudent investment cost" schools of public utility rate-making.

Governor Roosevelt did not reply to Chairman Prendergast

immediately. Instead he began a steady stream of publicity for his side of the case and began gathering facts to support it.

In October he wrote to J. Lionberger Davis, an old friend living in St. Louis:

Have you read the new book by Mosher on Public Utilities? The whole question, in my mind, is as to whether a public utility has the right to make any old profit that it can or not, in other words, as to whether there is any real distinction between a public utility company and a purely private business.

Mosher in his book asks the question along these lines. If a public utility company puts one million dollars into its plant, equipment, etc., raising $750,000 of the sum by issuing six percent bonds, and the other $250,000 by issuing common stock; and then two or three years later they prove that their plant and equipment, because of rises in construction costs, is worth two million dollars, are the common stockholders entitled to reasonable, i.e., eight percent dividends on $250,000 or on $1,250,000. Of course, the poor bond holders get none of the increase and the common stockholders get it all.

Of course, the answer is that 25 years ago when the whole question of public utility regulation came to the front, the basic theory of Governor Charles Evans Hughes and others at that time was that people who invest in public utility common stock should do so with two definite thoughts in mind: first, that through public regulation, cut-throat competition will be eliminated and dividends on their stock will be reasonably assured up to a reasonable amount, i.e., about eight percent; and secondly, that in return for this freedom from cut-throat competition they must not expect to get more than a reasonable return on the investment, and that savings in operating costs and ability to earn more than the eight percent should rightfully come back to the consumers in the form of reduced rates.

We have got a long way from that theory in the past 25 years.[45]

Defending his position in a letter to his uncle, Roosevelt listed the inadequacies he found in public utility regulation:

Nobody claims that government operation with all factors properly balanced is more businesslike than that of a private company, but the fact remains that where there is government operation the household consumer pays less in his monthly bills.... Nobody says that industrial power in New York State, for example, is being sold to the larger consumers at too high a price. The following points, however, are borne out by statistics:

1. There seems to be unnecessary discrimination against the smaller users of industrial power.

2. There is too wide a spread between household rates in different parts of the State.

3. The general profit to the private companies from household rates is too large.

4. Installation charges, especially in the farming districts, are prohibitive.

5. Contracts between household users and private companies cannot be understood even by the best lawyers.

The basic fact remains that the private companies have discriminated against household users of electricity and that publicly owned developments have not, and the further basic fact remains that by one method or another the return to investors in private companies has not been at a "reasonable rate" on the basis of prudent investment.

I hope that some day I can talk over this whole matter with you, for I have read literally hundreds of papers and documents on the whole subject and would love to talk it over with you.[46]

To get evidence to support his contentions Roosevelt asked Louis Howe to have a study made of comparative electric bills in Canada (served by publicly owned systems) and New York. He wanted the evidence: actual bills, or photographic copies of them, paid by small householders, large householders, and small businessmen. He suggested that comparisons be made for Niagara Falls, Ontario, and Niagara Falls, New York; between Toronto and Rochester; between a city at the limit of the Canadian hydroelectric transmission line and a similar city in New York; between the highest rate charged in Ontario and Quebec by a regulated private utility and the highest rate charged in New York.[47]

In an article in *Forum* Roosevelt detailed his criticisms of public utility regulation. He pointed out that public utilities operate under franchises from government for the performance of essential services to the public, and have, therefore, come under regulation. They are protected from competition and in return must provide adequate service and charge reasonable rates. Roosevelt contended that originally the intention was to establish rates which would provide a reasonable return on the actual investment, making allowances for depreciation and operating capital. But this prudent investment theory of rate-making had been lost sight of through vagueness in the laws, adverse legal decisions, and poorly staffed public utility commissions. Instead the utilities pushed, and the courts accepted the reproduction cost theory of rate-making, which, in periods of rising land values and costs, would provide very large profits on the original investment of the owners. Furthermore, mergers and holding companies had expanded stock issues beyond the value of the assets of the utilities: should consumers pay rates high enough to earn dividends on this water? The solution was double-barreled, said Roosevelt: better regulation and government-owned plants to act as a yardstick for the private companies.[48]

Prodding the legislature, Roosevelt told it that

Our antiquated Public Service Commission Law has proved itself unable to cope with the enormous growth and huge consolidations of public utility corporations and it has become evident that new methods of regulation, supervision and administration must be devised.[49]

Prodding Chairman Prendergast of the Public Service Commission, Roosevelt wrote him about the coming hearings on a telephone rate increase, a case in which the Federal courts had recently overruled the Commission and ordered an increase. Roosevelt put him squarely on the spot: the company intended to put the new rates into effect in five days, having the sanction of the court; but Roosevelt asked Prendergast "to resist the taking effect of the new rates" by "firm and aggressive action."[50]

Prendergast resigned in a huff, much to the delight of the Governor, who felt that under him "proper utility regulation was not being carried out."[51] Roosevelt appointed Milo R. Maltbie to succeed him. The Governor defended his position in the conflict with Prendergast, pointing out that it involved a difference of opinion on the basic purposes of the Commission:

In the days of Governor Hughes the Legislature created, to speak for the sovereignty of the people of New York State, the Public Service Commission. And, mind you, here is a distinction which also has been forgotten. In these latter days and in the past few weeks, you have read much about whether the Public Service Commission of this State is a quasi-judicial body. Well, it is not quasi-judicial, or any other kind of judicial. And my friend, my esteemed friend, who stepped out of the chairmanship of the Public Service Commission yesterday, in a speech in Albany the other day, said that it was the function of the Public Service Commission to sit upon a bench and hand out justice on the one side to the people of the State, and on the other side to the utilities; in other words a sort of arbiter between two contesting forces.

Historically, practically, legally and in every other way, Mr. Prendergast was dead wrong. The Public Service Commission is not a quasi-judicial body. The Public Service Commission is the representative of the Legislature, and, back of the Legislature, of the people. It is not dealing between two contestants. It is representing one side, the people of the State, definitely and clearly. And it has one function, not a function to choose between the people and the public utilities, but the sole function, as the representative of the people of this State, to see to it that the utilities do two things—first, give service, and secondly, charge a reasonable rate.[52]

On the same day he had written to Prendergast the Governor asked the legislature for a memorial to Congress asking passage of a law to remove litigation regarding public utility rates from the original jurisdiction of the Federal courts. Calling attention to the telephone rate case, he pointed out that the utilities had by-passed regulation by the Public Service Commission and review by the state courts. Instead, "by a scratch of the pen," hearings and trials of fact were transferred to a master appointed by a Federal court "who is unequipped by experience and training, as well as by staff and assistants, to pursue that searching inquiry into the claims of the company which the consuming public is entitled to demand." The master becomes the rate-maker, not the Commission, he said. In the interests of local self-rule and self-government, Roosevelt wanted the Federal courts to be courts of appeal only.[53]

In February, 1930, the Commission on Revision of the Public Service Commission Law brought in its reports, majority and minority. The six members of the legislature, all Republicans, were the majority; Governor Roosevelt's three appointees—Frank P. Walsh, Professor James C. Bonbright, and David C. Adie—were the minority.

The minority report was drawn up with the full agreement and approval of Governor Roosevelt. His appointees had consulted with him frequently and also with Felix Frankfurter, then teaching at the Harvard Law School. It began by charging that regulation of public utilities in New York State had been a complete failure. The Public Service Commission, designed originally to protect the public interest, had instead assumed a judicial role; it had accepted without question the reproduction cost theory of valuation, and had not seriously attempted to prevent rate increases. On the other hand, the report stated, wherever municipally owned competition existed, rates were lower. The minority report then recommended that "prudent investment cost" be the method of valuation, with each company signing a compulsory contract with the Public Service Commission setting forth the valuation for a period of years. It also urged that a People's Counsel be added to the staff of the Commission, that a better system of uniform accounts be used, and that competition be developed through municipally owned utilities.[54]

The majority report virtually agreed with the minority in that regulation had broken down and that the basic cause was the confused valuation procedure. But its recommendations were much weaker.

The majority recommendations were embodied in over thirty bills introduced into the legislature of which only eight were important. The legislature passed and the Governor signed a bill to give the Public Service Commission authority

over holding companies; a bill changing the method of appeal
from decisions of the Commission; and a bill creating a
Bureau of Valuation and Research. Two bills were mysteri-
ously lost in the closing rush of the final night of the session:
they provided for regulation of private water companies and
for submetering of electricity in large buildings. Three bills
were vetoed by the Governor: one provided a People's Counsel in the office of the Attorney General; F.D.R. vetoed it on
the ground that the Commission itself should act for the
people and such a counsel should be employed by the Commission. The valuation bill was vetoed because it failed to
set up proper standards for valuation and had even then
been watered down when spokesmen for the utilities opposed
it. The contract bill was vetoed because it provided for
voluntary, not compulsory, contracts; the utilities had already let it be known that they would sign valuation contracts
only against their will.[55] The remaining bills stemming from
the majority report and passed by the legislature, twenty in
number, were approved by the Governor. Four bills based
on the minority report were defeated. Governor Roosevelt
remarked, "the mountain labored and brought forth a
mouse." [56]

The following session of the legislature gave no results
whatever. Although Governor Roosevelt asked for enactment of the minority proposals in his annual message on
January 7, 1931, and repeated his request in a special message
on April 10, the Republican-dominated legislature paid no
attention.

In the meantime, however, the Public Service Commission
was acting strongly. For example, on May 1, 1930, it had cut
the rates paid by 900,000 home telephone users, but had
allowed business rates to be increased; the telephone company's valuation was reduced by over $35 million and its
revenue by $900,000. The company was criticized for high
cost operation by Chairman Milo R. Maltbie, into the bargain.
A new day in public utility regulation had come, in spite of

failure of the legislature to enact the changes in the law asked by the Governor.[57]

Roosevelt's power and utilities program earned him the enmity of big business in general and the utility interests in particular. Uneasiness among business circles caused the *Public Utilities Fortnightly* to ask the Governor "whether or not it will be possible for a privately owned public utility to earn a reasonable return on its investment in New York" or whether "it is the real purpose of the present administration there to secure ultimately the whole field of public utility service for governmentally owned plants."

Roosevelt replied strongly. Pointing out that the only alternative to regulation is government ownership, he called on the utilities to be less rapacious—or else:

I am firmly convinced that a proper system of public regulation will not endanger prudent unimpaired investment in public utilities, provided the management is efficient and constructive.

It may be safely asserted that one of the most important causes, if not the prime cause, of the present dissatisfaction with public regulation...is the attempt by those in control of utilities to obtain, not merely a fair return upon prudent unimpaired investment, but profits in excess of such an amount. This is the reason why reproduction cost has been so widely adopted in rate cases by utilities. They have not been content with a fair return upon investment. They have sown the wind; they may reap the whirlwind.

Private management does not have a right to existence in the face of a determination by the public to operate its utilities, but it does have a right...to protection against confiscation directly or indirectly.[58]

Shortly afterwards Roosevelt was attacked by Thomas F. Woodlock, columnist for the *Wall Street Journal,* who charged that the prudent investment theory was "a doctrine condemned alike by the Supreme Court of the United States and by considerations of elementary justice." He argued that in times of rising prices, if the return on capital does not go up the value of the capital is diminished, and this amounted to nothing less than confiscation. The Supreme Court had so held, said Woodlock, and Roosevelt knew it.[59]

A "faithful reader and critical admirer" of Woodlock answered him. Asserting that Governor Roosevelt was fully conversant with the law on this issue, he said that the Governor was appealing to the utilities as a business proposition to be content with a fair return on their prudent investment or else put up with government-operated competition: "Governor Roosevelt does not suggest that the utilities ought to be forced by law to base rates on prudent investment, but he does suggest that they might be forced by competition to get out of business unless they do so." The writer asserted that Roosevelt was no radical, nor was he advocating disobedience to the mandates of the Supreme Court, but that public opinion was a greater court than any. Roosevelt, he said, had not

... indicated his disbelief in capitalistic society or private initiative. On the contrary, he would have capital train itself into better condition by reducing unnecessary profits and improving its relations with the public. His position on public utilities is but a phase of this general viewpoint. Personally, I do not believe that Governor Roosevelt is a red. I do not believe he is even a blushing pink. I believe he has far more regard for capitalistic society than those who would stand idly by and see it commit suicide. I believe that the capitalistic ship of state would be far better in the hands of a skipper such as Roosevelt, who can really see shoals and bars, and fears not to discipline his own crew, than under the leadership of certain political navigators who persist in taking their bearings through rose-colored binoculars.[60]

Criticism from Wall Street balanced the earlier criticism of socialist Norman Thomas, who had written harshly of Roosevelt's Tammany Hall dedication speech in July, 1929, and of Roosevelt's power policies in general.[61] The Governor had replied with surprise:

I am somewhat surprised to learn that you "bitterly attack" my power program. I was under the impression that both you and the party of which you are the acknowledged head in this state were largely in agreement with me as to the need of a better regulation of our public utilities and of the securing of cheaper electrical rates for our people, particularly our householders.[62]

Thomas replied, of course, that his objective was full public ownership of the whole power system.[63]

While Governor Roosevelt was reviving public utility regulation and working toward state development of the St. Lawrence power sites, a similar fight was going on in Washington. Senator Norris had introduced a bill providing for Federal development of Muscle Shoals on the Tennessee River, for power and for production of fertilizers. In 1931 such a bill was passed by both houses of Congress and vetoed by President Hoover, who later termed it a "piece of socialism." [64]　Hoover felt that the proper function of government in the field of public utilities was regulation to protect the public; where power was produced as a by-product of navigation, reclamation, or flood control projects, the power should be sold to private firms for distribution, with regulation of rates and services by public service commissions. He vetoed the Norris Bill because its purpose was to put the government in the electricity and fertilizer business; the power generated at Muscle Shoals was not a by-product but the major purpose of the development. Instead, he asked for a commission to be set up by the states of Alabama and Tennessee to lease the Muscle Shoals properties and he called for construction of Cove Creek Dam (later Norris Dam) for the purpose of flood control.[65]

Roosevelt's position on Muscle Shoals was opposed to Hoover's. Roosevelt favored the Norris Bill and, although he was "definitely keeping out of Federal legislative questions," he let it be known that "Governor Roosevelt heartily approves of the government development of the big plant at Muscle Shoals." [66]

Indeed, the development of the Tennessee Valley under the New Deal may be considered a logical extension of Roosevelt's scheme for regional development in New York State. When he was Governor, F.D.R. dreamed of a rural-industrial society involving decentralization of industry in small cities and towns, to be promoted by development of electric power; rural life was to be improved by good roads and better schools, lower taxes for the farmer, and improvement of facilities for the marketing of his products; and an effort was to be made to rebuild and preserve the state's forests and to rationalize the use of land. In all of this the state government took the lead, but always on the assumption that local governments and individuals would cooperate voluntarily. Indeed, the program could go only as far as local governments and individuals wished. Although only parts of the program were implemented, it was the first attempt at comprehensive regional planning along modern lines by either Federal or state governments. Roosevelt's leadeship in the area of regional planning was one of his most important contributions to the reform philosophy that culminated in the New Deal.

CHAPTER X

Social Welfare Legislation, 1929-1932

GOVERNOR ROOSEVELT'S program of labor and welfare legislation was much less spectacular than his water power fight and considerably less successful than his agricultural program. As in the case of the power policies, Governor Smith had already broken the ground, had made the earlier spectacular advances, and had laid the foundation for the further legislation asked by Roosevelt. Nevertheless, the Republican-dominated legislature remained hard to budge, and Roosevelt asked for considerably more than he got.

One outstanding improvement over the previous administration was the appointment of Frances Perkins [1] as Industrial Commissioner. Under Perkins the work of the Department of Labor was greatly improved, especially in the speed with which claims under the workmen's compensation laws were settled, and she invigorated the drive for better working conditions for which the department was known.

The new Governor's legislative program as it related to labor went beyond not only his predecessor's, but also the party platform and his own campaign promises. In addition to the fulfillment of the pledges contained in the party platform, he asked for "further elimination of unhealthy living conditions in the congested areas" and "declaration by law that the labor of a human being is not a commodity or an article of commerce." [2] Of particular importance to labor was Roosevelt's renewal of the pledge of a law prohibiting the granting of temporary injunctions in labor disputes without notice of a hearing, and provision for jury trial of any alleged violations of such injunctions. Smith had not supported this proposal.

In a special message to the legislature devoted to labor legislation Roosevelt listed the measures that he considered most pressing, saying that "such demands can no longer be regarded other than as matters of an absolute right." They included a fair wage board for women and children, extension of workmen's compensation, the proposals limiting injunctions in labor disputes, legislation providing that labor is not a commodity, and a 48-hour week for women and children in industry.[3] The legislature would have none of this: it adopted two bills extending slightly the list of diseases covered by workmen's compensation, which the Governor signed after castigating the legislature for not making the bills broader,[4] and in another bill it reduced the amount of compensation paid in certain cases, which bill was vetoed by the Governor.

At the next session of the legislature the results were a little better. The Governor repeated his demands of the previous year and added a request for state regulation of private employment agencies.[5] The legislature approved some of the measures, including a bill to provide weekly half-holidays for women, another small increase in the number of diseases covered by workmen's compensation, and the important measure to restrict the use of injunctions in labor disputes.

The contest between the Governor and the legislature continued the following year, with Roosevelt calling for completion of his program and adding an additional request for a special body in the Department of Labor to enforce provisions of the laws relating to wages and hours.[6] The legislature responded by finally enacting a statute providing for an enforceable forty-eight hour week and a weekly half-holiday for working women, and nothing more. With the exception of a bill providing for the eight-hour day and prevailing wage rates on all state highway contracts, and another providing for a five-day week on all state public works, passed during the 1931 extraordinary session of the legislature, nothing else was done to fulfill Roosevelt's program to aid labor with which he began his administration.

In addition to the promotion of legislation favorable to labor, Roosevelt sought to strengthen collective bargaining procedures, particularly in the garment industry in New York City. Governor Smith had appointed an advisory commission in 1924 in an attempt to foster stable employer-employee relationships, but the effort failed in the face of a battle for control of the ladies' garment workers' union by communist and non-communist elements. A disastrous strike in 1926 almost destroyed the union, but after purging itself of communist influence it came back strongly with a short strike in July, 1929. Both the union and the employers' associations then asked Governor Roosevelt's intervention in fostering better relations in the industry.[7] The Governor cooperated by calling a "Cloak and Suit Conference" in New York City on December 12, 1929. The meeting was designed only as an informal discussion that would lead to closer relationships between manufacturers, retailers, and union and nothing specific developed from it.[8] The union then decided on a general strike in the industry to close the remaining sweatshops, beginning on February 4, 1930. The Governor immediately called a conference at Albany between representatives of the union and the employers' associations "in order to facilitate the conclusion of voluntary agreements between the parties." He expressed the hope that they would "work together heartily to bring into the less fair and progressive portions of the industry enlightened and progressive industrial standards."[9] A settlement was effected at this conference which provided for a full-time impartial chairman in the New York dress industry—a model system that remains today as the method used to settle disputes in the industry. But "aside from this the dressmakers gained nothing."[10]

In another branch of the clothing industry Lieutenant Governor Lehman took the initiative in promoting effective bargaining. In the millinery industry both the union and employers asked Lehman to initiate talks to arbitrate issues in dispute between them. This he did. Jules Weil, president of the Cloth, Hat, Cap and Millinery Workers Union, was invited to Albany on October 6, 1931, to promote an agreement to end racketeering in the industry and to develop collective bargaining. Following the meeting Raymond V. Ingersoll was asked to begin conferences between the two parties, with the result that a collective agreement was reached in April, 1932. The workers gained a five-day week and a few minor benefits. The union then struck briefly to organize the non-union shops, and succeeded in increasing both its membership and that of the employers' association.[11]

Thus, in two important branches of the clothing industry in New York City patterns of collective bargaining that were to persist for many years were developed during the Roosevelt governorship with active aid from Albany.[12]

Governor Roosevelt's reputation as a friend of labor, built up by sponsorship of labor legislation and of collective bargaining, was threatened only once. In 1930 the United States Congress passed the Hawes-Cooper Bill, which provided for regulation of prison-made goods sold in interstate commerce. Roosevelt criticized the bill as an unwarranted invasion of states' rights and questioned its constitutionality, only to arouse the ire of William Green, president of the American Federation of Labor. Green pointed out that goods made in New York prisons were not sold on the open market and that prison-made goods from other states were hurting New York labor, and asked that Roosevelt investigate the problem more carefully. Roosevelt retreated. He informed Green that he supported the purposes of the act, but objected to "the growing usurpation of federal privileges at the expense of the states." A few days later he told the State Federation of Labor that his position had been subject to "grotesque misrepresentation," adding:

No one more clearly realizes the evil of competition of prison labor with free labor than I. The best proof of how seriously I regard this matter is that I have added to the State-created Prison Commission a Governor's subcommittee to consider how we may keep our prisoners employed without competing with the labor of our free workmen.... It is almost unnecessary for me to add that I am wholly and irrevocably opposed to letting one state dump its prison-made goods on the free markets of another state.

By October the Governor was admitting even the constitutionality of the Hawes-Cooper Bill, "and I merely raised the point that the proposition ... might have been obtained through state agreements." [13] A few weeks earlier the Governor had appointed a special advisory commission on prison labor to work out plans for New York prisons so that prisoners could be given useful work that would not compete with free labor.[14] What had started out as a political attack on the Hoover administration ended up as an effort to repair Roosevelt's ties with organized labor.

While Governor Roosevelt was seeking to aid labor by passage of the legislation asked for by organized labor and by development of patterns of collective bargaining, he also promoted broader social welfare measures. Chief among these was old age insurance.

Roosevelt had called for a scientific study of the subject during the 1928 campaign. He repeated this demand in his first message to the legislature and called for the creation of a commission of nine members to present recommendations to the legislature.[15] The Governor insisted that "there is nothing socialistic in a program of this kind," and in his message to the legislature requesting the commission he explained the need for such legislation.

New social conditions bring new ideas of social responsibility.... We can no longer be satisfied with the old method of putting them [the aged] away in dismal institutions with the accompanying loss of self-respect, personality and interest in life.

Poverty in old age should not be regarded either as a disgrace or necessarily as a result of lack of thrift or energy. Usually it is a mere by-product of modern industrial life. An alarmingly increasing number of aged persons are becoming dependent on outside help for bare maintenance. While improved medical science has increased man's span of life, the rapid pace of modern industry has proportionately increased the number of years during which he is an unsought employee. . . . No greater tragedy exists in modern civilization than the aged, worn out worker who, after a life of ceaseless effort and useful productivity must look forward for his declining years to a poorhouse.[16]

Specifically, the Governor recommended an insurance system based on contributions by the worker and by the government, and warned against any method that "savors too much of a straight governmental dole." [17]

Several months later F.D.R. stated the principle that welfare legislation was the duty of the state, and that individuals were entitled to benefits as a matter of right, because of their contributions to the community:

There has been also a growing realization on the part of our people that the state itself is under obligations to those who labor, that the citizen who contributes by his toil to the wealth and prosperity of the commonwealth is entitled to certain benefits in return, which only the commonwealth can give. This principle . . . has been, I am proud to say, more clearly recognized, more firmly established in the State of New York than in any other political division of our country.

The time had now come to take one further step, as the state recognizes its obligation to "those . . . who work hard and faithfully through long years, until time lays its heavy hand upon them." [18]

The Commission on Old Age Security was established, with a majority of its members appointed by the Republican legislature, and reported a plan that the Governor could not accept fully. It recommended that the state assume half the cost of the care of needy persons seventy years of age and over, with administration in the hands of county and city governments. Local administration of old age relief was to be reviewed and supervised by the State Department of Social Welfare. It also recommended that institutional care of needy persons be improved. Thus, "outdoor" relief was permissible but not mandatory; it was a plan for relief rather than insurance; and wide variation in local systems was possible.

The recommendations were quickly translated into legisla-

tion. Needy persons seventy years of age or older were eligible
for a county-state pension if they had been citizens and resi-
dents of the state for ten years. The amounts of the pensions
were discretionary with the public welfare boards of the
counties and cities, but were not to exceed $50 per month.
Governor Roosevelt signed the bill reluctantly on April 10,
1930.

Roosevelt felt that the bill was only "an extension and
improvement of the old poor law" and was weakened by local
administration and the lack of provision for equal benefits in
all localities.[19] He was especially critical of the fact that it
was a mere pension, or "dole," and did not promote individual
savings:

The most successful systems are based on what might be called
a series of classes by which a person who has done nothing in his
or her earlier life to save against old age is entitled only to old
age care according to a minimum standard. Opportunity is offered, however, under those systems for wage earners to enter other
classifications, contributing as the years go by towards increased
incomes during their later years. In other words, a definite premium
should be placed on savings, giving to the workers an incentive to
save based on the prospects of not only food and shelter, but on
comfort and higher living standards than the bare minimum. All
of this has been omitted ... yet it is a fundamental principle of
old age security against want unless we are to accept merely a
dole system.[20]

He reported his objections to the people of the state by radio
a week later:

At the head of the list of accomplishments this year I would put
the Old Age Relief Law. . . . The bill, however, does not go as far
as I had hoped, for we must do more than see that old people merely
have food and lodging. I hope that next year the Legislature
will be able to work out a plan under some sort of contributory
system. . . . Furthermore, instead of an arbitrary age limit for the
beginning of relief, we shall probably come to some form of indeter-
minate period based on the actual ability of old people to take care
of themselves. In some cases this is well past seventy and in other
cases the time comes at a much earlier age. . . . [21]

In the 1930 campaign for the governorship F.D.R. outlined the old age security measures he favored.

I look forward to the time when every young man and young woman entering industrial or agricultural or business activity will begin to insure himself or herself against the privations of old age. The premiums which that young man or young girl will pay should be supplemented by premiums to be paid by the employers of the State as well as by the State itself. . . . They will be getting not charity, but the natural profits of their years of labor and insurance.[22]

At the next session of the legislature Governor Roosevelt characterized the old age enactment as "charity" and called for revision: "the next step to be taken should be based on the theory of insurance by a system of contributions commencing at an early age." [23] The legislature, however, failed to take any further action either in the 1931 session or that of the following year, when the Governor repeated his plea.

Governor Roosevelt was even less successful in obtaining unemployment insurance for New York State. The subject was a highly controversial one in those days and Roosevelt had to move cautiously. To illustrate: Frances Perkins advised the Governor that "while speaking upstate, you can safely promise . . . a study of the various systems of unemployment reserves, both public and private," adding, "I think I would go cautiously when talking about unemployment insurance by that name. 'Unemployment reserves' is safer and more educative for the present." [24] Unemployment insurance was not made an important issue in the campaign of 1930, although the Democratic platform pledged a commission to study the problem.

However, F.D.R. did endorse unemployment insurance in a speech at the Governors' Conference held in the summer of 1930, prior to that year's election. He argued that the nation would always have a serious unemployment situation, either actual or potential, unless a scientific and businesslike insurance system was developed. A five-day week, shorter hours, and public building programs would help in a depression emergency, but a permanent solution would lie only in insurance. He noted the various unemployment insurance systems adopted in other nations and declared that "unemployment insurance shall come to this country just as certainly as we have come to workmen's compensation for industrial injury, just as certainly as we are today in the midst of a national wave of insuring against old age want." The solution of the problem, he said, rested with the states and the Federal government, and required a true insurance system on an actuarial basis; it could not be a mere dole that would encourage idleness.[25]

After the 1930 election Roosevelt moved forward toward an unemployment insurance plan. To enlist the cooperation of neighboring states he called a regional Governor's Conference on Unemployment, which met at Albany on January 23-24, 1931.[26]

The conference was devoted not to problems of immediate relief, but to long-range solutions. Leo Wolman spoke on public works as a means of stabilizing business and Aaron Rabinowitz described quasi-public housing projects as part of a stabilization program.[27] But major emphasis was given to unemployment insurance. This part of the program was sparked by Professor Paul H. Douglas, of the University of Chicago, who introduced the subject, wrote memoranda summarizing the various speeches given, and worked out details of an unemployment insurance bill. He vigorously supported unemployment insurance, pointing out that in addition to reducing the relief load it would encourage stabilization by maintaining the income of the unemployed worker and encouraging stabilization measures by private employers, since under Douglas's plan the employer's contribution would vary with the number of unemployed from his firm.[28] Other talks were given on voluntary unemployment insurance plans then in operation, foreign experiences, and the use of the insurance principle.

One result of the conference was formation of an Interstate

Commission on Unemployment Insurance to study the various proposals. Meeting on May 28, 1931, four committees of experts were formed to study the essential features of a sound plan: its cost, European experience, American experience, and proposals for unemployment insurance.[29] The commission's report, made early in 1932, recommended "compulsory establishment of state-wide systems of unemployment reserves." Each employer would contribute 2 percent of his payroll to the reserve for his firm, and his liabilities would not extend beyond this amount. The employer's contribution would be reduced by half when the reserve amounted to $50 per employee and he would make no further contribution when the reserve reached $75 per employee. Employees would make no contributions to the reserves; benefits to them would be $10 per week or half of the weekly wage, whichever was lower, and the maximum benefit period would be 10 weeks in any twelve-month period. The state was to administer the funds. Professor Leiserson added the reservation that a general fund might be better than individual funds for each industrial plant.[30]

In the meantime, Governor Roosevelt had been seriously considering the various proposals. In February, 1931, he wrote to his wife's brother about it:

You have doubtless read that eight or ten of the large manufacturers in Rochester have put an unemployment insurance plan into effect. Yesterday Mr. Ecker, President of the Metropolitan Life, called on me and told me they are ready to go ahead with an experimental unemployment insurance policy, based on different forms of employment.... This shows, to my mind, that we can approach the problem from a businesslike point of view and work into it gradually instead of starting any wholesale plan like that in England.

I still think the employee should contribute something, though my social welfare friends in New York are leaving him out on the theory that it is too conflicting and difficult to put him in and that the administrative cost thereof would be excessive.[31]

A month later Roosevelt asked the legislature to appoint a commission of experts to investigate the subject and report to the 1932 legislature a plan providing a scientific system of unemployment insurance. He said,

Any nation worthy of the name should aim in normal industrial periods to provide employment for every able-bodied citizen willing to work. An enlightened government should look further ahead. It should help its citizens insure themselves during good times against the evil days of hard times to come. The worker, the industry and the State should all assist in making this insurance possible.

But he warned against a dole:

The dole method of relief for unemployment is not only repugnant to all sound principles of social economics, but is contrary to every principle of American citizenship and of sound government. American labor seeks no charity, but only a chance to work for its living. The relief which the workers of the state should be able to anticipate, when engulfed in a period of industrial depression, should be one of insurance, to which they themselves have in a large part contributed.[32]

Instead of an expert commission, the legislature formed a joint legislative committee, with only one appointee by the Governor. At its hearings testimony in opposition to unemployment insurance was heard from both the National Association of Manufacturers and the New York State Federation of Labor.[33] While the legislative committee deliberated, the final report of the Interstate Commission on Unemployment Insurance was made public and Governor Roosevelt transmitted its recommendations to the legislature, asking enactment of its plan. A bill to that effect was introduced in the 1932 legislature, but the Republican leadership would not cooperate. The joint legislative committee recommended postponement of any action, much to the disgust of the Governor's appointee to that committee.[34] Thus, the legislative session of 1932 ended with no action being taken on unemployment insurance.

Roosevelt's program for labor and social welfare legislation was largely unrealized when he left the governorship at the end of 1932. Nevertheless, it bolstered his reputation as a friend of labor, and its accomplishments were not meager. Workmen's compensation was extended somewhat and administration of the law was greatly improved. The forty-eight hour week for women in industry was finally enacted. The use of injunctions in labor disputes was restricted. Efforts to promote collective bargaining were made. And while the old age pension law that was enacted was much less than Roosevelt asked for, and no unemployment insurance law was passed, Roosevelt's advocacy of those two reforms foreshadowed their enactment when he became President. Roosevelt showed as governor that he was a friend of labor and a strong advocate of social insurance.

CHAPTER XI

The Election of 1930

THE ELECTION of 1930 came more than a year after the great stock market crash of 1929, at a time when the nation was faced with the prospect of a winter of increasing unemployment. Nevertheless, neither the Federal government nor any of the states had taken any major steps to provide relief. The depression was still young and few realized its severity.

In New York the first tentative steps to meet the problem had been taken. The Department of Labor had improved the organization of the State Employment Service, beginning even before the stock market break. An important step had been taken in March, 1930, with the appointment by Governor Roosevelt of a Committee on Stabilization of Industry, and through the joint efforts of the Committee and the Department of Labor all but one large industrial city in the state had a local emergency relief committee. Throughout the year 1930 the Department of Public Works had increased its expenditures for hospitals, prisons, highways, and bridges, with the avowed purpose of furnishing emergency employment. But these measures had not made much of a stir: the issues of the 1930 gubernatorial campaign revolved around Roosevelt's program for agriculture, power development, and labor legislation, and around the Republican charge of Tammany corruption.

The Republicans, although they had little hope of victory, nominated Charles H. Tuttle, Federal Attorney for the New York area, who made a major issue of "Roosevelt's subservience to Tammany."[1] There was a certain amount of substance in Tuttle's charge. Roosevelt, who made few tactical errors in politics, had made a serious strategic error in his relationship with Tammany. As soon as he became Governor he sought to mend his political fences with Tammany, and this meant the replacement of the pro-Smith Tammany leaders with men who were at least non-partisan in their relationships with Smith and Roosevelt. John F. Curry became the new Tammany leader, and together with Mayor James Walker of New York City "purged" the organization of the so-called Smith Democrats. Tammany returned to the predatory tactics of old: blatant padding of street-cleaning and sewer construction contracts, granting of a bus franchise to a favored company, secret increases in salaries for public officials, and sale of judgeships to the highest bidder. Although Roosevelt was outwardly neutral in the conflict between the Smith and Walker-Curry forces, he granted patronage to deserving New Yorkers through the Tammany leaders, and thereby strengthened the Walker-Curry group. Some of Roosevelt's appointments to the bench were particularly bad, and can be explained only as attempts to work with the Tammany leaders. Governor Roosevelt's actions might be defended on the grounds that he needed Tammany support for his legislative program. But if so, he could have used his influence to clean up Tammany a little, as Smith did.

F.D.R.'s attempt to use Tammany for his own ends did not succeed. When the scandals came to light just prior to the 1932 nominating conventions, Roosevelt was forced to take action, and Mayor Walker resigned. This earned F.D.R. the enmity of the Tammany leaders, and they went back to their old sweetheart, Al Smith, and supported him for the presidency. At the nominating convention in that year a majority of the New York delegates supported Smith to the bitter end, against their own Governor. But in 1930 Roosevelt was still trying for Tammany support, and this lent substance to Tuttle's charges against him.

The Democratic state convention at Syracuse, held from September 28 to 30, sought to ignore the scandals which were

already coming to light. Senator Robert F. Wagner, in the
keynote address, did ask the party to oust all those who
bought political office, but his main attack was on the Republican administration in Washington: he demanded constructive leadership to solve the problem of unemployment.[2]

The major planks in the party platform pledged creation
of a commission to study unemployment, development of
unemployment exchanges, and unemployment insurance and
employment stabilization; continued development of the
party's program for agriculture; and reform of the public
utility law along the lines asked by the Governor.

Although the Republican candidate began a very vigorous
campaign in which he made over 250 speeches, the response
was poor. The party had no positive program, and relied
almost exclusively on criticism of the Governor. Turnouts at
the Republican rallies were light and the results were obvious
even to the Republicans well in advance of election day: even
the New York *Herald-Tribune* virtually conceded the election
two weeks in advance.[3]

Governor Roosevelt, on the other hand, ran on his record,
and it was a good one. In his acceptance speech he reminded
the voters that in the 1928 campaign he had stood for a continuance of the reforms iniciated by Smith:

My theme then was that progressive government, by its very terms,
must be a living and a growing thing, that the battle for it is never
ending and that if we let up for one single moment or one single
year, not merely do we stand still, but we fall back in the march
of civilization.[4]

Speaking to the people of the state by radio ten days later,
Roosevelt castigated Hoover for "weakness and unwillingness
to look the situation in the face" as unemployment became a
greater and greater problem. He criticized the Federal census
of unemployment for not counting the partially employed,
and recounted the efforts of New York State to meet the
problem: increased expenditures for public works, preference
for state citizens in jobs offered by public works, and the work

of the Commission on Stabilization of Employment. "The State Government," he said, "is doing its best to improve a vastly difficult situation thrown on our door-step by the Republican Administration." [5]

In Buffalo, Roosevelt blamed Hoover for the depression, saying that he had done nothing to curb speculation. He criticized the President for making optimistic statements and doing nothing: "Although the times called for quick and decisive action by the Federal Government, nothing happened but words." Government projects should have been accelerated, said the Governor, especially public works such as roads, river and harbor improvements, hospitals, and public buildings. On the next day, in Rochester, Roosevelt asked improvement in the old age pension law that had been passed by the legislature earlier in the year. At Syracuse he detailed his power development program and showed that users of electricity in Ontario paid considerably less than did users in New York: this he attributed to weak regulation of private companies and the absence of competition from municipally operated plants in New York. Castigating the Republicans for subservience to the utility interests, he spoke at great length to explain in simple terms just how he wanted the state to develop its power resources, ending with a plea that it would not put the state into the power business. At Utica the Governor renewed his demands for labor laws and recounted all those that had been passed in the two sessions of the legislature since the previous election. At Albany he spoke again about improvements in the old age pension law and public utility regulation.[6]

Near the end of the campaign Roosevelt summed up the advances in social welfare legislation in New York State as a great and continuing conflict between "the army of reaction, of do-nothing, of special privilege" and "the army of liberal thought and progressive action." In dramatic terms he listed what he considered to be the important battles already won or in progress: wages and hours legislation and factory laws, better hospital facilities, prison reform, old age security, public utility regulation and public power development, rural tax reform, the multiple dwellings law for crowded cities, state parks, state aid to education, highway construction, and public health facilities.[7] All in all, a series of enactments designed to make the world a better place for the underdog.

Having summed up the achievements of his and Smith's administrations, the Governor turned to the pressing problem of the depression. He told the Advertising Club of New York that in the year since the stock market crash "we have had serious depression in our business and industrial life," but expressed the view that the economy could not go much lower. The major problem of recovery, he said, was one that could not be solved by legislation, by "commission fiat," or by charity; it could be solved only if each individual recognized his own responsibility to do something for recovery. To illustrate, he told how he planned to employ two additional workers on his Hyde Park "farm" that winter, creating jobs for two of the unemployed. Magnify this over the nation, he claimed, and the five million persons out of work could be employed and the economic situation greatly improved.

We need this one good turn to start the wheels moving, this one good turn on the part of those who have the power to do so to make their purchase of labor, of materials, of clothing, of the necessities, even the luxuries of life, now, instead of putting these purchases off until next summer. If these Americans who have the purchasing power will use that power now, we will raise immediately the economic level of the whole population.[8]

If anything, this ineffective "Boy Scout" method of meeting the depression problem was exactly what Roosevelt had criticized Hoover for doing. Immediately after the stock market crash Hoover had conferred with business leaders in an effort to obtain continuation of normal business spending —without great effect.[9] If we wished to be charitable we could consider Roosevelt's speech as an attempt to do something when it promised even the slightest hope of help in an exceedingly difficult situation. This speech does, however, illustrate the ineffectiveness of the philosophy of individual *noblesse oblige* in the face of the grave problems of modern industrial society.

Better answers to the depression problem were on the way, however. In one of the final speeches of the campaign, in Brooklyn on the last day of October, Roosevelt, in outlining his program for the next two years, placed special emphasis on "the problem of unemployment and business depression." Two measures, he hoped, would bring definite results: the study being made by the Committee on Stabilization of Industry, which was investigating employment exchanges, business planning, public works, and unemployment insurance; and continued efforts to reduce the cost of marketing.[10] These proposals, whether effective or not, at least represented effort by the state government to meet the problem, and were in sharp contrast to Roosevelt's *noblesse oblige* speech in New York just four days earlier.

Nothing could illustrate better that Roosevelt stood at a point in history that marked the transition from the philosophy of individualistic *noblesse oblige* to the philosophy of the welfare state than these two speeches. The first was clearly of the old tradition—and Roosevelt sincerely believed it. He was brought up in that tradition, he was educated in it. The second was in the newer tradition of the welfare state —and Roosevelt believed in it, too. But as has already been pointed out, the major difference between the two was one of method: the goal—a better life for the average person—was the same.

At any rate, Roosevelt won a tremendous victory, with 1,769,200 votes to Tuttle's 1,044,093. The margin of over 700,000 votes made him the logical Democratic presidential candidate for 1932.

CHAPTER XII

Depression Relief, 1929-1932

THE HOOVER ADMINISTRATION in Washington was not prepared for the depression and when it came was unable to foresee its severity. In this it was joined by practically all professional economists and forecasters.

What Hoover feared more than anything else was a financial crisis following the stock market crash. Most of the things he did in the first months of the depression were designed to avert such a calamity: this is the explanation for his series of moderately optimistic public statements that seem now to have been foolishness. What he was trying to do was avert the fear and pessimism that could lead to a financial panic and a great deepening of the depression. Thus, on October 25, 1929, he refused to comment on the stock market, but said, "The fundamental business of the country, that is, production and distribution, is on a sound and prosperous basis," while Treasury officials minimized the crash as being "the result of undue speculation." [1] In an effort to maintain the confidence of business and financial leaders, a series of conferences were held at the White House in November. The railroad presidents pledged continuance of normal maintenance and construction work; to a gathering that included the biggest names in American industry the President spoke of the seriousness of the situation, and asked that wages be maintained, that construction work be continued, and that the work week be reduced—all in an effort to cushion the shock; the construction and public utility industries were asked to cooperate and all but Samuel Insull agreed. A conference with labor leaders obtained the withdrawal of some demands for wage increases, and a conference of farm leaders expressed approval of these steps.[2] At the same time the Federal government increased its expenditures for public works for the coming year, and the governors of all states were asked to do the same.[3] In the meantime, the Federal Reserve authorities attempted to relieve the credit shortage by substantial open market purchases.

When the immediate danger to the financial institutions of the country seemed to have been averted, Hoover turned to the problem of unemployment relief. In October Hoover announced the formation of the President's Emergency Relief Organization to aid in the formation of local relief committees and to coordinate their activities. It was designed to use local and state resources for relief, in accord with Hoover's philosophy:

The basis of successful relief in national distress is to mobilize and organize the infinite number of agencies of self help in the community.... But after and coincidentally with voluntary relief, our American system requires that municipal, county, and state governments shall use their own resources and credit before seeking such assistance from the Federal Treasury.... I am willing to pledge myself that if the time should ever come that the voluntary agencies of the country, together with the local and state governments are unable to find resources with which to prevent hunger and suffering in my country, I will ask aid of every resource of the Federal Government.[4]

The day when voluntary and state-local relief funds became inadequate was not far off. In February, 1932, the Federal Farm Board began distributing through the Red Cross the supplies of surplus commodities it had accumulated, and in May of that year the Reconstruction Finance Corporation began to make loans to states unable to provide relief funds themselves.

In the meantime, expansion of public works continued, but only by dribbles. In the three years from 1930 to 1933 Federal expenditures on public works were increased only from $410,420,000 to $717,260,000, at a time when there was agitation for expenditures as high as $5 billion.[5] Hoover did not want money spent on unproductive public works; instead he wanted money spent on income-producing projects. To this end he asked in May, 1932, that authority be given the R.F.C. to lend up to $3 billion to state and local governments and to private business for work-producing construction projects that would bring in revenues with which to repay the loans.[6]

Laudable as it was to provide relief and increase public works and construction expenditures, Hoover reduced the effectiveness of these measures by trying to balance the budget. He sought reductions in government expenditures and increases in taxes, which fortunately were resisted by an "obstructionist" Congress. It was the President's belief that a primary necessity for recovery was the balanced budget that would promote confidence in the government. But a balanced budget would neither promote nor retard recovery and it was a futile gesture at a time when other of Hoover's policies sought to foster recovery by expanding Federal expenditures. All in all, the Federal debt increased by almost $3,500,000,000 during the Hoover administration—much against the President's will.

Finally came the financial crisis of 1931. Starting in June in central Europe, it spread rapidly, and Britain was forced off the gold standard in September. Seeking to alleviate the crisis, Hoover suggested a moratorium on intergovernmental debts, which was finally accepted by the governments involved on July 5.[7] He also proposed an international "standstill agreement" on short-term bank bills that was adopted later in the month.[8] To meet the crisis at home the President urged the formation of a series of government-sponsored credit institutions—the Reconstruction Finance Corporation to make loans to banks, railroads, and "public bodies"; Home Loan Banks to provide mortgage credit; Agricultural Credit Banks to make loans on crops and livestock; expansion of the Federal Land Banks; and other legislation to ease credit. And again the Federal Reserve System was attempting to promote easier credit.[9]

While all this was going on in Washington, what did the Governor of New York have to say? During the campaign of 1930 he criticized the President for not taking decisive action immediately after the 1929 crash, but did not specify what should have been done. He criticized the President for not expanding public works enough. Above all, there ran the thread of criticism that Hoover had dumped the problem on the laps of the states and avoided the responsibilities of the Federal government. It was the same disagreement over the functions of the Federal government that had cropped up in the 1927 Mississippi flood disaster.

But while Roosevelt criticized Hoover's relief policies, those adopted in New York State were similar in many respects to those adopted in Washington. Roosevelt sought to rely upon local relief facilities, and it was not until they were exhausted that the state provided relief on a substantial scale. Concurrently with the relief program went expansion of public works by the state and encouragement of public works by county and local governments. And Governor Roosevelt also attempted to reduce non-relief state expenditures and increase taxes, although he did not advocate a balanced budget as strongly as did Hoover.

In his second message to the legislature on the first of January, 1930, Roosevelt did not mention the rising unemployment in New York State. But by the end of March he had appointed a Committee on Stabilization of Industry to develop "a long time program for industrial stabilization and prevention of unemployment."

We do not expect miracles, but rather to assist the employers of this State in a gradual progress toward stabilization based on authentic American business experience and arising out of and adapted to their own industrial problem, and such methods as their good will and sound business judgment may develop.[10]

The Governor had clarified the problems to be worked out by the Committee in listing the major types of unemployment they had to consider: seasonal, technological, and cyclical.[11]

The Committee's work, however, was expected to have little

relevance to the immediate unemployment relief problem, so the Governor urged all local officials to take needed action. He outlined what he thought was necessary:

Collection of local statistics of unemployment.
Cooperation between local governments and private philanthropies.
Stimulation of "small job campaigns in every city and town ... so that the modicum of unemployment relief can be furnished locally."
Establishment of local employment clearing houses.
Expansion of local public works.

In addition, he wanted local committees to plan methods of stimulating local trade and industry, and full cooperation from industrialists in keeping their factories "operating at full or nearly full time throughout this crisis." [12]

Within a month the Committee on Stabilization of Industry made its preliminary report.[13] It recommended several emergency measures to employers, including retention of as many workers as possible, a speeding of maintenance and repair work, manufacturing for inventory "to the limit of academic wisdom," and a reduction of the work week. When workers had to be laid off the committee recommended keeping those with dependents as long as possible, payment of a "dismissal wage," and aid in finding employment elsewhere. For a long-range program the committee had little to offer: it suggested that the state and local governments postpone public works during prosperous times, holding them back until a depression came.[14]

It is clear that the measures proposed by the Governor and his stabilization committee were emergency measures designed to meet a temporary need only. Reliance on local officials and private businessmen, together with no planning of a comprehensive state-sponsored program of relief or employment, indicated that both the committee and the Governor expected the emergency to be of short duration. But as the emergency deepened during the summer and it became evident that the winter of 1930–31 would be one of great hardship, the attitude of those in charge of the state government shifted.

The Committee on Stabilization of Industry took on the job of coordinating local efforts to promote employment, and, inevitably, local relief efforts. Its report, submitted to the Governor on November 13, 1930, emphasized the immediate problem of how to meet the depression unemployment problem and said very little about long-range plans. The report, even so, left a great deal to be desired. As an indication of the current state of knowledge of the business cycle it reveals more of ignorance than anything else.

The report discussed four types of unemployment: "seasonal, cyclical, technological, and chronic." The most important type, according to the committee was the first:

> Seasonal unemployment seems to be the principal single cause of the total volume and is occasioned either by uneven purchasing by ultimate consumers or by weather conditions which affect production.... Fluctuations in industries producing consumers' goods create irregular demand for raw materials and spread seasonal unemployment through the textile, leather and other industries.
>
> Most of these irregularities can be traced back to changes in the weather....

Having found the culprit, the committee proceeded to examine the other types of unemployment. Regarding the business cycle it said:

> Despite the large amount of research into the nature of the business cycle, causes of depression and boom are complex, changing and accidental, and have not been any more definitely isolated than have the causes of cancer. We do, however, know far more about ways in which we might lessen the severity of these cyclical swings than we put into effect.

The committee felt that technological unemployment had been exaggerated, but caused suffering which must be mitigated. Chronic unemployment was attributed to maintenance by business firms of a labor reserve to meet their peak demands, and could be avoided by better organization of the labor market.[15]

Recognizing that "during periods of cyclical unemployment individual firms are to a large degree helpless to overcome the numerous factors that create depression" and that "the ultimate control of the business cycle is . . . a long way off," the committee pointed out that

The State and municipal governments are not as helpless in these emergencies as are private industries. They can time their public works so that an appreciable volume of additional work can be undertaken as private business slackens.

Another suggestion was for private firms to time their long-range construction projects to take advantage of low labor and material costs during depressions, and, during depressions, to reduce the work week rather than lay off part of the labor force. The committee was not very hopeful, however: "Cyclical fluctuations may be lessened in part by an intelligent public works policy, but their control lies outside the power of State and federal agencies." [16]

With this as background, the committee made its recommendations. The major stress lay on measures to be taken by private business to reduce seasonal unemployment and technological unemployment. It also advised extension of the state unemployment service, organization of local committees to promote employment, and share-the-work plans in industry. For the long run it wanted a state planning board to coordinate public works expenditures at all levels of government and to accelerate such expenditures during depressions, and it wanted industry to develop unemployment insurance plans. Finally, it sought "full and impartial investigation of this question," obviously realizing that its efforts were inadequate.[17]

The report of the committee was the signal for action to meet relief needs for the coming winter. The Governor made available National Guard and Naval Militia armories, with cots and blankets, for the housing of the unemployed and homeless, notifying all mayors and village presidents that "this use could occur only after the ordinary facilities of your locality have been exhausted." [18] The Committee on Stabilization of Industry was reappointed as an emergency commission to coordinate and encourage employment of persons out of work, to encourage the establishment of loan funds for the unemployed, and to coordinate local relief work,[19] and the membership of the committee was increased to include persons concerned with charity and relief. At the same time Roosevelt asked Lieutenant Governor Lehman "to act as a committee of one to survey and speed up as far as possible all of the public works of the State" so that "we can find ways economically to employ several thousand additional men during the winter months."[20] The Governor also wrote the chairman of his stabilization committee suggesting schemes to set up loan funds for the unemployed.[21]

Thus, in the second winter of the depression New York State relied primarily upon local relief facilities to meet the distress of the unemployed.

The only major effort of the state was in the area of expanded public works, but even that could not be maintained. In 1930 the Department of Public Works spent or obligated itself to spend $117,634,159,[22] which represented a substantial increase over 1929. The expenditures were increased to $131,-232,609 the following year,[23] but in the face of reduced tax revenues were cut by the legislature in 1932 to only $85,383,-431.[24] The major reductions were in highway and public building construction. The Governor sought to have the legislature restore the cuts, pointing out that 13,345 men would lose their jobs. As F.D.R. put it:

While the State should economize in unessential public works which do not give immediate, direct employment to large numbers of men, nevertheless it is incumbent on us to continue essential public works, especially where they do provide direct wages for many unemployed and simultaneously are a real economic and social asset to the State.[25]

Roosevelt's plea was in vain, however, and in one of the worst stages of the depression New York curtailed its expenditures.

The state could well have afforded much larger public works expenditures. Although tax revenues were falling, the State Comptroller reported that "at the present time, New York State's credit is higher than that of any other government in the world" and that the state could easily sell more than $30 million worth of bonds. The bonds could even be paid off within five years by higher income and inheritance taxes, thereby placing the relief burden on those best able to pay, he added.[26]

The Governor, however, had not fully accepted the principles of deficit financing. He did not ask for a bond issue to finance public works, but he did ask for one to finance relief.

By the close of 1930 it had become obvious that the depression was going to be longer and deeper than anyone had suspected. The relief efforts of local governments, coordinated by the state and supplemented by increased expenditures for public works, were not going to be enough to meet the problems of the continuing emergency. The stabilization committee was now the Governor's Commission on Unemployment Problems, and had given up all pretense of seeking long-range solutions and was concentrating on the problem of emergency relief. In January, 1931, it reported to the Governor on the status of local relief efforts: the report showed that in almost half of the cities of the state relief facilities were inadequate, that there was great variation in the quality of relief offered, and that, in general, administration of relief was inefficient. The report pointed out that most local relief administrations had old-fashioned conceptions of their duties and that standards almost everywhere were too low. Physical and mental health, earning power, and morale were beginning to deteriorate. The Commission concluded that more work relief rather than home relief was needed, along with better administration and coordination; it also asked for further expansion of public works projects.[27]

There were no changes in policy, however, until the fall of 1931, when it became obvious that local relief would not be sufficient to carry the load of what loomed as one of the most miserable winters in the history of the state. The State Board of Social Welfare and the State Charities Aid Association, in a joint report to the Governor, pointed out that in-

dividual savings and credit and assistance from relatives had
largely been exhausted as a cushion against want, and that
almost every city in the state had spent as much for relief in
the first half of 1931 as in the whole of 1930. Equally large
expenditures were expected in the second half of the year, yet
all the evidence pointed to the inadequacy of relief already
granted.[28] From New York City, the director of the Welfare
Council described an equally desperate situation, and asked
the Governor to call a special session of the legislature to
consider the problem.[29]

The Governor took up the suggestion and a special session
of the legislature met on August 25, 1931.[30] Roosevelt recommended five bills to the legislature. The first authorized a
Temporary Emergency Relief Administration of three members, serving without pay, and appropriated $20 million for
relief. The money was to be spent by the T.E.R.A. for work
relief during the winter months, either directly or through
local governments. If work projects could not be developed,
direct relief could be granted. The second increased the income tax by 50 percent for all income brackets. The third
authorized cities and counties to issue 3-year bonds for relief
and public works expenditures. The fourth provided for a
five-day week in all contracts for state or municipal public
works. The fifth provided that of the $20 million relief ap-
propriation a total of $548,000 be used to pay a soldiers'
bonus. After some resistance from the Republican-dominated legislature, the Wicks Bill, embodying the Governor's
program, was passed. New York became the first state to set
up a comprehensive state-administered relief system for the
unemployed.[31]

It quickly became clear, however, that a $20 million ap-
propriation would not last long. By the time the legislature
convened for its regular session in January, 1932, the Governor had to ask for an immediate appropriation of $5 million
more and approval of a bond issue of $30 million for sub-
mission to the voters in the 1932 election. Because tax

revenues could no longer support the relief needs of the state, and because of the seriousness of the situation, the Governor was willing to depart from his pay-as-you-go policy. Thus New York State adopted deficit financing not as a calculated policy to minimize the depression, but was forced into it against the will of the Governor and the legislature. It was a last resort in a worsening situation.[32]

Indeed, .n its broader aspects the policies of the state regarding depression relief represented drift—or if you wish, experimentation—rather than mastery. At first the state government sought to meet the depression emergency by coordinating the relief efforts of local governments and private charities, with some supplementary aid in the form of increased public works expenditures. When local efforts proved to be inadequate as the depression deepened, the state government took over the responsibility for relief, at first on a pay-as-you-go basis and later by means of a bond issue. The older ideal of local responsibility gave way to state responsibility in the face of the necessities of the situation.

On the national scene a similar shift was taking place. Hoover had placed responsibility for depression relief on the states, and when state resources were in danger of exhaustion, promoted the program of R.F.C. loans to states for work projects. Hoover thereby began the shift to Federal responsibility for relief that culminated in the New Deal's Federal Emergency Relief Administration.

CHAPTER XIII

Bank Failures, 1929-1932

WHILE RELIEF for the unemployed was the most important immediate problem of the depression facing Governor Roosevelt—and his policies evolved pragmatically as the nature of the situation changed—he also had to handle the problem of bank failures and their impact on the community. A number of large banks failed, involving the deposits of millions of small savers and thrift account holders: the City Trust Company failed in New York City early in 1929, the private bank of Clarke Brothers failed in Brooklyn a little later, and the Bank of the United States followed suit late in 1930, closely followed by New York's Chelsea Bank and the Binghamton State Bank.

In dealing with the problem of bank failures Roosevelt showed an inconsistency and vacillation that was quite unexpected from one who was the heir of the progressive tradition and the formulator of a state welfare and development program. In particular, his failure vigorously to push proposals to require that commercial banks treat thrift accounts in the same manner as savings banks handled savings accounts is difficult to reconcile with his concern for the welfare of the common man. The objections made by the bankers should not have deterred him from action to protect the small depositor.

The reason for Roosevelt's difficulty in handling the banking problem is not hard to find: his father was a banker, as was his favorite uncle, Frederic A. Delano; he himself had substantial experience as a financier, and had numerous personal relations with bankers. Under the circumstances it is not hard to understand why he did not take a particularly hostile attitude toward bankers, why he generally assumed them to be honest men of good will—in spite of such tirades as his Tammany Hall speech of July 4, 1929. Nevertheless, by the time of the 1932 election Roosevelt's attitude had changed and the inconsistencies of his position had been resolved as he worked through the necessities of the problem itself, and his views on banking were one with his other views on economic problems. An examination of the change in Roosevelt's policy toward the banks will tell us much about the way his economic thought developed within the context of a changing problem.

Shortly after Roosevelt assumed office the City Trust Company of New York closed its doors, beginning a political scandal of importance and starting the new administration on reform of the state banking laws. The City Trust Company was largely the creation of Francesco Ferrari, who came to America in 1912 and became a private banker dealing largely with the Italian-American population in New York City. In 1925 he organized the Harlem Bank of Commerce and became its president, and also became vice-president and later president of the Atlantic State Bank of Brooklyn; in 1928 these two concerns were merged into the City Trust Company. Upon Ferrari's death on February 1, 1929, rumors of improper use of funds appeared, and ten days later the bank closed its doors.

The State Superintendent of Banks, a Smith appointee named Frank H. Warder, was implicated, having accepted bribes to condone illegal acts and approve a weak financial structure.[1] Warder helped in the organization of a new firm, the Mutual Trust Company, to take over the affairs of the City Trust Company "on condition that the depositors be paid in full," and then resigned.[2] Roosevelt accepted the resignation and expressed approval of the "successful conclusion of the incorporation of the new company."[3]

But on April 22 the District Attorney of New York County

began an investigation of possible criminal activities in connection with the City Trust Company and it became known that Warder was preparing to leave the country.[4] Because the new State Superintendent of Banks, Joseph A. Broderick, did not have subpoena powers to keep Warder from leaving, a Commissioner, with power of subpoena and investigation, was appointed under the Moreland Act. Robert Moses, Secretary of State under Governor Smith, was chosen.[5]

Moses made a thorough investigation and in his report showed that the City Trust Company had built a very weak financial structure, committed illegal acts, and engaged in very bad banking practices, while Warder had accepted bribes from Ferrari on several occasions.[6] The most important aspect of the Moses report, however, was his series of recommendations for improving the performance of the State Banking Department and for revising the Banking Law. He suggested a reorganization of the Department and higher pay for its employees, that officials of the Department be prohibited from owning stocks or bonds in banks under their jurisdiction, that private banks be brought under state jurisdiction and the formation of new private banks be prohibited, that thrift accounts in commercial banks be made subject to the same laws that governed investment of savings bank accounts, that the law regarding the responsibilities of bank officers and directors be revised, and that the Banking Department be required to investigate original capital and increases in capital of banks to see that the capital was actually paid in and not fictitious.[7]

Shortly after the Moses report was submitted, Governor Roosevelt, instead of forwarding its comprehensive proposals for reform to the legislature, appointed a Commission on Revision of the Banking Law, composed of businessmen and bankers, to make recommendations before the next meeting of the legislature in January, 1930. F.D.R. remarked somewhat weakly: "I hope that the Banking Commission will tighten up a bit on the functioning of directors and officers of banks." [8] Yet he had appointed bank directors and officers to recommend the legislation.

Meanwhile, on July 1, 1929, Clarke Brothers, a private bank in Brooklyn, closed its doors. The members of the firm were indicted for using the mails to defraud and for conspiracy to defraud; by August 10 three had been convicted and sentenced to prison terms.

These events led Governor Roosevelt to ask the legislature in January, 1930, to tighten the Banking Law and increase the inspection staff of the Banking Department:

The meshes of the Banking Law have been woven so loosely as to permit the escape of those meanest of all criminals who squander the funds of hundreds of small depositors in reckless speculation for private gain. The entire Banking Law is in need of revision and the Banking Department needs immediately far more adequate inspection facilities.[9]

But no specific legislation was recommended.

Then on January 27 the Commission on the Revision of the Banking Laws made its report. It recommended a number of improvements in the organization of the Banking Department, placing of the employees of the Department under Civil Service, and higher pay for them. It felt that bank charters should not be granted as freely as in the past. The Commission disagreed with Moses's view that the laws regarding the duties and responsibilities of bank officers and directors be tightened up; and it did not desire the elimination of private banks, but rather that they be brought under the jurisdiction of the Banking Department. Most important, on the issue of thrift accounts there was further disagreement with Moses: the Commission did not feel that such funds should be subject to the same regulations as savings accounts, but desired a requirement that a reserve of 3 percent be held against deposits other than demand deposits for all banks not members of the Federal Reserve System.[10]

Legislation embodying the Commission's recommendations was introduced into the legislature, and by April 22 the Gov-

ernor had signed a number of amendments to the Banking
Law, calling them "some of the most necessary, important
and constructive banking legislation proposed in recent
years." [11]   Private banks were brought under the control of
the Banking Department, penalties for a bank that refused
to permit examination were extended, and bank directors were
to be notified by the Banking Department of the results of
examinations.

No effort was made, however, to segregate thrift accounts
in commercial banks.   This proposal had been made in the
Moses resport, but was rejected by the Commission.   Roosevelt at this time followed the lead of the latter group, supporting the relatively slight reforms proposed by the bankers
themselves.   But he changed his view by March of the following year.

The event that caused Roosevelt to change his opinion
about thrift accounts was the failure of the Bank of the United
States on December 11, 1930.   Over half a million depositors
found their savings unavailable when the bank closed its
doors, and there was demand for another Moreland Act investigation.   Depositors who held thrift accounts in commercial banks busied themselves in transferring them to savings banks.[12]   Two other banks closed their doors, the Chelsea
Bank in New York, and the Binghamton State Bank, with
further losses to depositors.

Soon after, on March 24, 1931, Governor Roosevelt asked
the legislature for protection of thrift accounts, arguing that
"in the mind of the average layman . . . there is no nice distinction between thrift accounts and savings accounts" and
that "any further delay is inexcusable, and in my opinion is a
breach of trust which the depositors of the State have in their
legislative bodies." [13]   At the same time F.D.R. accused the
bankers of blocking reform by a campaign of obstruction in
the legislature.[14]

The legislature answered this request by passing a bill to
permit investment of savings deposits in stocks, bonds, or

notes of water districts. The Governor vetoed the bill with
the comment that some of these obligations were "extremely
undesirable investments for savings banks." [15] The legislature
allowed the proposal to amend the law concerning thrift accounts to die in committee, in spite of a last-minute appeal
by the Governor to pass such legislation.[16]

When the legislature next convened on January 6, 1932—
in a presidential election year—Roosevelt urged a much
broader program of banking reform in his annual message.
He asked for an advisory council to help the Banking Department in its work, repeated his request for protection of
thrift accounts, and then added two new and important proposals. There was immediate need, said the Governor, for
revision of the laws of the state dealing with sale of securities
to the public to "differentiate between prospects and true
values" so that the public could know the "whole truth about
what in the past has been a package too often sold only because of the bright colors on its wrapper." [17]

Finally, Roosevelt brought up the issue of branch and chain
banking and concentration of control in the banking field:

We must by law maintain the principle that banks are a definite
benefit to the individual community. That is why a concentration
of all banking resources and all banking control in one spot or in
a few hands is contrary to a sound public policy. We want strong
and stable banks, and at the same time each community must be
enabled to keep control of its own money within its own borders.[18]

This last proposal was attacked especially strongly by banking interests, and F.D.R. explained his position further:

What I had in mind was not to prevent a trade area or county
system, but to prevent absentee landlordship. For example, a man
came to my office the other day from Syracuse to complain that
the savings bank of Middletown in Orange County was foreclosing
a lot of home mortgages in Syracuse, and would not go along with
the methods adopted in regard to these mortgages by the Syracuse
savings banks. In other words, there is a lot of resentment against
the way strangers handle a situation in an area they know nothing
about.[19]

Only one of F.D.R.'s recommendations was enacted into law: the legislature provided a modified version of the advisory board the Governor had requested. Roosevelt felt uneasy about bankers being required on the board, even as a minority, on the grounds that "representatives of objects of governmental regulation should not do the regulating." [20] This was in sharp contrast to his actions earlier, when he appointed bankers to the committee recommending banking legislation. But since the Governor was not obliged to accept the recommendations of the board, Roosevelt was willing to sign the measure. The legislature took no action on F.D.R.'s other proposals concerning thrift accounts, securities issues, and branch or chain banking.

By 1932 Roosevelt's views on banking conformed to his broad economic philosophy emphasizing the welfare of the average person. His earlier position on the bankers' side of the question had shifted. In addition, several elements of broader New Deal policies had appeared in Roosevelt's proposals for banking legislation during his governorship. Protection of thrift accounts was to become guarantee of bank deposits, and regulation of securities issues and exchanges on a national scale was to be accomplished under the New Deal.

CHAPTER XIV

What Can Be Done about Depressions?

As THE BAD TIMES became worse, Governor Roosevelt sought to find policies that would meet the larger depression problem, not only at the state level, but in the area of national policy.

His mail was full of suggestions, many of them of the crackpot variety, for ways to end the depression. A recurring theme was the proposal to place the unemployed on farms where they would be able to raise their own food,[1] and one correspondent wrote from a hobo jungle near Sacramento that a back-to-the-land movement was the only alternative to destruction of the "capitalistic" Federal government by a proletarian revolution.[2] Other proposals were to limit wage earners to one per family,[3] and to shorten the work day in order to spread work.[4] One man sent F.D.R. a U.S. Department of Commerce pamphlet entitled "You Can Make It For a Profit," describing how to make furniture and other objects out of wood, with the suggestion that the unemployed could put themselves to work.[5]

Roosevelt was actively looking for ways out of the depression. He had appointed his Committee on Stabilization of Industry in 1930, but, as we have seen, the Committee didn't think much could be done about cyclical swings in economic activity and as the depression worsened it was gradually transformed into a relief organization.

Nevertheless, Roosevelt's curiosity about depression remedies continued. In May, 1931, he lunched with Sir George Paish, who had just completed his book, *The Way to Re-*

covery, and who asked Roosevelt to write a foreword to it.[6] He read Sir Arthur Salter's *Recovery: The Second Effort,* and thought it was "exceedingly interesting." [7]

In 1931 Roosevelt invited Norman Lombard, then executive vice-president of the Stable Money Association, to attend the Governors' Conference on Unemployment at Albany and present his views on recovery.[8] Lombard wrote a paper on "The Relationship Between Unemployment and Business Depressions and Monetary and Credit Policies," which he sent to Roosevelt in January, 1931, and which formed the basis for his discussion at the conference.[9]

Lombard began with the proposition that the supply of money and credit should be more effectively kept in line with the sound needs of business; if this were done the industrial machine would work more smoothly. Other remedies were necessary too, but monetary reform was essential. He phrased the argument in terms of the value of gold:

> If measures can be taken to stabilize the purchasing power of gold, to that extent will unemployment be reduced. Fluctuations in the purchasing power of gold, or of money, affect unemployment as follows: When gold increases in value that means that the general level of prices falls (because gold will buy more), and, when gold decreases in value, the general level of prices rises (because gold will buy less).[10]

The evils of falling prices (depression) and rising prices (boom) were discussed, with Lombard maintaining that in order to prevent unemployment and unhealthy booms it was necessary "to stabilize the general level of prices, i.e., the purchasing power of money." Lombard recognized that while changing the monetary base had been proposed as a means of stabilizing the value of money, the supply of credit was more important. He concluded with the statement that "stabilization of the purchasing power of our unit of value should be the primary aim of monetary credit policy." [11]

Lombard did not advocate the use of Fisher's "compensated dollar" as a means of stabilizing the price level. He proposed the use of credit controls that were already available,[12] and suggested that F.D.R. take that position at the Governors' Conference.[13]

In January, 1931, Lombard wanted to control business fluctuations by stabilizing the level of prices. But during the depression prices had fallen to very low levels. Should they be stabilized there? It was becoming obvious to proponents of stable money that stabilization at prosperous levels was considerably different from stabilization at depression levels. Thus, interest shifted to efforts to raise the price level and then stabilize. This became the goal of the Committee for the Nation, formed by a number of businessmen in the summer of 1932.[14] A major part of the Committee's proposal was the raising of the price of gold by 75 percent in order "to bring the commodity price level to a 1926 base," [15] and such action was urged on the New Deal early in 1933.

The transition from Lombard's view to that of the Committee for the Nation is a simple one. Lombard maintained at the 1931 Governors' Conference that price stability depended upon a stable value for gold. But if the problem were viewed as one of raising prices, then the price of gold should be raised. This is exactly the twist given to the idea by Professors Warren and Pearson and the Committee for the Nation. Indeed, the continuity of ideas is paralleled by a continuity of organization: when the Stable Money Association could no longer support itself it donated what assets it had to the Committee for the Nation "in the expectation that as soon as reflation was completed, the Committee would take up the project of stabilization as its major objective." [16]

One connection between Roosevelt and these ideas was Irving Fisher himself. Although Fisher was never a close adviser of Roosevelt's at any time, in September, 1932 he sent the Governor galley proofs of his book *Booms and Depressions* and later a specially prepared copy a month in advance of publication. The Governor, off on a campaign trip through the West, took the proofs along with him.[17]

It was not Irving Fisher, but Professors George F. Warren and Frank A. Pearson of Cornell University who were most influential in bringing ideas of monetary manipulation to F.D.R.'s attention.

The theory of Warren and Pearson was expressed in a series of articles published in *Farm Economics* in the years 1931-33, and later in their book, *Prices*. According to their theory the general level of prices was determined by the ratio of monetary stocks of gold to the physical volume of production.[18] Thus:

For the thirty year period 1885 to 1914, monetary stocks of gold in the United States had to increase at the same rate as the physical volume of production in the United States in order to maintain stable commodity prices. If gold stocks increased more rapidly than the production of other things, prices rose; if gold increased less rapidly, prices fell.[19]

Warren and Pearson felt that declining commodity prices were the result of a rising value of gold: gold had an excessive value in the postwar period because of increased demand for the metal as many nations returned to the gold standard. As long as the monetary unit was tied to gold it, too, would have an excessive value, and commodity prices would remain low.

What were the remedies? Warren and Pearson argued that "when a nation suspends gold payments, it can establish any internal price level that it desires." Three methods could be used: "forcibly maintaining the dollar at a low gold value," "reducing the amount of gold in the dollar," or "substituting another metal for all or a part of the gold in the dollar." [20]

Once the price level had been raised by this method it was to be stabilized by the use of a "compensated dollar." Warren and Pearson in 1933 took over Fisher's idea:

If prices rose 0.1 percent in a week, the weight of gold purchasable by a dollar would be increased 0.1 percent until any rise was corrected. If prices fell 0.1 percent, the weight of the gold purchasable by the dollar would be decreased 0.1 percent.... This would make the dollar have the same value at all times. It would be independent of the business cycle.[21]

Henry Morgenthau, Jr., had studied under Warren at Cornell, and it was he who first brought the professor to the attention of Governor Roosevelt. As early as December, 1930, Warren visited Roosevelt at Warm Springs, and he became an important adviser on agricultural matters. The Governor was familiar with the articles by Warren in *Farm Economics*,[22] and in May, 1932, he wrote that "I am doing a lot of studying down here on the fluctuating dollar. If we don't do something for stabilization, we will be headed for real trouble." [23]

Ideas of raising prices by raising the price of gold—or what is the same thing, devaluing the dollar—were in the air during the early thirties, and Roosevelt was familiar with them. He had read Salter's book, he had heard Lombard's discussion of the relationship between gold and prices, Fisher's ideas had been put before him, and he was familiar with the arguments of Warren and Pearson. Roosevelt may not have been converted to the ideas of Warren and Pearson in 1932, but he certainly was familiar with them and with others of a similar nature.

Price "reflation" was to become a major basis of the New Deal's recovery program. In a press conference on April 13, 1933, shortly after taking office as President, Roosevelt stated that "the whole problem before us is to raise commodity prices," and continued in off-the-record remarks:

The general thought is that we have got to bring commodity prices back to a recent level, but not to the 1929 level except in certain instances. You take, for instance, city real estate in 1929. It was then altogether too high, and you ought not to bring city real estate back to the 1929 level.... On the other hand, farm commodity prices were comparatively low in 1929 and have been going down since rather steadily for five or six years [*sic*]. So that it has got to be a definitely controlled inflation.... It has got to be a controlled price level.[24]

Later, in a "fireside chat" on October 22, Roosevelt said:

Finally, I repeat what I have said on many occasions, that ever since last March the definite policy of the Government has been to restore commodity price levels. The object has been the attainment of such a level as will enable agriculture and industry once more to give work to the unemployed ... to make possible the payment of public and private debts more nearly at the price level at which they were incurred ... to restore a balance in the price structure so that farmers may exchange their products for the products of industry on a fairer exchange basis ... [and] to prevent prices from rising beyond the point necessary to attain these ends. The permanent welfare and security of every class of our people ultimately depends on our attainment of these purposes.[25]

The problem of "reflation" was very much under discussion in 1931 and 1932, and monetary measures to achieve it were only one method that had been proposed.

Discussions of how to raise farm prices had been going on for years, for the crop surpluses of the twenties prevented farmers from sharing in the prosperity of the twenties to the same extent as other groups. The earlier proposals had been based on the idea that tariffs could be effective in raising farm prices. The idea was to maintain a domestic price higher than the world price by the amount of the tariff plus shipping costs. Numerous methods were proposed to achieve this goal. The McNary-Haugen Bills, first introduced in 1925 and vetoed by President Coolidge in 1927 and 1928, were built around the "equalization fee" principle: a Federal board would buy surplus crops at the domestic price and sell them abroad at the lower world price; losses would be met by an equalization fee paid by all producers. Since only a portion of the crop would be sold abroad, the equalization fee paid by the farmer would be less than the gain from selling the major portion of the crop at high domestic prices. The McNary-Haugen plan was widely supported and had the endorsement of the Farm Bureau Federation. Roosevelt had written favorably of one variation of this plan in 1926.

A second plan "to make the tariff effective" was the export-debenture plan. It proposed a bounty on exports of farm products to be paid in the form of "debentures" that could be used by importers in paying customs duties. The domestic price would be unable to fall below the world price plus the export bounty, while farmers who were paid the bounty in debentures could sell them to exporters. This plan, which would have raised prices to the consumer and at the same time offered a substantial stimulus to production of crops for export, was presented in Congress as a substitute for the McNary-Haugen plan in 1926 and 1927, but was not adopted. It was endorsed by the National Grange, but its support in Congress came primarily from opponents of any price-raising plan, who supported it as a political maneuver.

A third proposal was the "domestic allotment" plan, first proposed in 1926. A portion of the crop of a primary agricultural product, say wheat, would be designated for domestic use. The government would then issue allotment certificates based on that amount, entitling the seller to collect an amount equal to the tariff on the product; these certificates would be issued to the farmers on the basis of their acreage. Thus the farmer would be paid an amount equal to the world price plus the tariff only on that part of the crop consumed in the United States. For any crops over and above his domestic allotment the farmer would obtain only the world price. Proposed originally by W. J. Spillman of the Department of Agriculture, it was modified by Beardsley Ruml and Professor John D. Black of Harvard to make the allotment certificates transferrable, and modified still further by M. L. Wilson of Montana State College, who included a processing tax to pay for the scheme and voluntary crop-restriction by the farmers in order not to increase output of surplus crops.[26] By 1932 Wilson's version of the domestic allotment plan began to attract considerable attention, and it became the basis for several bills introduced in the last session of Congress under President Hoover.

While the Middle West was clamoring for higher farm prices, the Republican administrations of Coolidge and Hoover sponsored cooperative marketing of farm products as a means of lowering costs of distribution and increasing the return to the farmer—a commendable long-range program, but not one to satisfy the demand for immediate remedies—and sought to provide more liberal credit facilities for farmers. The Mc-Nary-Haugen and export-debenture plans were rejected as "price fixing." Nevertheless, even Coolidge and Hoover could find no other solution than price stabilization. In 1926 a government corporation was set up to buy cotton at a fixed price, and $10 million was appropriated for this purpose. And in 1929 the Federal Farm Board was organized, and provided with $500 million with which to hold surpluses off the market by loans to cooperatives. The Board's attempt to raise wheat prices was an obvious failure by early 1930, and its attempt to encourage voluntary acreage restriction succeeded only in arousing the ire of the farmers. The farmers' organizations went back to their advocacy of the McNary-Haugen and export-debenture plans and the newer domestic allotment scheme.

While all this was going on, the Governor of New York was concentrating on his own state and deliberately making no statements on questions of national policy. However, he was sceptical of the possibilities for success of the Federal Farm Board and thought that tariff reductions on manufactured goods were of more importance to farmers.[27] In 1930 he was already thinking in terms of crop reduction:

I wish you would give me your thought on a matter which has interested me greatly for a year. . . . Is there any possible device to be worked out along volunteer lines by which the total wheat acreage of the nation could gradually be decreased to the point of bringing it in line with the actual national consumption figures? [28]

But in 1931, when interviewed for *The Country Gentleman*, he did not have much faith in any of the price-raising schemes and said nothing of acreage restriction. The interviewer wrote:

In his opinion the debenture plan, applied to wheat, could possibly have worked for a time some years ago. With a worldwide overproduction of wheat and the many restrictions in foreign markets he does not feel it would work now. He believes also that the

Federal Farm Board's stabilization attempt defeated its chief end —the improvement of the market for the American grower.

"The accumulated holdings that the Board acquired as a result seem to me to have perpetuated the surplus situation and delayed the eventual adjustment," he said. "All such expedients for artificially sustaining prices or impeding the natural movement of commodities seem to have failed wherever they have been attempted."

But if all the proposed remedies were ineffective, what was to be done: Roosevelt's answer was that if general prosperity were restored, the farmers' main problems would be solved:

"Right now the farmer's well being is bound up with that of all the rest of us," he said. "The main thing needed now is to get trade moving again, people buying of one another and selling to one another. Commodity prices are not likely to rise until a demand is created by this sort of process." [29]

There were two reasons for Roosevelt's lack of interest in farm relief plans: they applied to an agricultural problem that was of minor importance in New York, and F.D.R. himself was more interested in long-range land-use planning. The great crop surpluses of the twenties and early thirties were largely a problem of those midwestern and southern areas that produced wheat, corn, cotton, and other staples in large quantities. New York farmers, concentrating on fruits, dairy products, and truck farming, had little "exportable surplus" in the normal times of the twenties comparable to the surpluses produced in the Midwest and South.[30] Furthermore, Roosevelt was more interested in regional planning and a long-range program for agricultural betterment than he was in the short-run problem of depression relief for farmers. When he was governor he left the latter subject for his Agricultural Advisory Commission to solve. But the Commission itself had little to offer. In January, 1932, it reported that the milk situation, extraordinarily complicated, should be investigated by a joint legislative commission. As for the problem of mortgage foreclosures and the failure of local banks in many rural areas, it recommended that the Governor support four proposed measures that would permit farmers in the state to take advantage of the credit facilities of the Federal Intermediate Credit Bank for the northeastern states. The Governor immediately supported these two proposals and they were both enacted during the 1932 session of the legislature.[31]

In spite of his lack of interest in farm relief measures and farm price support plans, he recognized that loss of purchasing power on the part of the farmer was a major factor in the depression. In his famous "forgotten man" speech in April, 1932, he pointed out that farm purchasing power was greatly diminished and argued that "one of the essential parts of a national program of restoration must be to restore purchasing power to the farming half of the country." [32]

A little later, Roosevelt again stressed the need for increasing farm purchasing power and emphasized the long-run problems of resource use rather than the immediate problem of farm prices:

The farming interests represent half our population. They have lost buying power and this has been largely responsible for depressing industry. We must at once take the farm board out of speculation in wheat and cotton, try out a new plan to insure getting surplus crops out of the country without putting the government in business, and set up machinery to save the mortgaged farm by cutting down amortization and lowering interest rates. These immediate steps must be followed by a land utilization survey in order to eliminate marginal lands and start a very large reforestation and flood control program. Finally we must give assistance to those families in cities who may wish to return to good land. I use these as illustrations of the broad planning and active leadership which must extend to all the other problems, because it is clear that the solution lies not in opportunism or in last minute remedies but in going to the source of the trouble.[33]

It seemed to many observers in the early thirties that the basic problem of industry was also overproduction and surpluses that were driving prices down. There was talk of the need to "adjust production to demand" and a number of proposals were made for schemes to regulate production in manufacturing.

Early in 1931 Roosevelt was already thinking about proposals to restrict "abnormal consumption" and "abnormal production" during good times:

There are, of course, certain industries which, with a little more organizing, can put the rule into practice. It is even easier to do so with raw materials, such as oil, coal and copper. The copper producers are all working it out pretty well, and the oil and coal producers are almost ready to follow suit. I am inclined to think that the same methods can be extended to the production of crops, such as wheat and cotton, during the next decade.

These raw material industries, however, while they can restrict or increase production, have very little control over consumption. It is, therefore, the manufacturing industries on whom the real task falls. That brings up the question of how far the credit system should be extended to the consumer himself.

Personally, I felt from 1922 on that the terrible campaign in favor of installment buying by the individual consumer was the most dangerous thing we had to contend with, but I must be honest in saying that the present depression has not thrown back as many installment wares into the hands of the sellers as I had expected.[34]

A few months later he queried a friend, then traveling in Europe, about the problem of overproduction. The reply to Roosevelt's letter suggested repeal of the Sherman Act and giving the Federal Trade Commission power to license large combinations in the various industries, while production of raw material products could be regulated by the states as a conservation measure.[35]

The most important proposal designed to stabilize industry by controlling production was made by Gerard Swope of General Electric Corporation in September, 1931. Swope proposed that trade associations be set up in each industry and that their chief function be the establishment of codes of fair practice designed to stabilize prices and coordinate production and consumption. He felt that full reports to the Federal Trade Commission would serve to prevent exploitation of the public. At the same time he proposed a comprehensive system of social insurance to be run by the trade associations and to include unemployment insurance, old age pensions, workmen's compensation, and disability insurance. But the heart of the plan involved "the establishment of balance between production and consumption through control of production within the association." [36]

The "Swope Plan" came in for a great deal of discussion in the succeeding months. A number of business leaders spoke favorably of it, as did Nicholas Murray Butler and Karl T. Compton. Stuart Chase suggested that it be applied first in the electrical equipment industry as an experiment, while Charles F. Abbott of the American Institute of Steel Construction proposed suspension of the anti-trust laws to permit operation of the plan. William Green of the American Federation of Labor served notice that it would require the co-operation of labor as an equal partner, while Norman Thomas denounced it as a "capitalistic nostrum" and later as "a kind of Fascism." The plan was approved at its annual meeting by the United States Chamber of Commerce, which, after polling its members, recommended relaxation of the anti-trust laws to permit trade associations to regulate production and the establishment of an economic council by industry to coordinate the activities of the individual associations.[37]

Meanwhile William G. McAdoo had suggested the creation of a Federal "Peace Industries Board" designed to adjust national production to national consumption,[38] and the Senate Committee on Manufactures set up a subcommittee headed by Senator LaFollette to investigate the feasibility of a National Economic Council designed to stabilize the economy.[39] Among other proposals for government control of industry was Justice Louis D. Brandeis's suggestion that control by the states could be based on the legal doctrine of public convenience and necessity.[40] The lines were being drawn in the conflict between proponents of private control and government control of industrial production.

All of this talk of planning and control was anathema to President Hoover. His views on planning had been presented in "A Twenty Year Plan for America" published in *American Review of Reviews* for July, 1931. Hoover recognized that the depression had temporarily halted the expansion of the American economy, but he had "an American plan" to take care of a twenty million increase of population in the next twenty years. The plan encompassed building cities, factories, highways, parks, schools, colleges, churches, and other facilities to take care of the population increase, along with an increase of 20 percent in agricultural production and 25 million horsepower of electricity. "We plan more leisure for men and women and better opportunities for its enjoyment," said Hoover. The plan was to be fulfilled by American free enterprise and American initiative: "This plan will be carried out if we just keep on giving the American people a chance. Its impulsive force is the character and spirit of our people." [41]

When the Swope Plan was proposed Hoover immediately rejected the idea. In a memorandum written at the time he wrote:

This plan provides for the consolidation of all industries into trade associations, which are legalized by the government and authorized to "stabilize prices." There is no stabilization of prices without price-fixing, and this feature at once becomes the organization of gigantic trusts such as have never been dreamed of in the history of the world. . . . It means the repeal of the entire Sherman and Clayton Acts, and all other restrictions on combinations and monopoly.[42]

Roosevelt, on the other hand, spoke favorably of planning, but his utterances were so lacking in specific proposals that one wonders if he himself knew exactly what kind of planning —other than the regional land-use planning he advocated for New York State—he believed in.

In his "forgotten man" address in April, 1932, he spoke of "a plan to meet our present emergency," comparing the depression emergency to World War I. He rejected government deficit spending as one of the "illusions of economic magic":

People suggest that a huge expenditure of public funds by the Federal Government and by State and local governments will completely solve the unemployment problem. But it is clear that even if we could raise many billions of dollars and find definitely useful public works to spend these billions on, even all that money would not give employment to the seven million or ten million people who are out of work. Let us admit frankly that it would be only a stop-gap. A real economic cure must go to the killing of the bacteria in the system rather than to the treatment of external symptoms.[43]

The essentials of a plan to meet the emergency, Roosevelt felt, would lie, first, in restoration of the farmer's purchasing power, second, in freer credit to the farmer, home-owner, and small businessman, and third, in revised tariffs that would permit foreigners to sell more goods in America.[44]

This rejection of government spending as a remedy followed closely on a letter from Bernard Baruch, to whom F.D.R. had written asking for his ideas on the depression. Baruch insisted that without a balanced budget other measures would be of no avail and that a sound government security and a sound money system were absolutely necessary for recovery. While he recommended that the Federal budget be reduced to $3½ billion—because the government could afford no more —he did recommend a bond issue of $2 billion, the proceeds of which would be lent to the states and cities for self-liquidating public works like bridges and slum clearance. Federal taxes should be raised, said Baruch, to pay the interest on any such bond issue and keep the Federal budget in balance.[45]

Roosevelt was convinced that planning was necessary if depressions were to be avoided in the future, but when he spoke in St. Paul on April 18, 1932, he was still looking for the proper plans and could speak only in general terms:

The plans we may make for this emergency, if we plan wisely and rest our structure on a base sufficiently broad, may show the way to a more permanent safeguarding of our social life to the end that we may in a large number avoid the terrible cycle of prosperity crumbling into depression. In this sense I favor economic planning, not for this period alone, but for our needs for a long time to come.[46]

Of all of Roosevelt's speeches early in 1932, the one that best illustrates his search for solutions to the depression problem is his speech at Oglethorpe University on May 22. Here he laid before the graduating class all of his basic ideas regarding long-range reforms within the capitalist system necessary to diminish or eliminate economic instability. He started out with the necessity for planning:

As you have viewed this world of which you are about to become a more active part, I have no doubt that you have been impressed by its chaos, its lack of plan. Perhaps some of you have used stronger language. And stronger language is justified.

Roosevelt pointed out that "our industrial advance" has been accompanied by haphazardness, "gigantic waste," "duplication of productive facilities," "scrapping of still useful equipment," "mortality in commercial and industrial undertakings," and "waste of natural resources." Much of this, he said, could be avoided by a "larger measure of social planning."

Roosevelt spoke with scorn of "the theory that the periodic slowing down of our economic machine is one of its inherent peculiarities—a peculiarity which we must grin, if we can, and bear because if we attempt to tamper with it we shall cause even worse ailments."

This attitude toward our economic machine requires not only greater stoicism, but greater faith in immutable economic law and less faith in the ability of man to control what he has created than I, for one, have.

While F.D.R. recognized that post-World War maladjustments and monetary problems throughout the world were important aspects of the problem, he thought that the most important phase of the problem, in the long run, would be "controlling by adequate planning the creation and distribution of those products which our vast economic machine is capable of yielding."

In addition to advocating some kind of planning, Roosevelt believed that the basic trouble was an insufficiency of buying power. The place to start would be an increase in consumption, and for the long run, a more equitable distribution of income:

No, our basic trouble was not an insufficiency of capital. It was an insufficient distribution of buying power coupled with an over-sufficient speculation in production. While wages rose in many of our industries, they did not rise proportionately to the reward to capital, and at the same time the purchasing power of other great groups of our population was permitted to shrink....

I believe that we are at the threshold of a fundamental change in our popular economic thought, that in the future we are going to think less about the producer and more about the consumer. Do what we may have to do to inject life into our ailing economic order, we cannot make it endure for long unless we can bring about a wiser, more equitable distribution of the national income.

But if Roosevelt thought that planning and greater equality of income were basic reforms necessary to avoid future depressions, he had to admit at the end of his Oglethorpe speech that he was as puzzled as was everyone else concerning immediate plans:

The country needs and, unless I mistake its temper, the country demands, bold, persistent experimentation. It is common sense to take a method and try it: If it fails, admit it frankly and try another. But above all, try something.[47]

While Roosevelt did not go beyond a general advocacy of planning in his speeches of early 1932, he did think he knew where to start in working out plans—it was the general area of consumption that he felt was crucial. If consumption spending were stimulated he felt that the economic machine could move at a more rapid pace.

He did not believe in Say's law of markets: that production of goods created the purchasing power with which to buy the goods:

I am glad that you do not believe in that modern school of economics which holds that the more you produce the more the public will consume, thus in effect discovering the hitherto unknown method of pulling oneself up by one's bootstraps.[48]

Instead, he always emphasized that consumption had to be stimulated in any effort to induce prosperity. In his "forgotten man" speech in April, 1932, he had pointed out that unless the purchasing power of the farmer were restored, "the wheels of railroads and of factories will not turn." [49] The same theme was repeated in his address at Oglethorpe University a month later.[50] Nevertheless, Roosevelt had not yet taken the step, obvious to economists after Keynes, of accepting government spending as a means of restoring purchasing power. This was not to come until after he became President.

Roosevelt's search for measures to bring about recovery from the depression was not very successful. By the spring of 1932 he had not worked out anything more than a few general ideas. He had dabbled in proposals to manipulate the price of gold and knew what they meant, and he was aware of proposals for "reflation" of the price level. But schemes to raise farm prices did not find Roosevelt an enthusiastic supporter in spite of his belief that the purchasing power of the farmer had to be increased. He had inquired into the idea of "adjusting production to consumption," but took no part in the discussions about whether that job should be undertaken by the government or by private industry. It was not until the campaign of 1932 that he spoke in favor of industry-sponsored plans. Roosevelt did speak favorably of planning to promote recovery and prevent future depressions, but he spoke only in the most general terms. Of one thing he was certain, however: a workable recovery plan would have to start with stimulation of consumption, especially by the farmer, while underlying his whole attitude was a willingness to experiment with any proposals that seemed sensible.

CHAPTER XV

The "Brain Trust"

IN PREPARATION for the 1932 campaign Roosevelt brought together a group of expert advisers that later was dubbed "the brain trust." Originally devoted to the drafting of speeches and statements, this group developed during the campaign and after the election into a continuing "seminar" on measures applicable to the depression emergency. It had nothing to do with the getting of votes and the building of political fences, but concentrated on basic policy matters. Although it had a core of permanent members, many persons were called in for special purposes from time to time.

Roosevelt's official family was organized on a functional basis and special efforts were made to prevent an overlapping of authority. Among F.D.R.'s closest advisers were Louis Howe, his faithful general handy man, and Basil O'Connor, his law partner. In 1932 Howe and O'Connor were constantly consulted on political matters and at times on policy matters. In charge of the gathering of delegates and votes—the job of getting Roosevelt nominated and elected—were Edward J. Flynn, political boss of the Bronx, and James A. Farley. These two men worked closely with Howe. None of these men, however, were equipped to do the necessary job of developing policies for the depression emergency, both for use as campaign material and for presentation to Congress by the new administration.

The original brain trust was composed of Samuel I. Rosenman, counsel to the Governor, and Columbia University professors Raymond Moley, Rexford G. Tugwell, and Adolf A. Berle. Rosenman, who had a vast knowledge of New York

State politics, tended to devote himself to political affairs rather than economic policy after Roosevelt's nomination, while at the time he was moving out of the "brain trust" picture Hugh S. Johnson was moving in. But the major members of the group remained Moley, Tugwell, and Berle.

These men had the job, at first, of drafting speeches for the pre-convention campaign for the presidential nomination. In performing this function they did not foist upon Roosevelt ideas that were new to him, but rather sought to help the Governor "crystallize his own ideas and inclinations, reflect them accurately, extend them where necessary, and present them congruously." [1] Moley described how F.D.R.'s speech accepting the nomination was written:

Its preparation was the work of weeks. Hence, immediately after his return from Warm Springs the two of us began a conversational review of the ideas that had been presented to him in the meetings at Albany and in the memoranda of May 19th. From these two or three talks I was able to get a general notion of what ideas he wanted to emphasize and what to play down.... He asked me, early in June, to prepare a speech memorandum containing an exposition of the ideas he wished to make his own....

The result was a document in speech form approximately nine thousand words long. While it was taking shape, I consulted him frequently by telephone and in person. I also showed parts of it to Rex [Tugwell], Adolf [Berle], Sam [Rosenman], and Louis [Howe], asking for their advice on one point or another....

When I had finished, in the third week of June, I took the document to Albany. The Governor read it with care, making penciled corrections here and there and indicating, in the margins, points that he wanted to strengthen, passages to "boil," as he phrased it, and things that should be omitted for the sake of brevity. This draft I took back to New York, where I revised it in accordance with his instructions.[2]

Samuel I. Rosenman, who remained a "ghost-writer" for Roosevelt longer than anyone else, has given a vivid description of the interaction between Roosevelt and his writers in the production of a major address.[3] The process included numerous drafts, each one of which was gone over carefully by Roosevelt, who often wrote sections of the speech himself, argued vigorously over certain points with his writers, and in the end had the last word. As Rosenman put it:

I do not mean to imply, of course, that any of the people who helped in the preparation of speeches would try to impose their own views on the President or to slip them in. Even if they had tried, they would have failed. We always informed him of any contrary view expressed to us by one of his associates, and it would be fully and frankly discussed. . . .

The President would listen and he would argue. When the reasons had all been given, and he had heard all our own arguments, it was he who would make the final decision.[4]

Rosenman acknowledged that the speeches as finally delivered were Roosevelt's, no matter who the "collaborators" were:

He had gone over every point, every word, time and again. He had studied, reviewed, and read aloud each draft, and had changed it again and again, either in his own handwriting, by dictating inserts, or making deletions. Because of the many hours he spent in its preparation, by the time he delivered a speech he knew it almost by heart.[5]

The members of the brain trust—or at least the important ones who did more than merely provide information on a special problem—were chosen because they reflected Roosevelt's own viewpoint. Ernest K. Lindley, who himself largely wrote the Oglethorpe Commencement Address of May 22, 1932,[6] wrote that

Mr. Roosevelt had developed his political philosophy long before the depression began and long before he met any member of his brains trust. The brilliant gentlemen in that group were among those who helped to apply Mr. Roosevelt's philosophy to the specific conditions of 1932-33. Mr. Roosevelt did not recruit his professorial advisers to provide him with a point of view; he drew them to him because their point of view was akin to his own.[7]

Moley is in accord with Lindley's view,[8] and Rosenman agrees that Roosevelt chose advisers and speech writers who shared his views.[9]

The key men of the brain trust—Raymond Moley, Rexford G. Tugwell, and Adolf A. Berle—were all then teaching at

Columbia University. Of these men Moley was a political scientist, Tugwell an economist, and Berle a lawyer who had delved deeply into economics. All three were agreed that the Federal government must take a more positive role in economic life.

Of the three men, Tugwell has been most closely associated with that idea. Born in 1891 in western New York, he had a career of teaching economics at the University of Pennsylvania, the University of Washington, and Columbia. As a student he had come under the influence of Simon N. Patten, vigorous critic of the orthodox economics of the early twentieth century.[10]

The major theme that ran through Tugwell's writing in the twenties and early thirties was that modern industrial techniques and the application of scientific knowledge to industry made possible the development of a true economy of abundance—and that such a trend could be greatly advanced by rationalization of industry under the leadership of government. In *Industry's Coming of Age* he presented a detailed account of the trend toward increased productivity and its causes and made an eloquent plea for further advances along that line.[11] He argued that large-scale operations and the combination movement had contributed to increased productivity by effecting large savings and superior coordination and that large-scale enterprises should, therefore, be encouraged. "The productive mechanism under integration of industry," if wisely managed, "can adjust the flow of materials into its plants, and out of them into the hands of consumers, in as nearly perfect a fashion as our facilitating mechanisms are prepared to allow."[12] Trade associations should likewise be encouraged insofar as it increased productivity and rational and set higher standards for the industry involved. According to Tugwell, combination was not something to be abhorred, as in the Louis D. Brandeis fashion, but should be encouraged: it could facilitate exchange of information and more efficient use of resources.

The maturity of industry and its moving away from competition to combination and rationalization made voluntary or automatic controls inadequate. "Government controls ought to be brought to bear where voluntary ones break down, where, in fact, the interests of the public conflict with those of a super-coordinated industry." [13] Rationalized industry should be encouraged and made to serve social rather than individual ends, argued Tugwell, and we must take advantage of social rather than selfish motives in the interest of a better moral world. All of this could be achieved only if there were a plan for the reasonable but forceful shaping of industry to the needs of society.[14]

Tugwell developed an explanation of the depression derived from his theory of increasing productivity and the economy of abundance. In "The Principle of Planning and the Institution of Laissez Faire" [15] he placed particular emphasis on scientific management and integration of industrial processes as a means of promoting abundance, but pointed out that the economy was not ready for the flood of goods produced:

If we had had eyes to see the implications of Taylor's work we should have known that the vast expansion of production which must follow would clog all the old channels of trade, swamp the mechanisms of an artificially limited commerce, and end in a period of violent reconstruction.[16]

Tugwell followed this overproduction-underconsumption explanation of the depression with the argument that a policy of *laissez faire* was "anachronistic" in an economy of scientific management, that "confusion and disorder will prevail whenever the wilful pursuit of business privileges, as we still know them, chokes the smooth interchanging flow logically belonging to the system of industry." [17] Planning was the solution to the problem, and Tugwell advocated creation of a national economic council to act as a planning agency.[18]

In addition to advancing productive efficiency, Tugwell argued that accumulation of undistributed corporate surpluses was an important cause of overproduction-underconsumption.

Business firms accumulate surpluses as a defense against bad times, but this prevents the reduction of prices and the increase in real purchasing power that could avoid bad times, he argued.[19]

Tugwell summed up his views on planning in *The Industrial Discipline and the Governmental Arts,* published in 1933.[20] In it he argued that an effective system of planning by the Federal government could be instituted within the existing constitutional and institutional framework. Some changes would be needed: Federal incorporation of business firms, a tax on undistributed profits to drive them into the capital market where their allocation could be controlled, and a central governmental agency to draw up production plans and fix prices in conjunction with trade associations in the major industries. Using these instruments, the private business system could be coordinated and directed toward the attainment of higher output and greater productivity.[21]

Tugwell's views echoed a number of ideas held by Roosevelt, although Tugwell expressed them in greater detail and with greater vigor than did F.D.R.: the growing maturity of the American economy, underconsumption-overproduction as the root of the depression, the value of planning to achieve a better life. Most important, both men saw the need for a Federal program that would stabilize the economy and inevitably mean rejection of the *laissez-faire* ideal.

Adolf A. Berle, Jr., made a different type of contribution to the deliberations of the brain trust. Brought in originally as an expert on credit and corporation finance, he contributed a wealth of information on the concentration of economic power that supplemented both Tugwell's ideas on planning and Roosevelt's aversion to the financiering, irresponsible business leader.

Berle was born in Ohio in 1895. He graduated from Harvard at the age of eighteen and from law school at twenty-one. After working in Louis D. Brandeis's law office he served in the army in World War I and was later an expert on the

staff of the American Commission to negotiate peace with
Germany. After World War I he lectured on finance at
Harvard and taught law at Columbia. While in the latter
post he was recruited by Moley for the brain trust.

Berle had just completed, with economist Gardner C. Means,
The Modern Corporation and Private Property when he began
working with Roosevelt. That work was an elaborate description of the structure and control of the modern corporate
system. It showed that over 38 percent of all business wealth,
apart from banking, was concentrated in the hands of only
200 giant corporations and that those corporations were in
turn dominated by small groups of managers or financiers.
The vast number of stockholders—the nominal owners—had
lost control of their property through the use by management
of loose charters of incorporation, voting trusts, non-voting
stock, the holding company, and other legal devices. "Control
is maintained in large measure apart from ownership" in the
200 largest non-financial corporations.[22]

The rise of the giant corporation and the separation of
ownership and control had important implications, according
to Berle and Means. In the first place, the traditional doctrine of the role of profits in the economy had to be amended.
In the nineteenth century the manufacturer or businessman
owned real property, as distinguished from paper claims to
property; he lived near his business and generally carried
direct responsibility in management; the profits accrued to
him and motivated his business decisions. But under the
new corporate system the owners, having given up the responsibility of management, no longer were the sole recipients
of profits—the management function began to be a recipient
of profit. The clear motivation of profits had become blurred
and the traditional theory of profit motivation could no longer
be maintained.

In the second place, the traditional theory of private
property was changing. The owners, having given up the
responsibility of management, were not solely entitled to

profits; nor should the interests of the managers be dominant, for they generally held only a very small ownership interest in the corporation. The rise of the giant corporation had brought to the fore the claims of the community as a whole, and the corporation must serve the interests of all society:

Neither the claims of ownership nor those of control can stand against the paramount interests of the community.... It remains only for the claims of the community to be put forward with clarity and force.[23]

Berle and Means did not discuss the role of government in the situation they described. Indeed, they did not specify in any detail the kind of action required to meet the problems they had raised. But one implication of their argument is clear: if the profit motive no longer acts as a spur to private enterprise in the manner in which it is supposed to act, and if the public interest in the affairs of large corporations has become vital, there must be some substitute for the profit-price system. It is at this point that the ideas of Berle and Tugwell dovetailed. Tugwell's belief in rationalization and government planning provided the solution to the questions raised by Berle and Means. His concept of planning was a logical supplement to Berle's analysis of the modern corporation, although in *The Modern Corporation* Berle did not take that position.

In a later book Berle accepted the implication of his analysis —that substantial government intervention was necessary in order to protect the public interest. In *Liquid Claims and National Wealth* (co-authored with Victoria Pederson) it was pointed out that the proportion of paper claims to wealth (securities of various sorts) had increased in recent years at a rate much faster than national wealth had increased. The rise in importance of liquid claims to wealth meant that a decline in their value could have a depressing effect on business. Such a decline may result from the operation of natural forces in the economy and have disastrous results:

The operation of so-called "natural" forces is perhaps theoretically healthy from the technical point of view of economics. But they may make life and government and social order impossible. It is then not a question of permitting the natural forces to operate; to do so might bring down the whole structure.[24]

The authors rejected "a mere *laissez-faire* policy" of permitting private interests to take the only steps to protect the community, and called for a conscious policy "to diminish the necessary area of liquidity." [25]

Berle cogently summed up his viewpoint in an article in the New York *Times* Sunday Magazine in the fall of 1933. He recognized that the "old economic forces still work and they do produce a balance after a while. But they take so long to do it and they crush so many men in the process that the strain on the social system becomes intolerable." He characterized the New Deal as a "gigantic attempt to mold an individualist, capitalist system into a directed economic effort," not by revolution but by "the more difficult course of moderation and rebuilding." [26]

The other members of the brain trust can be treated in more summary fashion, for they contributed less to the economic thought of F.D.R. Raymond Moley was one of the original members of the brain trust; indeed it was he who brought Tugwell and Berle to the attention of Roosevelt early in the spring of 1932. Moley had been born in Ohio in 1886, and after graduating from college became a school teacher in his native state. However, he found time to attend Columbia University and during World War I he taught at Western Reserve University. In 1923 he went to Columbia to teach government and became a professor of public law in 1928. His special field of knowledge was crime and the administration of justice: he was a consultant for crime surveys in Illinois, Pennsylvania, and Virginia during the twenties and held the post of research director of the New York State Crime Commission in 1926 and 1927. When Governor Roosevelt was looking for experts to staff his Commission on the Administration of Justice in 1931, Moley was a logical choice, and he became research director of the Commission. From that post he gradually became a closer adviser of the Gov-

ernor and in 1932 got together with Basil O'Connor and
Samuel I. Rosenman to recruit the brain trust.

Moley's function in the group was more that of a catalyst
and organizer than originator of economic policies. His special
ability was to keep the discussions of the group relevant to
the current political situation, and his knowledge of government was invaluable to the others. Roosevelt's conversation
with Moley just before F.D.R. left for the 1932 Governors'
Conference illustrates Moley's role in the brain trust. Roosevelt wanted the group to work out material for use in the
coming campaign, and told Moley:

Rex [Tugwell] could go on with his farm thing, though he'd be
good on other things too. Berle could work up something on debt
and finance; you know—RFC and mortgage foreclosures and the
stock market. And you put in whatever you want to and pull the
whole thing together so it makes sense politically.[27]

In addition to Moley, Tugwell, and Berle, Samuel I. Rosenman and Basil O'Connor often took part in the discussions of
the brain trust with Roosevelt prior to F.D.R.'s nomination,
but when the job of the group became less and less that of
writing speeches and more and more that of exploring the
unknown ground of anti-depression policy, they gradually
dropped out. Their place was filled, after the nomination,
by Hugh S. Johnson.

Johnson was born in Kansas in 1881, went to West Point,
and served in the Army until 1919. It was he who wrote and
administered the World War I draft act. After the war he
joined with George N. Peek in running the Moline Plow
Company and in developing one of the earliest plans for relief of agriculture in the postwar period. He allied himself
with Bernard M. Baruch in 1929 and is reputed to have been
one of the "bears" who anticipated the stock market crash
of that year. In 1932 he was one of Baruch's assistants in
the "stop Roosevelt" movement at the Democratic convention, but immediately offered his services to the successful
candidate. A businessman and speculator, he had little in-

terest in the reforms advocated by Berle and Tugwell, but he did feel that substantial aid to agriculture and a rebuilding of consumer purchasing power were essential to recovery. His special talent was a vigorous, colorful prose style; his major contribution to the brain trust was incisive analysis of the Hoover policies.[28]

These, then, were the brain trusters—Moley, Tugwell, Berle, Rosenman, O'Connor, Johnson. Their first job was to prepare campaign materials for Roosevelt, but they soon discovered that a basic policy to meet the depression emergency had to be developed *de novo*. There were few guideposts to policy for them to follow, since the more orthodox economists had not integrated into their thinking the modern economic trends that had so impressed Berle and Tugwell. Thus, the job of developing economic policies to meet the problems of industry, agriculture, labor, and financial institutions had to be started from the beginning. And if the candidate were fully to understand the policies, if he were to make them truly his own, he would have to take part in the discussions himself. The most important member of the brain trust was Roosevelt himself.

Moley had described the meetings at Albany between Roosevelt and his advisers:

The routine was simple enough. Sam [Rosenman], "Doc" [O'Connor], and I would take one or two men on the late-afternoon train to Albany, arriving in time for dinner. The talk at the table would be pleasant, casual and generally inconsequential. But once we had moved out of the dining room to the study ... random talk came to an end. Roosevelt, Sam, or I would throw a question at the visitor, and we were off at an exciting and exhausting clip.

The Governor was at once a student, a cross-examiner, and a judge. He would listen with rapt attention for a few minutes and then break in with a question whose sharpness was characteristically blurred by an anecdotal introduction or an air of sympathetic agreement with the speaker. Sooner or later, we would all have at the visitor, of course. But those darting questions of Roosevelt's were the ticks of the evening's metronome. The intervals between them would grow shorter. The questions themselves would become meatier, more informed—the infallible index to the amount he was picking up in the evening's course. . . .

By midnight, when the time came to dash for the train to New York, Sam, "Doc" and I would be done in; the visitor (who would not realize for some days, in most cases, that he had been squeezed dry) would look a trifle wilted; and the Governor, scorning further questions, would be making vigorous pronouncements on the subject we had been discussing, waving his cigarette holder to emphasize his points.

This performance we repeated again and again through the spring and summer.[29]

Tugwell has described the same series of conferences, calling them "the preparation of a president," and emphasizing that many times the participants were investigating areas that had not previously been definitively studied. He points out that both Roosevelt and the brain trusters were trying to find answers—that were not forthcoming—to the depression problem.

Mr. Roosevelt's mind was struggling all these months, evidently to crystallize some program which would be more than the re-establishment of old institutions and their reform. We did not supply it for him; and he could not put it together from what he had available or what anyone else could supply. This was the one needful thing; and he could not dig it out of us.[30]

This failure was not due to lack of study, however:

He often got down in the scholar's dirt with the rest of us and worked, worked hard at the specific task of knowing what government at Washington had to be and to do in the circumstances which were looming up. This work was by no means always relevant to campaigning. And it never seemed to him overeasy to learn, nor did the solutions he examined appear to have the satisfactory simplicity of common sense. The whole process was quite like that which every true scientist faces at some time or other when he finally reaches the boundaries of what is known.[31]

Rosenman points out that "Roosevelt had nearly always read something on the subject, and usually had some undigested opinions about it. He did not hesitate to express them and to invite criticism." [32]

These meetings performed several functions. In the first place, they enabled Roosevelt to clarify his own thinking on the major economic problems, tendencies, and forces of the time. Secondly, they brought him up-to-date on most viewpoints and proposed solutions for the problems; there were few proposals that the brain trust discussions seem to have missed. In the third place, they opened up new avenues of policy that had not been considered previously. As Rosenman put it,

Sometimes we differed among ourselves. Then our ideas and arguments, pro and con, would be "batted out" before him [Roosevelt], discussed and debated. New lines of thought would be stimulated. It was the kind of "home-work" in governmental thinking which Roosevelt enjoyed, which he used a great deal in the White House, and from which he always profited. Out of it his own thinking was brought into sharper focus. Sometimes it knocked down newly formed ideas of his own; sometimes it opened up entirely new avenues which would later broaden into action.[33]

When Roosevelt went on a vacation to Warm Springs in April, 1932, he asked his brain trust to continue working in his absence. The object was to prepare memoranda on various phases of the economic problem, developing specific measures that could be the basis of an effective program for Roosevelt to consider and upon which he could build. A series of memoranda was developed by the group and carried to Roosevelt at Warm Springs by Rosenman on May 19. The preparation of these statements forced the brain trusters to define their basic beliefs, to work out the fundamentals on which any coherent policy must rest:

First ... we proceeded on the assumption that the causes of our ills were domestic, internal, and that the remedies would have to be internal, too.

Second was the belief that there was need not only for an extension of the government's regulatory power to prevent abuses (stock market regulation and the abolition of child labor, for instance) but for the development of controls to stimulate and stabilize economic activity ("planning" for agriculture and the concentration of great powers in the Federal Reserve Board, for in-

stance). The former, designed to curb economic power and special
privilege, did not depart in principle from the lines of policy laid
down in the administrations of Theodore Roosevelt and Woodrow
Wilson. But the latter carried us pretty far from ancient moorings.

Third, was the rejection of the traditional Wilson-Brandeis
philosophy that if America could once more become a nation of
small proprietors, of corner grocers and smithies under spreading
chestnut trees, we could have solved the problems of American life.
We agreed that the heart of our difficulty was the anarchy of concentrated economic power.... We believed that any attempt to
atomize big business must destroy America's greatest contribution
to a higher standard of living for the body of its citizenry—the
development of mass production. We agreed that equality of
opportunity must be preserved. But we recognized that competition, as such, was not inherently virtuous; that competition...
created as many abuses as it prevented.[34]

The memoranda of May 19 were used extensively in
preparation of F.D.R.'s nomination acceptance speech, as well
as other major speeches of the campaign.[35]

But while the memoranda of May 19 may have defined a
set of basic assumptions and beliefs, the anti-depression
policies developed in them were of limited value: they attacked the problem in piecemeal fashion by suggesting remedial action for specific areas in the economy where weaknesses had shown up, rather than an over-all program that
would get to the heart of the depression problem. Many of
the suggested remedies were long-range reforms that would
not have important immediate effects.

Tugwell, for example, wrote a memorandum on "International Economic and Financial Policies." [36] Three issues
in that general area, he argued, were of dominating importance: tariffs, intergovernmental debts, and international
monetary problems. High tariffs, it was felt, were a major
cause of the world depression, and the United States should
take the lead in negotiating reciprocal tariff reductions. Such
a policy would reduce the burden on distressed consumers,
lower costs of production both for industry and the farmer,
and stimulate exports. The intergovernmental debts that

were a heritage of World War I were, in Tugwell's view, a second major source of the world depression, and the United States should be willing to reduce them in exchange for reduction in the German reparations and disarmament. As far as international monetary problems were concerned, Tugwell felt that sound currencies were indispensable and that a quick return to the gold standard by nations that had left it was essential. He also suggested an international conference to work out methods of averting financial dangers in the world economy and cooperation between central banks to prevent flights of capital.[37]

Meanwhile Berle and Louis Faulkner recommended a number of long-range reforms which were designed to strengthen the economy against the threat of future depressions. They suggested publicity of corporate finances and of stock transactions by officers or directors of corporations, control by a Federal board over issuance of new securities, and the development of branch banking to strengthen the banking system. They also recommended Federal regulation of large corporations where two or less controlled more than 50 percent of an industry, and a system of old-age, sickness, and unemployment insurance. In the international field, they felt that Russia offered a large market for both manufactures and farm products and that international negotiations could result in reduction of war debts owed to the United States in exchange for European tariff reductions and reduction in reparations.[38]

Although the depression remedies proposed by the brain trusters were not comprehensive in nature, some thought was given to broad factors contributing to the depression. Tugwell, for example, felt in 1932 that disparities among groups of prices were most responsible for continuation of the depression. As he explained it, during periods of stability each group in the economy produces some good or performs some service which has a price that will permit others to buy that product with the revenues derived from their production.

However, when there is a rapid change in the general price level, some prices change more than others, thereby upsetting the previous relationships and reducing the buying power of some groups. He felt that in 1932 the economy was adjusting to a price level lower than that of the late twenties and the maladjustments accompanying that movement were the factors that prevented recovery in business activity. On one side retail prices and public utility rates were too high, while on the other side agricultural prices were too low. General inflation was not the answer, but rather an adjustment that was controlled and planned.[39]

Tugwell was obviously groping both for reasons why the depression continued and for broad remedies. His failure, and the failure of the other brain trusters, to find proper answers led them into depression remedies that sought to improve conditions in particular areas of the economy—such as agriculture; or to solve particular problems—such as mortgage foreclosures on homes or the financial difficulties of the railroads.

But if the brain trusters failed to find a basic theme around which to build a coherent anti-depression policy, they were merely reflecting the inability of the economics profession as a whole to do it. Among economists there was no generally accepted explanation of the causes of depressions—systematic study of the problem was still quite recent—and consequently there were no easily recognizable policies that could be followed. Roosevelt and the brain trust found themselves trying to do in a few short months what the economics profession should have been doing for decades.

CHAPTER XVI

The Campaign of 1932

THROUGHOUT the 1932 campaign Roosevelt castigated Hoover for doing nothing about the depression, which, according to F.D.R., Hoover's policies had helped to bring on. Typical of these attacks was Roosevelt's campaign speech at Columbus, Ohio, on August 20:

So I sum up the history of the present Administration in four sentences:

First, it encouraged speculation and overproduction, through its false economic policies.

Second, it attempted to minimize the crash and misled the people as to its gravity.

Third, it erroneously charged the cause to other Nations of the world.

And finally, it refused to recognize and correct the evils at home which had brought it forth; it delayed relief; it forgot reform.[1]

This was the theme of the whole Democratic attack on Hoover, reiterated again and again during the campaign. The attack reached its peak in Baltimore on October 25, when Roosevelt characterized his four points of criticism as "the 'Four Horsemen' of the present Republican leadership: The Horsemen of Destruction, Delay, Deceit, Despair." [2]

Nevertheless, in the field of promoting recovery from the depression the Hoover administration was not inactive, although its policies seem quite mild when compared with those of the New Deal. Hoover did not stand idly by, but took positive action. Immediately after the crash of 1929 he sought to promote voluntary cooperation in maintenance of business capital expenditures, stabilization of wage rates, and a shortening of the work week. The Reconstruction Finance

Corporation sought to provide capital to hard-hit business firms, especially banks, railroads, and insurance companies; and this was certainly positive government action to strengthen the credit structure. At the same time the Federal Reserve System sought to help by making large open-market purchases. For agriculture, the Federal Farm Board tried to raise prices of staple crops by buying surpluses in the market, and this experiment served to indicate that price-raising schemes that did not entail production restriction were doomed to failure. Finally, the annual deficits that Hoover abhorred and Roosevelt condemned represented positive anti-depression action, albeit unwilling, on the part of the Hoover administration.

The Hoover policies can hardly be considered part of a policy of *laissez-faire,* of reliance on the rugged individualism of nineteenth-century America. They were, instead, the first steps toward the more comprehensive policies of the New Deal. As one writer has observed,

Without this reconnaissance work, the country would hardly have been convinced that the need justified a bolder policy. It would not have been prepared to support the more adventurous experimenting of the New Deal.[3]

An example of the "reconnaissance work" for the New Deal done by the Hoover administration was Hoover's effort to reform the securities exchanges by relying on voluntary action by the exchanges themselves. On October 13, 1930, he told the officials of the New York Stock Exchange that unless they reformed their rules to eliminate abuses, Federal regulation would be inevitable. Little, however, was done by the Exchange.[4] And in the 1932 campaign Hoover could only say that "there is no Federal law or regulation of the sale of securities and ... there is doubtful constitutional authority for such law."[5] The evident inadequacy of such an approach made possible the further steps that were taken by Roosevelt after he became President.

Hoover's reconnaissance work was primarily in the area of finance and credit. His emphasis on financial remedies was consistent with the ideas of orthodox economics that, as Say's Law described it, there could be no general overproduction and that the cause of economic dislocations would be found in the area of exchange rather than in production or distribution. In particular, this view was popular before World War I—it underlay, for example, Sprague's analysis of financial crises that was taught to F.D.R. at Harvard.

When it came to proposals for government activities in the area of production and distribution, Hoover was generally to be found in opposition. He was not happy about the Farm Board's excursion into influence over production and prices. He wanted no planning by government, but his support of "voluntary cooperation" in industry—short of agreements on price—showed that he was not wedded to the atomistic competition implied in the economists' version of the *laissez-faire* economy. In the area of development of natural resources Hoover was quite willing for the Federal government to undertake great flood control, navigation, and reclamation projects. He was a strong supporter of such projects in the Mississippi Valley, in central California, and on the Colorado and St. Lawrence Rivers. Where electric power was generated as a by-product, he was willing to have the Federal government produce the power if it were distributed by regulated private companies, but he opposed government projects that were primarily for purposes of electric power production.

In the field of welfare Hoover favored old-age pensions financed through private insurance companies, and he opposed unemployment insurance in the hands of government, while favoring such insurance through private insurance companies.[6] Hoover was silent on the subject of unemployment insurance in the early thirties.

While Hoover's actions in many respects represented an extension of government activity in economic affairs, he remained a spokesman for the *laissez-faire* ideal:

The only method by which we can stop suffering and unemployment is by returning people to their normal jobs in their normal homes, carrying on their normal functions of life. This can only be done by sound processes of protecting and stimulating the existing economic system which we have in action today.[7]

In contrast with Hoover, Roosevelt advocated a considerable increase in government welfare activities and in Federal programs that would affect prices, production, and distribution.

Roosevelt was convinced that the depression meant that America would turn again to the liberal-progressive path and that numerous reforms would come. In the spring of 1930 he wrote:

There is no question in my mind that it is time for the country to become fairly radical for at least one generation. History shows that where this occurs occasionally, nations are saved from revolutions.[8]

At the same time he expressed fear of both leftist and rightist political movements:

We face in this country not only the dangers of communism, but the equal danger of the concentration of all power, economic and political, in the hands of what the ancient Greeks would have called an Oligarchy.[9]

Basically, F.D.R. took a middle-of-the-road, reforming position. In 1931 he wrote:

We are going through a difficult period and I think that everybody in the country realizes this fact. There will be many changes in the next few years, and many readjustments to meet the new conditions but, in the final analysis, the fundamentals are the same as they always have been.[10]

The fact that conditions of the early thirties would lead to expansion of the powers of the executive branch of the government, and that the possibility of dictatorships in Europe was imminent, was also realized by Roosevelt. Just returned from a quick trip to Europe, he wrote in the summer of 1931:

I sometimes get really disturbed when I see the very difficult economic and political conditions that seem to exist throughout Europe. We are as a whole in a period of real danger to our type of civilization and because of the confusion the time will soon be ripe for some form of definite leadership not only here but in every European country.[11]

These sentiments were developed in many speeches during the 1932 presidential campaign. Roosevelt continually called for a change, but not just any change: he saw the need for liberal reforms. For example, speaking at the Brown Palace Hotel in Denver, on September 15, he said:

The world marches forward, very often towards more liberal solutions of new problems, for short period of time [sic], and then it is very apt to stop and adjust the new things that have come about. We are about to enter into a new period of liberalism in the United States, and we need it.[12]

Candidate Roosevelt set out to develop in his campaign a liberal program of reform to meet the demands of the electorate. Indeed, he presented in his campaign addresses almost all of the elements of the New Deal's program-to-come. Few people followed his campaign closely enough to realize this; one of the few who did was his opponent, President Hoover.

Roosevelt's speech accepting the nomination at Chicago on July 2, 1932, set the tone of the campaign. It promised no specific measures, but couched in general terms the candidate's outlook. Roosevelt promised reconstruction of a middle-of-the-road character, neither reactionary nor radical:

Wild radicalism has made few converts....
To meet by reaction that danger of radicalism is to invite disaster. Reaction is no barrier to the radical. It is a challenge, a provocation. The way to meet that danger is to offer a workable program of reconstruction.[13]

Roosevelt then pointed out that a basic cause of the depression was the failure of consumer purchasing power to keep pace with production:

In the years before 1929 we know that this country had completed a vast cycle of building and inflation ... expanding ... beyond our natural and normal growth. Now it is worth remembering, and the cold figures of finance prove it, that during that time there was a little or no drop in the prices that the consumer had to pay, although those same figures proved that the cost of production fell very greatly; corporate profit resulting from this period was enormous; at the same time little of that profit was devoted to the reduction of prices. The consumer was forgotten. Very little of it went into increased wages; the worker was forgotten, and by no means an adequate proportion was even paid out in dividends— the stockholder was forgotten.

As a result, "enormous corporate surpluses piled up" which "went chiefly in two directions: first, into new and unnecessary plants which now stand stark and idle; and second, into the call-money market of Wall Street, either directly by the corporations, or indirectly through the banks."

Then came the crash. You know the story. Surpluses invested in unnecessary plants became idle. Men lost their jobs; purchasing power dried up; banks became frightened and started calling loans. Those who had money were afraid to part with it. Credit contracted. Industry stopped. Commerce declined, and unemployment mounted.
And there we are today.[14]

Having stated his general position on reform, and attributed the depression to lack of purchasing power in the hands of consumers, Roosevelt then turned to more specific problems. He advocated economy in government, and approved public works as a means of stimulating employment only if the projects were self-sustaining and could be financed by bond issues. For the farmer, he advocated reforestation of marginal lands and some arrangement to reduce surpluses and raise farm prices by the amount of a reasonable tariff.

I am sure that the farmers of this Nation would agree ultimately to such planning of their production as would reduce the surpluses and make it unnecessary in later years to depend on dumping those surpluses abroad in order to support domestic prices. . . .
Farm leaders and farm economists, generally, agree that a plan based on that principle is a desirable first step in the reconstruction of agriculture.[15]

Roosevelt also promised the farmer lower interest rates and longer maturities for his mortgages.

He attacked the Republicans on the ground that theirs was a *laissez-faire* policy.

Our Republican leaders tell us economic laws—sacred, inviolable, unchangeable—cause panics which no one could prevent. But while they prate of economic laws, men and women are starving. We must lay hold of the fact that economic laws are not made by nature. They are made by human beings.[16]

Stressing that the people of America wanted work and security, Roosevelt ended with that famous sentence:

I pledge you, I pledge myself, to a new deal for the American people.[17]

Four weeks after his acceptance speech Roosevelt spoke about the Democratic platform in a radio address from Albany. The men who drafted the Democratic party platform in 1932 —and most of them were pledged to support Roosevelt for the nomination—wrote a document designed more to avoid the loss of votes than to attract them. The platform found the cause of all the economic troubles in the Republican administration; by implication, the economic system was fundamentally sound but improperly directed and all that was needed was a change in leadership. No important economic changes were envisaged, although the platform pledged the "rehabilitation" of silver along with a sound currency. It advocated a balanced budget and reduction of government expenditures, Federal aid to the states for unemployment relief, expanded public works, shorter hours for labor, insurance for the unemployed and the aged under state laws, refinancing of farm mortgages, extension of farmers' cooperatives, antitrust enforcement, protection of the investing public, removal of government from all fields of private enterprise, regulation of holding companies, more rigid supervision of banks, and encouragement of foreign trade. The most important plank of the platform, in the eyes of the delegates, had little to do with economic problems: repeal of the prohibition amendment got more applause at the convention than all of the other planks combined.[18]

In his acceptance speech Roosevelt stated that he accepted the Democratic platform "100 percent," [19] and he repeated that pledge in his radio address of July 30. He put special stress on the budget deficits of the last few years of the Hoover administration and on the Democratic pledges of a balanced budget and a sound currency. Roosevelt tried to meet the problem of how to provide relief and still balance the budget:

> We face a condition which, at first, seems to involve either an unbalanced budget and an unsound currency or else failure of the Government to assume its just duties....
>
> This dilemma can be met by saving in one place what we would spend in others, or by acquiring the necessary revenue through taxation. Revenues must cover expenditures by one means or another. Any government, like any family, can for a year spend a little more than it earns. But you and I know that a continuation of that habit means the poorhouse.[20]

Aside from the comments on government expenditures Roosevelt largely devoted himself to a reading of the platform. However, he did emphasize the problems of the tariff and war debts and measures to reduce speculation and business financial manipulations.

Roosevelt then turned his attention to the job of outlining a program to meet the depression emergency. It was a program that reflected his liberal-reforming attitude, and was designed primarily to improve conditions in specific areas of the economy that showed the greatest weakness. At the same time, Roosevelt had something for almost everyone—for the farmer, for the businessman, and for the worker.

The farmer came first, both because Roosevelt felt that an increase in farm purchasing power was necessary for an increase in consumption expenditures and because he wanted to make an appeal for the farm vote, especially in the middle-western centers of progressivism.

With the organization of the brain trust in 1932 Roosevelt had begun to consider more seriously the various plans for the relief of agriculture then current. Tugwell was assigned the special job of investigating them, and in the memoranda of May 19, 1932, discussed at some length the domestic allotment proposals. Late in June Tugwell attended a meeting in Chicago on agricultural problems, sponsored by the Giannini Foundation for Agricultural Economics, at which the plan was discussed. There he met M. L. Wilson, the chief sponsor of domestic allotment. Wilson was immediately invited to come to New York to confer with Tugwell and Moley: "ne explained in detail what the 'Voluntary Domestic Allotment Plan' (the name of the new scheme) was, the extent of its support among farm organization leaders, and its political and economic possibilities."[21] Taken to see Roosevelt at Albany, Wilson explained his plan to F.D.R. before the major speech of the campaign on agricultural policy.

That speech was given in the heart of the midwest farming area, at Topeka, Kansas, on September 14, 1932. Roosevelt emphasized that the farm problem was many-sided and that no single solution would be adequate. In this connection he reviewed his farm policies as Governor of New York: tax relief, state aid for roads, schools, and rural health services, the state soil survey, and other legislation. The heart of the problem, he argued, was that the farm population's share in national income had fallen from 15 percent in 1920 to about 7 percent in 1932; throughout the period farm families represented about 22 percent of the population. The depression in agriculture spread to other areas of the economy: to the fifty million persons "immediately concerned with the present and future of agriculture" and to "another fifty or sixty million people" engaged in business or industry whose "lives and futures are profoundly concerned with the prosperity of agriculture."

Our economic life today is a seamless web. Whatever our vocation, we are forced to recognize that while we have enough factories and enough machines in the United States to supply all our needs, those factories will be closed part of the time and those machines lie idle part of the time if the buying power of fifty million people on the farms remains restricted or dead as it is today.[22]

After stating the problem Roosevelt divided his solutions into long-range and short-range policies. Taking up the former, he proposed planning for agriculture as the basis of any solution:

We must have, I assert with all possible emphasis, national planning in agriculture.[23]

He would reorganize the Department of Agriculture to make it the effective instrument of such planning, which would emphasize planned use of land and, in the eastern states, reforestation of marginal lands that could not be profitably farmed. As another element in a long-range farm program, Roosevelt advocated revision of the tax structure so that it would bear less heavily on farmers.

But his listeners in the wheat belt were much more interested in the immediate problems of farm surpluses and the farm debt burden, and Roosevelt moved rapidly on to his short-range program of farm relief. First, he promised refinancing of farm mortgages to provide lower interest payments and an extension of principal payments, to be accomplished by extension of Federal credit to holders of farm mortgages. Secondly, he promised tariff reductions to "restore the flow of international trade; and the first result of that flow will be to assist substantially the American farmer in disposing of his surplus." [24]

Restoration of foreign markets would take time, however, and Roosevelt proposed to give the farmer "in the shortest possible time the equivalent of what the protected manufacturer gets from the tariff." [25] He then proceeded to outline, in general terms, the basic principles of a workable plan for farm relief. "I seek to give to that portion of the crop consumed in the United States a benefit equivalent to a tariff sufficient to give you farmers an adequate price." As F.D.R. outlined it, the plan would have the following characteristics:

First: The plan must provide for the producer of staple surplus commodities a tariff benefit over world prices which is equivalent to the benefit given by the tariff to industrial products....

Second: The plan must finance itself....

Third: It must not make use of any mechanism which would cause our European customers to retaliate on the ground of dumping....

Fourth: It must make use of existing agencies and, so far as possible, be decentralized in its administration....

Fifth: It must operate as nearly as possible on a cooperative basis....

Sixth: The plan must be, insofar as possible, voluntary. I like the idea that the plan should not be put into operation unless it has the support of a reasonable majority of the producers of the exportable commodity to which it is to apply. It must be so organized that the benefits will go to the man who participates.[26]

Roosevelt closed his Topeka speech with a vigorous attack on Hoover's farm policies, and pointed out that the President had opposed all of the plans proposed to raise farm prices.

President Hoover's position on farm relief stood in sharp contrast with that of candidate Roosevelt in the 1932 campaign. The Republican platform that year had pledged support for "any plan which will help to balance production against demand, and thereby raise agricultural prices, provided it is economically sound and administratively workable without burdensome bureaucracy." [27] But Hoover specifically opposed such plans in his campaign speeches. More than a month before Roosevelt's Topeka speech he spoke in Washington in terms that were interpreted by farm leaders as opposition to all of the then current farm relief proposals:

There is no relief to the farmer by extending government bureaucracy to control his production and thus curtail his liberties, nor by subsidies that bring only more bureaucracy and ultimate collapse. I shall oppose them.[28]

Hoover's opposition was reiterated in his major farm policy address at Des Moines, Iowa, on the fourth of October, 1932:

I come to you with no economic patent medicine especially compounded for farmers. I refuse to offer counterfeit currency or false hopes. I will not make any pledge to you which I cannot fulfill.[29]

The President even disavowed the attempt of the Federal

Farm Board to raise prices of staple crops that was undertaken in 1929 and 1930:

> I wish to state frankly the difficulties that have arisen.... They
> arise mostly from the stabilization provisions, which never were
> and are not now the major purpose of the Farm Board. Even
> indirect purchase and sale of commodities is absolutely opposed to
> my theory of government....
> Experience has shown that the patent weakness of such actions
> is the damaging aftermath which accompanies disposal of these
> products. I am convinced that the act should be revised in the
> interest of the farmer, in the light of our three years of experience,
> and this proposal should be repealed.[30]

What Hoover did offer the farmers was the same old
remedies that the Republican party had found successful in
attracting farm votes during the twenties: a high protective
tariff on farm products and encouragement of cooperative
marketing. To this he added stimulation of foreign trade
through the obtaining of special concessions from foreign
nations in return for a scaling down of war debts, and a continuing effort to promote home markets by aiding recovery
from the depression. Hoover, too, advocated a study of land-
use patterns, reduction of farm taxes, and provision of greater
credit to farmers. But on this last question of mortgage foreclosures he offered less positive Federal action than did Roosevelt: he would offer credit through Federal land banks and
through the R.F.C., while Roosevelt would make that credit
conditional upon longer mortgages and lower interest rates.

In short, Hoover's Des Moines speech offered the farmers
nothing new, while Roosevelt showed that he was willing to
go well beyond anything that had yet been tried in the way
of farm relief.

Roosevelt placed special emphasis on the refinancing of
farm mortgages, devoting a whole campaign address to that
topic on October 21 at Springfield, Illinois. Three things were
necessary for the relief of agriculture, he said. First in importance was an increase in farm prices, and he referred to
his Topeka speech as offering a plan to achieve that goal

"worked out in cooperation with the wisest leaders of agriculture itself." [31] Second was a reduction in farm taxes. And third was a readjustment of the farmer's debt burden. Roosevelt promised to use Federal credit and the President's influence over the Federal land banks to reduce interest rates and extend the life of mortgages in order to reduce principal payments. He pledged that in cases where farm property had been seized by creditors in default of mortgage payments, the original owners would be given preference when the properties were sold. The Federal government, in other words, was to step into the farm mortgage market and see to it that the farmer was given a chance to obtain funds on easier terms.

In his discussion of the farm problem Roosevelt emphasized the influence of the tariff. His argument in this respect was outlined in detail at Sioux City, Iowa, on September 29. He attacked the Tariff Act of 1929 as a major cause of accumulated farm surpluses as well as the decline in farm purchasing power, because it raised prices that farmers had to pay.

He pointed out that high tariffs increased the cost of the things bought by farmers, but did not increase the selling price of farm products:

The principal cash crops of our farms are produced much in excess of our domestic requirements. And we know that no tariff on a surplus crop, no matter how high the wall—1,000 percent, if you like—has the slightest effect on raising the domestic price of that crop.

The high tariff, furthermore, had forced other nations to protect their own markets from American-made goods by trade restrictions of all kinds, and American firms began to set up plants in foreign countries. The "Grundy" tariff, he argued, "put more men on the street here" and "more people to work outside our borders." A further effect was inability on the part of foreigners to pay their American debts and buy American goods, because they could not sell here:

They just could not buy our goods with their money. These goods then were thrown back upon our markets and prices fell still more.

Summing up the effects of the Republican tariff policy, Roosevelt said that it

... has largely extinguished the export markets for our industrial and our farm surplus; it has prevented the payment of public and private debts to us and the interest thereon, increasing taxation to meet the expense of our Government, and finally it has driven our factories abroad.

Roosevelt promised that "the excessive rates in that bill as it became law, must come down," and that "international negotiation is the first, the most practical, the most common-sense, and the most desirable method."

We must consent to the reduction to some extent of some of our duties in order to secure a lowering of foreign tariff walls over which a larger measure of our surplus may be sent.[32]

In a later address over the radio on October 6, Roosevelt reiterated his proposal to negotiate tariff reductions reciprocally with foreign nations:

We shall try to discover with each country in turn the things which can be exchanged with mutual benefits and shall seek to further this exchange to the best of our ability....

More realistic mutual arrangements for trade, substituted for the present system in which each nation attempts to exploit the markets of every other, giving nothing in return, will do more for the peace of the world and will contribute more to supplement the eventual reduction of armament burdens, than any other policy which could be devised.[33]

Roosevelt found that his position on the tariff was not popular in many circles. People began writing in about specific tariffs, asking if Roosevelt proposed to reduce them. Republican orators began to suggest in the Middle West that he would reduce tariffs on farm products, and Hoover wanted to know just which tariffs were too high. Afraid of losing his gains in the Midwest, Roosevelt sought to assure the farm bloc that tariffs on farm products would not be reduced; at Baltimore on October 25, sandwiched into a rousing attack on the Republicans, he said:

My distinguished opponent is declaring in his speeches that I have proposed to injure or destroy the farmers' markets by reducing the tariff on products of the farm. That is silly. Of course I have made no such proposal, nor can any speech or statement I have made be so construed....

No tariff duty should be lowered to a point where our natural industries would be injured....

It is absurd to talk of lowering tariff duties on farm products....

I know of no effective excessively high tariff duties on farm products. I do not intend that such duties shall be lowered.[34]

In order fully to placate the farmer Roosevelt sent a telegram to the five large farm organizations just a few days before the election, saying, "Let me make it clear that I have consistently stood for a policy of tariff protection that will adequately insure the domestic market for our American Farmer." [35]

The industrial areas of the nation were equally uneasy about Roosevelt's tariff statements. If farm tariffs were not to be lowered, then it seemed that tariffs on manufactured products would be. Roosevelt sought to reassure the worker that he would not be harmed by any tariff reductions promoted by Roosevelt:

I have advocated a lowering of tariffs by negotiation with foreign countries. But I have not advocated, and I will never advocate a tariff policy which will withdraw protection from American workers against those countries which employ cheap labor or who operate under a standard of living which is lower than that of our own great laboring groups.[36]

Roosevelt had been forced to contradict himself, and it was obviously an attempt on his part to avoid alienating votes. His true position was made evident later, when he appointed Senator Cordell Hull to the vital post of Secretary of State. Hull was an advocate of tariff reduction and reciprocal trade agreements.

Roosevelt supplemented his program for agriculture with a corresponding program for business. But first he pointed out that much was wrong with the organization and methods of

American business. Speaking at Columbus, Ohio, on August 20, in an address in large part devoted to criticism of the Hoover administration, he criticized the concentration of control in American industry:

Appraising the situation in the bitter dawn of a cold morning after, what do we find?

We find two-thirds of American industry concentrated in a few hundred corporations, and actually managed by not more than five hundred individuals.

We find more than half of the savings of the country invested in corporate stocks and bonds, and made the sport of the American stock market.

We find fewer than three dozen private banking houses, and stock-selling adjuncts of commercial banks, directing the flow of American capital.

In other words, we find concentrated economic power in a few hands, the precise opposite of the individualism of which the President speaks.[37]

The public required protection against the financial manipulations of this business oligarchy, and Roosevelt would have the Federal government provide that protection. He proposed a series of measures that were to become the basis of much New Deal legislation concerning securities exchanges and banks. Included were true information to be made available to the public concerning the purposes of new security issues and the companies issuing them; Federal regulation "of holding companies that sell securities in interstate commerce"; Federal regulation of securities exchanges; more rigid supervision of banks; Federal government discouragement of speculation and use of the Federal Reserve Banks to that end; and the separation of commercial and investment banking.[38]

One area of the business community offered special problems—the railroads. Commercial banks, savings banks, and insurance companies had substantial investments in railroad bonds, and a large proportion of the railroad companies were faced with imminent bankruptcy. In addition, an efficient transportation system was an absolute necessity. Roosevelt devoted a major campaign address to railroad problems at

Salt Lake City on September 17. He pointed out that railroads had to compete with motor carriers operating over highways provided for them by the public—the motor carriers should, like the railroads, be regulated by the Federal government, he said.

Secondly, the railroads had often been required "to compete unreasonably with each other":

In regulating the railroads, we preserved the policy that at all times, between principal points, there must be competing railroad systems. There is a great deal to be said for that policy, ... so long as there is traffic enough to support the competing lines. As long as you have that traffic, the competition helps to insure efficiency. But as the railroads have been allowed to increase their capacity far beyond traffic needs, the wastes of competition have become more and more insupportable.

Roosevelt phrased the problem in the following terms: "Shall we permit them—in fact, force them—to bankrupt each other? Or shall we permit them to consolidate and so to economize through reducing unprofitable services? In other words, shall we permit them to divide traffic and so eliminate some of the present waste?"

Two other aspects of the railroad problem needed attention, Roosevelt asserted. One was "unnecessary or duplicated facilities" and the other was the "epidemic of railroad holding companies whose financial operations were, to say the least, not generally beneficial to the orderly development of transportation."

In order to solve the problems of the railroad system national planning was essential.

All that I have said should indicate that one chief cause of the present railroad problem has been the typical cause of many of our problems—the entire absence of any national planning for the continuance and operation of this absolutely vital national utility....

It is necessary that a single railroad should have a recognized field of operation and a definite part to play in the entire national scheme of transportation. It is necessary that each rail service should fit into and be coordinated with other rail services and with other forms of transportation.

Roosevelt proposed a national survey of transportation needs to determine the most efficient methods and to develop a national policy designed to "encourage that growth and expansion which are most healthful to the general welfare."

Candidate Roosevelt's program for the railroads envisaged use of the powers of the Federal government to obtain compliance with national policy on the part of the privately owned railroad companies. Specifically, he proposed financial help to the railroads to readjust their top-heavy financial structures, this help to be conditional upon the cooperation of the railroads in fulfilling their part of the national transportation plan. He would also revise the laws concerning railroad receiverships; extend the regulation of the Interstate Commerce Commission to cover motor carriers and railroad holding companies; and press to a conclusion the plans for railroad consolidation developed by the I.C.C. in the twenties. A change in the policy of the I.C.C. was also necessary, he felt: it ought not to require competition if traffic were insufficient to support competing lines, "recognizing, of course, the clear and absolute responsibility for protecting the public against any abuses of monopolistic power." [39]

Turning from railroads to public utilities in general and electric power in particular, Roosevelt summarized the attitudes that had been formed in his terms as Governor of New York. His speech on utilities was delivered in Portland, Oregon, on September 21. In order to emphasize his attitude toward public utility regulation, Roosevelt spoke of the common-law doctrine that businesses affected with the public interest must be operated to provide the public with adequate service at reasonable cost, and at the same time making possible the safe investment of private capital in them. He endorsed regulation of utilities by commissions, but insisted that the commissions were not umpires "between complaining consumer or the complaining investor on the one hand, and the great public utility system on the other hand." Rather, the regulatory commission "must act as agent of the public, upon its own initiative as well as upon petition, to investigate the acts of public utilities relative to service and rates, and to enforce adequate service and reasonable rates." [40] This type of regulation would protect both the consumer and the investor against "the unscrupulous promoter who levies tribute equally from the man who buys the service and from the man who invests his savings in this great industry."

Roosevelt proposed that reforms be made in public utility regulation. His eight-point program included full publicity on proposed security issues by public utility corporations, on ownership of utility bonds and stocks, and on all intercompany contracts; regulation and control of holding companies by the Federal Power Commission; regulation of securities issued by utilities; abolition of the reproduction cost theory of rate-making and use of the actual prudent investment theory; and "legislation making it a crime to publish or circulate false or deceptive matter relating to public utilities, or public utility commissions." He expressed opposition to government ownership of all public utilities:

I do not hold with those who advocate government ownership or government operation of all utilities. I state to you categorically that as a broad general rule the development of utilities should remain, with certain exceptions, a function of private initiative and private capital.

One exception was the right of any community to set up a municipally owned and operated utility service if a private utility were not serving the community adequately. Even the possibility of such action would force a private company to provide adequate service at reasonable rates, he thought.

Another exception, and much more important, was that state or federally owned power sites should be developed by government itself, although "private capital should, I believe, be given the first opportunity to transmit and distribute the power." Roosevelt emphasized four great sources of power in four different sections of the country that should be developed on a large scale by the Federal government; they were Boulder Dam on the Colorado River, Muscle Shoals on the Tennessee River, the St. Lawrence River, and the Columbia River.

Each one of these, in each of the four quarters of the United States, will be forever a national yardstick to prevent extortion against the public and to encourage the wider use of that servant of the people—electric power.[41]

Having indicated that the government would take the lead in developing a more efficient transportation system that was, nevertheless, to remain privately owned and operated, and that public utilities were to be more closely regulated at the same time that great hydroelectric power developments were to be undertaken by the Federal government, Roosevelt then turned to the more general problems of industry. Speaking before the Commonwealth Club of San Francisco on September 23, he laid down the principles that were to lead to the N.R.A. less than a year later.

He began with an historical introduction on the theme of the mature economy, recounting the conquest of the frontier and the growth of industry. But inevitably the development of the giant corporation and the close of the frontier raised serious problems for America:

The turn of the tide came with the turn of the century. We were reaching our last frontier; there was no more free land and our industrial combinations had become great uncontrolled and irresponsible units of power within the state.

It was impossible, said Roosevelt, "to turn the clock back, to destroy the large combinations and to return to the time when every man owned his individual small business," yet "the highly centralized economic system" could become "the despot of the twentieth century." Furthermore, equality of opportunity has been reduced by the closing of the frontier and the squeezing out of the small businessman by the large corporation in area after area of the economy.

In this modern corporate world a reappraisal of values was needed, asserted F.D.R. Instead of building new industrial plants and exploiting a frontier, we had

the soberer, less dramatic business of administering resources and plants already in hand, of seeking to re-establish foreign markets for our surplus production, of meeting the problem of underconsumption, of adjusting production to consumption, of distributing wealth and products more equitably, of adapting already existing economic organizations to the service of the people.

In such circumstances the role of government must be a changed one. Government should "assist the development of an economic declaration of rights, an economic constitutional order."

Then, in the most general terms, Roosevelt spoke approvingly of demands by business spokesmen "to limit the freedom of action of each man and business group within the industry in the common interest of all" and for some form of organization "which will bring the scheme of things into balance, even though it may in some measure qualify the freedom of action of individual units within the business."

The implication is, briefly, that the responsible heads of finance and industry, instead of acting each for himself, must work together to achieve the common end.

Government's role in this scheme of business cooperation was "to apply restraint" and to "protect the public interest." [42]

What candidate Roosevelt had done was to endorse in general terms the principles behind the Swope Plan and the proposals made by the Chamber of Commerce of the United States to permit industry to limit competition in an effort to coordinate production and distribution. However, he did not name the plans themselves. Roosevelt showed his willingness to have businessmen order their own house by cooperation, but he insisted that government take part as guardian of the public interest.

The basic principle of the "New Deal," as it applied to business, was to be cooperation under government direction, rather than competition. The principle was restated later in the campaign when F.D.R. spoke over the radio to the Roosevelt Business and Professional Men's League on October 6. Emphasizing the interdependence of all economic groups in American society, Roosevelt asserted that the primary goal of government is to guard the welfare of its citizens. Achievement of that goal required a "balance among productive processes" to obtain "stabilization of the structure of business."

That such a balance ought to be maintained by cooperation within business itself goes without saying.[43]

Later in the same address Roosevelt emphasized that business must be judged on the basis of its contribution to society:

We must set up some new objectives; we must have new kinds of management. Business must think less of its own profit and more of the national function it performs. Each unit of it must think of itself as a part of a greater whole; one piece in a large design.

Having made his appeal to the farmer and the businessman, Roosevelt turned to the worker. His task here was made easy by the unemployment, underemployment, and threat of unemployment that faced the urban wage earner. Much less of a specific program for that group was presented in the campaign, but Roosevelt did make three speeches that elaborated the measures he favored to promote social welfare and to solve the problem of unemployment.

At Detroit on October 2 he discussed his "philosophy of social justice through social action." That philosophy, F.D.R. declared, called for the reduction of poverty by attacking its causes. He called attention to the development of public health measures, workmen's compensation acts, aid to crippled children, old age insurance, and other advances of the previous decades. He asserted that "there are lots of new steps to take" and specifically mentioned unemployment insurance as one of them. But in this address Roosevelt spoke largely in generalities, emphasizing his basic philosophy that the major function of government is to promote the welfare of the citizens.

More specific measures were outlined in a radio address from Albany on October 13, and in a speech at Boston on October 31. Roosevelt stated his belief that the primary responsibility for unemployment relief lay with the local community and that when local funds were inadequate the state should provide them. But the obligation extended to the Federal government "when it becomes apparent that states and communities are unable to take care of the necessary relief work." He also advocated a program of state unemployment insurance and a nationally coordinated system of unemployment exchanges. He added that "there has been long overdue a reduction of the hours of work and a reduction of the number of working days per week." [45]

Throughout the campaign Roosevelt had repeatedly affirmed his belief that a more equal distribution of income was necessary if purchasing power was to be maintained. Such a position was a necessary corollary of his underconsumption-overproduction theory of the origins of the depression. It was not until late in the campaign, in one of his lesser-known speeches, that he explained what he meant by his references to a better distribution of income and how it was to be brought about. At Chicago, on October 1, he said:

As I have often made clear, underneath my economic policies is an attitude toward economic life. I have tried to set forth what I conceive to be a re-ordered relationship among all the factors in the economic scale....

I pointed out in San Francisco that our task is to meet the problem of underconsumption, of adjusting production to consumption, of distributing wealth and products more equitably.... Theoretically we could distribute purchasing power by confiscating everything and dividing equally, but you and I know that wealth would not stay distributed if we tried it in this way.

The way to distribute wealth and products more equitably is to adjust our economic legislation so that no group is unduly favored at the expense of any group or section. Where our laws assist or permit any group to exploit other groups the exploited ones can no longer buy. Government must systematically eliminate special advantages, special favors, special privileges wherever possible, whether they come from tariff subsidies, credit favoritism, taxation or otherwise.[46]

Nothing shows better how far Roosevelt was from the socialists than this statement.

Roosevelt, then, built an anti-depression program to solve specific problems of agriculture, industry, and the worker. In agriculture, measures were to be taken to solve both financial and production problems. In industry, the financial problem of the railroads was to be attacked, public utility regulation tightened up, and issuance of new securities regulated. And industry was to be permitted to control production through trade associations under the supervision of the government. The worker was promised adequate relief if he were unemployed and Federal encouragement of state systems of unemployment insurance. It was a program designed to strengthen weak areas in the economy, and to appeal to all the major economic interest groups. It was also a program that would not materially change the basic economic structure of the nation.

In one area Roosevelt did not follow through with the implications of his ideas. That area was public works. His statements on the subject in the campaign were not consistent. In some addresses he showed that he favored large Federal expenditures for public works, as, for example, in his advocacy of Federal power development on the Columbia, Colorado, Tennessee, and St. Lawrence Rivers.

In his speech of October 13 on the unemployment problem he advocated that governments accumulate funds in prosperous times to be used for public works in times of depression, but he took an equivocal stand on the use of public works to relieve unemployment:

All public works, including Federal, must be considered from the point of view of the ability of the government treasury to pay for them. There are two ways of paying for public works. One is by sale of bonds. In principle such bonds should be issued only to pay for self-sustaining projects or for structures which will without question have a useful life over a long period of years.

The other method of payment is from current revenues, which in these days means in most cases added taxes. We all know that there is a definite limit to the increase of taxes above the present level.

Instead of pledging a large-scale program of public works, Roosevelt compromised.

I am confident that the Federal Government working in cooperation with states and cities can do much to carry on increased public works and along lines which are sound from the economic and financial point of view.[47]

In Boston at the end of the month, however, Roosevelt took a stronger stand. He repeated his view that recovery must start with an increase in consumer spending:

It is essential to increase purchasing power in order that goods may be sold. There must be people capable of buying goods in order that goods may be manufactured and sold.

He added that the Federal government could stimulate recovery through public works expenditures:

In addition to providing emergency relief, the Federal Government should and must provide temporary work wherever that is possible ... in the national forests, on flood prevention, and on the development of waterway projects....

The Federal Government should expedite the actual construction of public works already authorized.

But counterbalancing these utterances was Roosevelt's speech of October 19 at Pittsburgh on the Federal budget. In it he likened the government budget to that of any family, pointing out that both must live within their incomes. Either one could have small deficits for a time, but continuation of deficits would lead to bankruptcy. He delivered a blistering attack on Hoover because of the Federal deficits of the preceding three years and promised that when he was elected there would be a program of rigid economy in government that would enable the Federal government to balance its budget without raising taxes. But Roosevelt was careful to add that

If starvation or dire need on the part of any of our citizens make necessary the appropriation of additional funds which would keep the budget out of balance, I shall not hesitate to tell the American people the full truth and ask them to authorize the expenditure of that additional amount.[49]

Roosevelt had rejected the borrow-and-spend arguments—but he left a loophole in his rejection.

Although Roosevelt's position on public works was not consistent, he did foreshadow in his campaign speeches most of the measures of the early New Deal, including agricultural relief (AAA), supervision of the securities exchanges and the sale of securities (SEC), legislation to save farm mortgages from foreclosure (FCA), Civilian Conservation Corps (CCC), Tennessee Valley Authority (TVA), legislation to save small home owners from mortgage foreclosure (HOLC), establishment of the National Recovery Administration (NRA), and legislation for the relief of railroads and revision of the railroad bankruptcy laws. All of this legislation implied a greatly expanded role for the Federal government in the regulation and direction of economic activity.

In particular, Roosevelt's program in 1932 represented much greater acceptance of the principle of planning than the American people had been accustomed to in the past. F.D.R. had spoken of planning in broad, general terms prior to his nomination, and his record as Governor included a comprehensive program of land-use planning. In the 1932 campaign he broadened his advocacy of the planning principle by applying it to many areas of the economy. In addition to reforestation of marginal lands and government power development as the keystone of regional development—applications of the regional plan idea—the candidate advocated planning for agriculture to maintain farm purchasing power and planning for industry to balance production and distribution. For railroad transportation he also advocated planning, directed and financed by government. Each one of these types of planning, as F.D.R. described them in the campaign, envisaged a different combination of government and private decision-making; all were variations on the same theme, however—the private enterprise economy was to be strengthened by a substantial amount of government intervention in the making of economic decisions.

Most of the political commentators and editorial writers of 1932 were not aware that Roosevelt's campaign speeches contained an outline of such a program, nor did they realize the implications of a changed role for government in the economy. Perhaps they did not analyze Roosevelt's campaign speeches or penetrate the generalities in which some of his more important proposals were cloaked. There was one observer, however, who did understand that the 1932 election was likely to be a turning point in economic policy, a turning point that would mark the replacement of the businessman as the dominant decision-maker in the economy and the substitution of the Federal government in his place. That observer was Herbert Hoover.

Hoover sought to communicate this knowledge to the voters, but the warning was cloaked in such an emotional economic patriotism that few listened. Speaking at Madison Square Garden on October 31, Hoover argued that he stood for the true American ideal, while the proposals of Roosevelt constituted a rejection of those ideals.

This campaign is more than a contest between two men. It is more than a contest between two parties. It is a contest between two philosophies of government.

We are told by the opposition that we must have a change, that we must have a new deal. It is not the change that comes from normal development of national life to which I object, but the proposal to alter the whole foundations of our national life which have been builded through generations of testing and struggle, and of the principles upon which we have builded the nation.[50]

Hoover asserted that the true liberalism on which America had been built assured freedom to the individual and equal opportunity; it gave free play to the initiative and enterprise of the individual, and had resulted in the great advances in

material well-being of the past 150 years. The depression was
only a temporary interruption of this progress. Further advances would be made in the modern world by voluntary cooperation by individuals, and not by an increase in governmental powers:

It is in the further development of this cooperation and a sense of
its responsibility that we should find solution for many of our complex problems, and not by the extension of government into our
economic and social life. The greatest function of government is
to build up that cooperation, and its most resolute action should
be to deny the extension of bureaucracy.[51]

Hoover contended that the actions of the Democratic majority
in Congress and Roosevelt's campaign speeches foreshadowed
a series of measures that would destroy the traditional American system: large expenditures for public works that would
bankrupt the Federal government, inflation that would destroy savings and all the financial institutions of the country,
power developments that would put the Federal government
into competition with private enterprise, a competitive tariff
that "would wholly alter our American system of life," and
an expanded role for government that would alter the traditional relationship between Federal, state, and local governments.

Hoover correctly saw that Roosevelt would expand the
powers of the Federal government in seeking to achieve what
F.D.R. had called his "philosophy of social justice":

If these measures, these promises, which I have discussed; or these
failures to disavow these projects; this attitude of mind, mean anything, they mean the enormous expansion of the Federal Government; they mean the growth of bureaucracy such as we have never
seen in our history.[52]

Hoover realized that the election of Roosevelt would mean
the triumph of the idea of the "positive state"—expanded
regulation, welfare legislation, and planning—over the ideal
of the *laissez-faire* state" supported by Hoover. The electorate chose Roosevelt by a vote of 22,821,857 to 15,761,841.

CHAPTER XVII

The Economic Philosophy of Franklin D. Roosevelt, 1932

THE ECONOMIC PHILOSOPHY of Franklin D. Roosevelt, as it had developed by 1932, may be summarized briefly, and in general form. The private enterprise–private profit economy should not be abolished, but retained. However, its operations were not always benevolent and did not always promote the general welfare; hence those operations must be improved and supplemented by state and Federal government efforts whenever the need arose.

This economic philosophy was years in developing. Its beginnings lay in the *noblesse oblige* philosophy of the Hudson River gentry: less fortunate members of the community should be helped by the more fortunate. Roosevelt, however, was to go well beyond this philosophy. He became a spokesman for the idea that society owed a debt to those who suffered economic misfortunes: provision should be made for those persons as a duty of society and as a right of the individual, rather than as charity.

At Harvard Roosevelt had courses in economics that were centered on the economic problems of his time, courses that emphasized the growth of big business and economic concentration, the monetary problems of the period, and the growing maturity of America as the frontier disappeared. His professors were advocates of economic reform who took the attitude that the economic system was not to be judged on the basis of abstract principles alone, but on its performance as judged by its contribution to human welfare. Although it is difficult to estimate just what Roosevelt took from his

Harvard courses, one thing is clear—the courses themselves were part of that intellectual-political ferment that was leading to Progressivism.

Roosevelt emerged from college when the Progressive movement was in its early stages. The theme of that movement was political and economic reform in the interest of the common man, and it emphasized that concentration of economic power was the major reason for the failure of American democracy to realize fully its potentialities. Roosevelt's schooling in progressivism made these two points major elements of his economic-political philosophy. In his early political career F.D.R. was in the progressive tradition, fighting bossism and big business, supporting welfare legislation, advocating conservation and other liberal causes. He was influenced by the example of his "Uncle Ted" Roosevelt; he supported the progressivism of Woodrow Wilson.

The ideas of progressivism were applied by Roosevelt in his career as Assistant Secretary of the Navy, where he had practical experience in dealing with monopoly in industry and in working with a pro-labor policy. His statements about economic problems were much more sophisticated after his Navy Department experience than they were before it. Of importance, too, in these years, was economic mobilization in World War I, which gave some idea of what the modern industrial economy can accomplish when directed by government leadership toward the achievement of a particular goal.

The tradition of progressivism was carried on by Governor Smith of New York in the twenties, taking the form of a program of welfare legislation. F.D.R. was one of Smith's strongest supporters. It was in these years that Roosevelt emerged as a party leader who emphasized the economic basis of political parties and sought to base the policies of the Democratic party on a truly "progressive" program that would promote the welfare of the common man.

Roosevelt was fundamentally a reformer who accepted the general framework of economic institutions of his time. He accepted the concept of private enterprise—but wanted to improve the performance of business. As early as 1914 he had differed with his superior, Secretary of the Navy Daniels, over the purposes of the government's armor plate plant: while Daniels wanted a plant large enough to produce all the government's requirements, if necessary, F.D.R. wanted only a pilot plant that would act as a "yardstick" to judge the performance of the navy's suppliers. In the twenties F.D.R.'s work with the American Construction Council indicated the type of reform he thought was necessary in business: business-men themselves could improve the performance of industry by cooperation, and public service could become the goal of responsible business leaders. In this way business itself could set its own high standards, and reduce the influence of the speculator, the promoter, and the monopolist. Roosevelt was not troubled by the possibility that the trade association might develop into an organ of monopoly. What Roosevelt condemned about modern American business enterprise was the development of monopoly and the concentration of eco-nomic power—as, for example, in his Tammany Hall speech of July, 1929. He was not anti-business, but was opposed to monopoly and financial promotions.

One of the most interesting aspects of Roosevelt's economic thought was his advocacy of land-use planning. Beginning with a strong interest in farming that arose in the rural en-vironment at Hyde Park, he was an early advocate of con-servation and reforestation. His desire to preserve and strengthen rural life appeared at an early date, and was sup-plemented by acquaintance with the regional plan idea as it was applied to cities. Government development of water power resources, advocated by Governor Smith, was likewise promoted by Roosevelt. During the latter's terms as gov-ernor these threads emerged as a regional plan for New York, comprising a comprehensive land-use survey, reforestation, road construction and building of regional markets, electrifi-cation, and dispersal of industry into rural areas.

Supplementing F.D.R.'s reforming attitude toward business and agriculture was his advocacy of social welfare legislation: laws protecting the worker, unemployment insurance, and old age insurance.

Roosevelt's advocacy of reform was always tempered by political considerations as he sought the best methods of promoting his ideas in the particular circumstances of the moment. Although his individual utterances are not good guides to his thinking, there was, nevertheless, a considerable degree of consistency in his actions and statements. The road to reform, as Roosevelt trod it, was not always straight and narrow, but its windings were always in a consistent direction.

While Roosevelt's economic philosophy found its greatest strength in long-range reforms, particularly welfare legislation and land-use planning, it found its greatest weakness in finding policies to meet the depression emergency. There was little enough in progressivism or in the desire to help the underdog—or, indeed, in the orthodox economic thinking of the late twenties and early thirties—that would lead to effective anti-depression policies.

Roosevelt's economic thought did contain the germ of a comprehensive attack on the depression: his underconsumption theory of depression origins. His proposals to raise farm purchasing power and provide a better relief system for the unemployed were considered by Roosevelt to be means by which consumer spending could be increased. But if he had carried his underconsumption theory to its logical conclusion he would have advocated a large program of public works, and this he did not do.

By far the most important aspect of Roosevelt's program in 1932 was its acceptance of the principle of planning. F.D.R. did not advocate a system of comprehensive, central planning for the entire economy. But he did show a willingness to experiment with different kinds of planning to meet the needs of different areas of the economy.

The American people in 1932 had been prepared for such an approach by two developments. In the first place, government intervention in economic affairs had been growing for decades. Beginning with intervention in a few areas of the economy on a piecemeal basis—public utility regulation, acts regulating working conditions in factories, and the beginnings of conservation programs—the nation moved into the area of monetary controls with the Federal Reserve Act of 1914 and into the beginnings of farm relief in the twenties. With the onset of the depression Hoover went even further, attempting especially in the area of finance and credit to take effective action against the depression.

In the second place, the depression itself was so severe, and recovery from it seemed so far off, that many persons lost faith in the idea that a normal, natural recovery would quickly come. Maybe the freely operating market economy would ultimately bring about a recovery, but it would take so long and be so costly that the nation could not trust itself to the process. F.D.R. himself expressed this idea in his speech at Oglethorpe University on May 22, 1932, when he advocated planning to avoid depressions. Roosevelt recognized the mood of the nation, that it was willing to experiment with new and fairly drastic methods of ordering economic life, and developed several types of planning in the early New Deal.

The principle of land-use planning expressed by Roosevelt as Governor appeared in the early New Deal in the Tennessee Valley Authority and its program of cooperation between a government corporation, local government, and individuals for river valley development. The Civilian Conservation Corps of the early New Deal was another form given to F.D.R.'s ideas of land-use planning.

In the 1932 campaign Roosevelt accepted the principle of planning as a means of raising farm prices; the result was the AAA legislation of 1933, encompassing benefit payments to farmers and restriction of output. Planning for agriculture was to be done by the Federal Department of Agriculture, with approval by the farmers.

In industry, trade associations were to "adjust production and consumption" through codes of fair practice supervised by government. Roosevelt's work with the American Construction Council in the twenties was a partial step in that direction, and his endorsement of the major principles of the Swope Plan at the Commonwealth Club in San Francisco on September 23, 1932, was the preamble to restriction of output and maintenance of prices by trade associations under the NRA codes.

All of these forms that were given to the principle of planning encompassed varying amounts of government direction, voluntary participation, and compulsory participation. They were experiments in new forms of social control, variations on the theme of planning in economic affairs. Aside from emergency banking legislation, the most striking aspects of the program of the "hundred days" of March-June, 1933, were NRA and AAA, and perhaps the most lasting monument of the early New Deal will be TVA.

The "positive state" as it was developing in the Roosevelt program encompassed more than planning in several forms, however. The framework within which private enterprise could operate was to be more closely defined and Federal regulations extended, i.e., railroad bankruptcy laws and securities regulation. Welfare legislation was to be extended, through unemployment and old age insurance. The debtor was to be aided by government provision of farm credit and loans to home owners. An expanded program of unemployment relief was to be adopted. In many ways other than planning the Federal government was to take greater responsibility for the functioning of the economy.

Clearly, the Roosevelt program enunciated in 1932 and developed in the early New Deal represented a turning point in economic policy. Although it had its antecedents, including a number of measures adopted during the Hoover administration, it represented an important advance of government intervention into new fields, using a variety of new techniques. The "positive state" was advancing on all fronts: regulation of business activity, welfare legislation, planning.

Herbert Hoover, who discerned this aspect of Roosevelt's New Deal, did not clarify matters by his charge of socialism. Roosevelt's program was far from the fundamental beliefs of the socialists: he did not advocate Federal ownership of basic industries or comprehensive planning of economic life, nor did he reject the profit system as the motivating force for production and distribution. Hoover misstated the problem, and Roosevelt's answer that he was not a socialist disposed of the criticism as far as Roosevelt was concerned.

Nevertheless, a real problem remains: would Roosevelt's "positive state" preserve conditions in the economy within which private enterprise could operate with vigor and health? Roosevelt thought that it would, indeed, that such action as his program represented was essential to the preservation of private enterprise. Nevertheless, the problem remains, more than twenty years later. Is the "positive state" a temporary stopping place on the road to socialism, or is it a true alternative?

Notes

INTRODUCTION

1. Broadus Mitchell, *Depression Decade* (New York, Rinehart, 1947), p. 124.
2. George Soule, *Economic Forces in American History* (New York, William Sloane, 1952), p. 494.
3. Richard Hofstadter, *The American Political Tradition and the Men Who Made It* (New York, 1948, reprinted 1954), Ch. XII. Hofstadter's view is in many respects a revival of a certain type of attack on Roosevelt made by his political opponents of the thirties, embellished with a number of carefully selected quotations and incidents. Compare the statement by Francis R. Stoddard, a New York Republican and long-time political opponent of Roosevelt's: "I would say that he [F.D.R.] was an opportunist who did every act from the standpoint of how much it would benefit him politically; he had no standard of right and wrong in the ordinary sense." "Reminiscences of Francis R. Stoddard," Oral History Research Project, Columbia University, p. 122.
4. Frances Perkins, *The Roosevelt I Knew* (New York, Viking Press, 1946), pp. 225-26. Most economists shared Roosevelt's bewilderment: the early reviews of Keynes's *General Theory of Employment, Interest and Money* (1936) are notable for their concern with small points and lack of comment on the central ideas. See Seymour Harris (ed.), *The New Economics* (New York, 1948), pp. 29-38.
5. Perkins, *The Roosevelt I Knew*, p. 34.

CHAPTER I: THE ROOSEVELT FAMILY BACKGROUND

1. New York *Tribune*, Dec. 9, 1900.
2. Bellamy Partridge, *The Roosevelt Family in America: An Imperial Saga* (New York, Hillman-Curl, 1936), pp. 46-47.
3. Rev. Edward P. Newton, *Historical Notes of St. James Parish* (Poughkeepsie, A. V. Haight Co., 1913), p. 44.

4. A more detailed description of Warren Delano as a China trader, the sources of his wealth, and his investments may be found in Daniel W. Delano, Jr., *Franklin Roosevelt and the Delano Influence* (Pittsburgh, James S. Nudi Publications, 1946), pp. 157-71, especially pp. 158-63.

5. Elliott Roosevelt (ed.), *F.D.R.: His Personal Letters* (New York, Duell, Sloan and Pierce, 1947-50), II, 274-75. Hereafter cited as *Letters*. Reproduced by permission of the publishers.

6. The Roosevelts also took annual trips to Europe so that James Roosevelt could visit the spas. On one of these trips F.D.R. was placed in the Nauheim Volkschule "to improve his German." On another he and his tutor went on a bicycle trip through France.

7. Tutorial Notebook, Sept. 29, 1891, Roosevelt Library.

8. Tutorial Notebook "Anglais," May, 1893, Roosevelt Library. Spelling and punctuation by F.D.R.

9. Franklin D. Roosevelt, "The Roosevelt Family in New Amsterdam before the Revolution" (Harvard College sophomore thesis, 1901, Roosevelt Library), p. 7.

10. An interesting discussion of the connection between *noblesse oblige* and democracy in Franklin D. Roosevelt's family heritage is to be found in "What's to Become of Us," *Fortune*, VIII, No. 6 (Dec., 1933), 114-17.

11. Arthur M. Schlesinger uses the term "Jeffersonian Aristocracy" and points out that in the early nineteenth century "political power had shifted . . . to a landed aristocracy . . . functioning as the guardian and protector of the masses" and "moved rather by a lofty spirit of public service and a sense of *noblesse oblige* than by unfaltering acceptance of democratic dogma." See Arthur M. Schlesinger, *New Viewpoints in American History* (New York, Macmillan, 1922), pp. 84-85.

12. Partridge, *The Roosevelt Family*, pp. 26-27; Karl Schriftgiesser, *The Amazing Roosevelt Family* (New York, Funk, 1942), pp. 108-21, 177-83; "Papers of Members of the Roosevelt Family, 1715-1863," Roosevelt Library.

13. Vernon L. Parrington, *Main Currents in American Thought* (New York, Harcourt, Brace, 1927), III, 7.

CHAPTER II: ROOSEVELT'S FORMAL EDUCATION IN ECONOMICS

1. Sermon by Rev. Endicott Peabody, October 14, 1900, in *Consecration of St. John's Chapel, Groton School* (Boston, T. R. Marvin and Son, 1900), pp. 25-26.

2. Joseph Dorfman, *The Economic Mind in American Civilization* (New York, Viking Press, 1949), III, 239.

3. The Groton School Catalogue for 1896-97 describes the course as follows: "Political Economy. Fundamental Principles of Political Economy. Lectures and Discussions. No textbook used."

There is no record of who actually taught the course, but Henry H. Richards, Alumni Recorder of Groton School, is "reasonably sure that the course in question was given by Guy Ayrault." (Richards to the author, Nov. 29, 1952.)

4. Mill had abandoned the theory in 1869 in a review of Thornton's *Labour and Its Claims*, but retained it in later editions of his *Principles of Political Economy*. Francis A. Walker's book *The Wages Question* (1876) sounded the death knell of the wages fund doctrine.

5. F.D.R. to Sara Roosevelt, Jan. 23, 1900, *Letters*, I, 379.

6. F.D.R. to Sara Roosevelt, Nov. 10, 1899, *ibid.*, p. 358.

7. F.D.R. to Sara Roosevelt, Jan. 11, 1900, *ibid.*, p. 374.

8. F.D.R. to Sara Roosevelt, Jan. 21, 1900, *ibid.*, p. 378.

9. *Ibid.*, pp. 160-65.

10. F.D.R. valued very highly his debating experience at Groton. After he became President he gave annual prizes to the foremost debaters in the Senior and Junior debating societies there. (Endicott Peabody to F.D.R., May 26, 1936; F.D.R. to Peabody, June 11, 1938, Roosevelt Library.)

11. *Letters*, I, 240-41, 253-55, 282-86.

12. *Ibid.*, p. 434.

13. *Ibid.*, p. 34.

14. For the four years Roosevelt accumulated the following semester hour credits: history, 36; English, 25; economics, 18; government, 18; geology, 9; French, 6; Fine Art, 6; philosophy, 3.

15. Andrew later became chief research economist for the National Monetary Commission (1908-12) which recommended reform of the banking system, and was Assistant Secretary of the Treasury under President Taft.

16. Required reading for the semester was:

John Stuart Mill, *Principles of Economics:* pp. 17-27; Book I, Chs. 3-6 (except pp. 94-103 and 110-27), 8, 10; Book II, Chs. 3, 11, 14-16; Book III, Chs. 1-5, 7-13.

Arthur Twining Hadley, *Economics: An Account of the Relations between Private Property and Public Welfare:* Chs. 3, 7 (except sections 318-28), 9, 10 (sections 346-52 only).

See G. M. Blakney, *Tutorial Outline for Economics I (1901-02)*, Harvard Archives.

17. G. M. Blakney, *Tutorial Outline for Economics I (1901-02)* p. 34, Harvard Archives.

18. Required reading for the second half-year was:

Mill, *Principles:* Book III, Chs. 17-18, 20-21, 25 (Sections 3-4); Book V, Ch. 4 (Sections 5-6), Ch. 10 (Section 1); Book I, Ch. 9 (Sections 1-2).

Hadley, *Economics*, Sections 467-93 and Ch. 6.

Charles F. Dunbar, *Chapters on the Theory and History of Banking*, Chs. 1-7 and 9-12.

See *Self-Tutoring Notes, Economics I, 2nd half 1902*, Harvard Archives. These tutorial notes contain summaries of Andrew's lectures to the class of which Roosevelt was a member.

19. *Self-Tutoring Notes, Economics I, 2nd half 1902*, p. 37.

20. *Ibid.*, p. 40.

21. Frederick J. Turner, "The Significance of the Frontier in American History," reprinted in *The Frontier in American History*, New York, Henry Holt, 1920, p. 2.

22. For the views of Turner at this time, see "The Problem of The West," "The Middle West," and "Contributions of the West to American Democracy," reprinted in *The Frontier in American History*, pp. 126-56, 205-21, 243-68.

23. Notebook of Albert G. Waite for History 10B, Spring, 1904, Harvard Archives. This notebook contains lecture notes for the classes Roosevelt attended.

24. William Z. Ripley (ed.), *Trusts, Pools and Corporations* (Ginn, Boston and New York, 1905), pp. xix-xxx.

25. William Z. Ripley, "The Capitalization of Public Service Corporations," *ibid.*, p. 148.

26. The Notebook of Albert G. Waite for Economics 9B, Economics of Corporations, 1904, Harvard Archives, gives us a picture of the course Roosevelt had as well as Ripley's approach and main ideas. The required reading included substantial portions of Jeremiah W. Jenks's *The Trust Problem*, E. S. Meade's *Trust Finance*, Richard T. Ely's *Monopolies and Trusts*, and John A. Hobson's *Evolution of Modern Capitalism.*

From time to time additional assignments were made, of two types. First, scholarly and scientific studies: articles in the *Economic Journal*, *Quarterly Journal of Economics*, *Political Science Quarterly*, and the *Journal of Political Economy*, the text of the Northern Securities decision of 1904, and parts of the U.S. Industrial Commission Report on Trusts. Second, popular works, some of them of a muckraking type: Ida Tarbell's and G. H. Montague's books on the Standard Oil Company, an article by Lincoln Steffens in *McClure's Magazine*, and John Moody's *Truth about the Trusts*.

27. *Railroads: Finance and Organization* (New York, Longmans, Green, 1915); and *Railroads: Rates and Regulations* (New York, Longmans, Green, 1912).

28. The Notebook of Albert G. Waite for Economics 5, Economics of Transportation, 1903-4, Harvard Archives, contains a summary of the course Roosevelt had. It follows, basically, the contents of Ripley's two books on the subject published some years later. The textbook used was Emory R. Johnson's *American Railway Transportation*, with generous additional reading assigned in Arthur Twining Hadley's early classic in the field, *Railroad Transportation*, Charles Francis and Henry Adams's *Chapters of Erie*, numerous articles in the professional economic journals as well as in more popular magazines, and parts of the report of the U.S. Industrial Commission.

29. Hadley had shown twenty years earlier that when fixed charges are high and competition forces returns to a level that just covers operating costs, the normal reaction of the firms involved will be to eliminate the price-cutting by agreement or merger. Arthur Twining Hadley, *Railroad Transportation* (New York, Putnam, 1885). Ripley agreed with this argument.

30. Notebook of Albert G. Waite for Economics 5, 1903-4 Harvard Archives; Ripley, *Railroads: Finance and Organization*, pp. 594-607.

31. The Notebook of Albert G. Waite for Economics 8A, 1904, Harvard Archives, contains full notes for the classes attended by Roosevelt.

32. Including chapters and articles by John Stuart Mill, J. Laurence Laughlin, Francis A. Walker, Frank W. Taussig, J. F. Johnson, and others.

33. Andrew's position that the general level of prices and the price of gold move together was close to the orthodox economics of his time. J. Laurence Laughlin argued that there was a definite relationship between the general price level and the value of gold (Joseph Dorfman, *The Economic Mind in American Civilization*, III, 274), and Fred M. Taylor wrote in 1906 that raising the price of gold would quickly result in a higher price level (*ibid.*, p. 394). None of these men advocated a deliberate revaluation of the dollar to control prices, but that idea appeared in the theories of Warren and Pearson in the early thirties and in the gold policies of the early New Deal.

34. *History of Crises under the National Banking System* (Washington, Govt. Printing Office, 1910) and *Banking Reform in the United States* (Cambridge, Mass., Harvard, 1911).

35. The Notebook of Albert G. Waite for Economics 8B, 1903,

Harvard Archives, gives a summary of the course a year before Roosevelt took it. Chief assigned readings were in Charles F. Dunbar's *Theory and History of Banking*, Walter Bagehot's *Lombard Street*, George Clare's *Money Market Primer*, Charles A. Conant's *History of Modern Banks of Issue*, and Sprague's *New York Money Market*. The students were to write two papers: the first on the London money market, explaining the cause of the fluctuations in the discount rate for any six weeks since 1889; the second on the New York money market, doing the same for 60-day "sight bills." Sources to be used were the financial newspapers and journals.

36. *Ibid.*, pp. 57-59.

37. *Ibid.*, pp. 285-87. These are Waite's words, not Sprague's.

38. F.D.R. could have taken courses dealing with various aspects of economic theory and the history of economic thought (taught by Taussig, Carver, Andrew, Bullock, and Gay), economic history (taught by Gay, Sprague, and Bullock), business-oriented courses in accounting and insurance (taught by Cole and Wambaugh), or courses on labor (Ripley), international trade (Sprague), public finance (Bullock and Taussig), and agriculture (Carver).

39. Interview with James P. Gifford, Associate Dean of the Law School, Sept. 20, 1952; Frank Freidel, *Franklin D. Roosevelt: The Apprenticeship* (Boston, Little, Brown, 1952), p. 76.

40. *Letters*, II, 64-65.

41. *Ibid.*, p. 85.

42. Other courses taken by F.D.R. in his first year (1904-5) with the teacher and the textbook were:

Pleading and Practice. Henry S. Redfield. Ames, *Cases on Common Law Pleading;* Perry, *Common Law Pleading;* Thompson, *Cases on Equity Pleading and Practice.*

Contracts. Charles T. Terry. Keener, *Cases on Contracts.*

Domestic Relations and Law of Persons. James B. Scott. Smith, *Law of Persons.*

Equity. James B. Scott. Keener, *Cases on Equity.*

Real and Personal Property. George W. Kirchwey. Gray, *Cases on Property*, Vol. 1; Kirchwey, *Readings in Real Property.*

Torts. Francis M. Burdick. Burdick, *Cases on Torts;* Pollock, *Torts.*

43. For an analysis of Burgess's views see Bernard E. Brown, *American Conservatives: The Political Thought of Frances Lieber and John W. Burgess* (New York, Columbia University Press, 1951).

44. F.D.R., "Notebook on Constitutional Law," unnumbered page, Roosevelt Library.

45. *Ibid.*, p. 41.

46. Roosevelt also took the following courses in his second year (1905-6):

Agency. Jackson E. Reynolds. Wambaugh, *Cases on Agency.*

Equity. William C. Dennis. Ames, *Cases on Equity*, Vols. 1-2.

Pleading and Practice. Henry S. Redfield. Thompson, *Cases on Code Pleading and Practice; New York Code of Civil Procedure.*

Negotiable Paper. George F. Canfield. Ames, *Cases on Bills and Notes.*

Quasi Contracts. James B. Scott. Scott, *Cases on Quasi Contracts.*

Real and Personal Property. George W. Kirchwey. Gray, *Cases on Property*, Vols. 2 and 3.

47. Joseph H. Beale, Jr., and Bruce Wyman, *Cases on Public Service Companies, Public Carriers, Public Works and Other Public Utilities* (Cambridge, Mass., Harvard Law Review Publ. Assn., 1902). Roosevelt's copy is in the Roosevelt Library.

48. *Ibid.*, p. 83. This dissenting opinion of Field's was the basis of the decision in *Smyth vs. Ames.* Roosevelt must have missed the discussion of *Smyth vs. Ames*, because that case is not annotated or underlined and there is a notation that it should be carefully studied.

49. Penciled notes by F.D.R. on *I.C.C. vs. Detroit, Grand Haven and Milwaukee Ry.* (1897), Roosevelt Library.

50. Penciled notes by F.D.R. on *I.C.C. vs. Alabama Midland Rr.* (1897), *ibid.*

51. Freidel, *Franklin D. Roosevelt: The Apprenticeship*, p. 76.

52. Roosevelt's third year (1906-7) law courses were:

Corporations. George F. Canfield. Keener, *Cases on Corporations.*

Evidence. William C. Dennis. Thayer, *Cases on Evidence*, (2nd ed.).

New York Trusts and Perpetuities. George F. Canfield. No textbook.

Partnership. Francis M. Burdick. Burdick, *Cases on Partnership*; Burdick, *Partnership* (2nd ed.).

Wills and Administration. Henry S. Redfield. Gray, *Cases on Property*, Vol. 4.

Conflict of Laws. J. B. Moore. Beale, *Cases on the Conflict of Laws.*

International Law. J. B. Moore. Scott, *Cases on International Law.*

Municipal Corporations. Frank J. Goodnow. Abbot, *Cases on Public Corporations*; Smith, *Cases on Municipal Corporations*.

Information on Roosevelt's law school courses was obtained from the Registrar, Columbia University. A list of his professors and textbooks was obtained from *Columbia University Bulletin of Information: School of Law* (New York, Columbia Univ., 1904, 1905, 1906).

CHAPTER III: FRANKLIN D. ROOSEVELT, PROGRESSIVE

1. Frances Perkins, *The Roosevelt I Knew* (New York, Viking Press, 1946), p. 9.

2. Interview with Mrs. Franklin D. Roosevelt, Aug. 16, 1951.

3. Chilly Harvard student Franklin D. Roosevelt, more interested in the political than the economic aspects of his "Uncle Ted's" intervention, wrote: "In spite of his success in settling the trouble, I think that the President made a serious mistake in interfering—politically, at least. His tendency to make the executive power stronger than the houses of Congress is bound to be a bad thing, especially when a man of weaker personality succeeds him in office." (*Letters*, I, 481.)

4. Leo Wolman, *Ebb and Flow in Trade Unionism* (New York, National Bureau of Economic Research, 1936), p. 16.

5. Theodore Roosevelt, *An Autobiography* (New York, Scribner's, 1912), p. 300.

6. Theodore Roosevelt, *The New Nationalism* (New York, Outlook, 1910), pp. 3-33.

7. *Ibid.*, pp. 23-24.

8. For a description of the Republican split in New York in 1910 see George Mowry, *Theodore Roosevelt and the Progressive Movement* (Madison, University of Wisconsin Press, 1946), pp. 134-55.

9. Frank Freidel, *Franklin D. Roosevelt: The Apprenticeship* (Boston, Little, Brown, 1952), p. 92.

10. Campaign speech at Hyde Park, Nov. 5, 1910, Roosevelt Library.

11. Campaign speech at Phillipstown, Nov. 2, 1910, summarized in the Cold Spring *Recorder*, Nov. 4, 1910; F.D.R. to the Editor, Hudson *Republican*, Nov. 7, 1910, p. 8.

12. Diary of F.D.R. for Jan. 1-3, 1911, entry for Jan. 1, Roosevelt Library.

13. Statement to the Press, Jan. 17, 1911, published in New York *Times* and Albany *Knickerbocker Press*, Jan. 18, 1911.

14. Quoted in the Toledo (Ohio) *News-Bee,* Jan. 23, 1911. Charles Murphy was the Tammany "boss."

15. Draft of speech given in the State Senate, April, 1911, Roosevelt Library; New York *Evening Globe,* Feb. 6, 1911; New York *American,* April 2, 1911.

16. F.D.R. to the Editor, New York *Times,* Sept. 6, 1912.

17. F.D.R. introduced a resolution requesting the United States Senators from New York to seek passage of a constitutional amendment to that effect. "Resolutions Proposed by the Hon. Franklin D. Roosevelt in the Senate of the State of New York," Roosevelt Library.

18. Speech before the Saturn Club, Buffalo, N.Y., Dec. 23, 1911, typescript and written notes in Roosevelt Library. A measure to provide for direct primaries was passed during the 1911 session of the legislature.

19. F.D.R. to the President of the Dutchess County Equal Suffrage League, Poughkeepsie *Daily Eagle,* May 30, 1911; F.D.R. to Miss Anna G. W. Dayley, Feb. 1, 1911, Roosevelt Library; F.D.R. to Miss Abbie Leach, May 24, 1911, Roosevelt Library.

20. Henry Salant to F.D.R., April 11, 1931. Salant had been a member of the State Senate at the same time as Roosevelt. In this letter, written eighteen years after the event, he recalled F.D.R.'s participation in the effort to annul the grant to the Aluminum Company.

21. F.D.R. was also a member of the Committee on Railroads and Canals in 1911-12 and Railroads, Codes, and Military Affairs in 1913. *Manual for the Use of the Legislature of the State of New York* (Albany, J. B. Lyon, 1911, 1912, 1913).

22. William G. Hannan, "Legislative Bills Proposed by the Hon. Franklin D. Roosevelt in the Senate of the State of New York," typescript in Roosevelt Library; F.D.R. to Joseph P. Chamberlain, Oct. 29, 1912, Roosevelt Library.

23. F.D.R. to H. S. Rivenburgh, Feb. 22, 1912, Roosevelt Library.

24. Poughkeepsie *Evening Enterprise,* March 4, 1912.

25. Franklin D. Roosevelt, "Growing Up By Plan," *The Survey,* LXVII, No. 9 (Feb. 1, 1932), 483.

26. F.D.R.'s interest in local farmers was described by Mrs. Roosevelt in an interview with the author, Aug. 16, 1951.

27. F.D.R. to Dr. Thomas E. Bullard, Feb. 18, 1913, Roosevelt Library.

28. Hannan, "Legislative Bills"; F.D.R. to Pierre Jay, Feb. 28, 1913, Roosevelt Library; F.D.R. to Leonard G. Robinson, March

12, 1913, Roosevelt Library; F.D.R. to Welcome H. Lawson, March 12, 1913, Roosevelt Library.

29. "Addresses of the Honorable Franklin D. Roosevelt, October-November 1928," typescript in Roosevelt Library, p. 94.

30. Hannan, "Legislative Bills"; F.D.R. to Frank Evans, March 28, 1912; F.D.R. to E. Graham Wilson, March 28, 1912; F.D.R. to A. G. Watson, Jan. 14, 1913; F.D.R. to J. F. Sheahan, Feb. 4, 1913; F.D.R. to Thomas L. Delahunty, Feb. 11, 1913; Thomas D. Fitzgerald (Chairman of the Legislative Committee, N.Y. State Federation of Labor) to F.D.R., Nov. 1, 1912; F.D.R. to Rev. Walter Laidlaw, March 27, 1912; F.D.R. to W. J. Nichols, March 25, 1912; F.D.R. to Peter J. Brady, May 25, 1911, Roosevelt Library.

31. F.D.R. to Otto J. Merkel, May 8, 1911, Roosevelt Library.

32. F.D.R. to Peter J. Brady, May 16, 1911, Roosevelt Library.

33. Perkins, *Roosevelt I Knew*, p. 14. Perkins concluded that F.D.R. at this period "had little, if any concern about specific social reforms" (*ibid.*, p. 13). This view is accepted by Bernard Bellush in his doctoral dissertation "Apprenticeship for the Presidency" (Columbia University, 1950), who says, "he [F.D.R.] had little more than a fundamental belief in good, clean, honest government" (Ch. 1, p. 3). Bellush claims that at this period F.D.R. "was quite disinterested in social and labor legislation" (Ch. 7, p. 37). This view is at variance with F.D.R.'s record in the State Senate.

34. John R. Commons and associates, *History of Labor in the United States* (New York, Macmillan, 1926-35), III, 478.

35. Abram I. Elkus to F.D.R., Feb. 6, 1913; F.D.R. to Elkus, Feb. 13, 1913, Roosevelt Library.

36. F.D.R. to Alburtis Nooney, Jan. 23, 1912, Roosevelt Library.

37. F.D.R. to George H. Putnam, March 17, 1911, Roosevelt Library.

38. F.D.R. to James L. Cowles, March 10, 1911; F.D.R. to William B. Millard, March 10, 1911, Roosevelt Library.

39. F.D.R. to A. M. Traver, March 11, 1912; F.D.R. to Oswald Garrison Villard, Jan. 30, 1913, Roosevelt Library.

40. Frederic A. Delano to F.D.R., undated letter, probably about April, 1911, Roosevelt Library.

41. Reported in the Troy (New York) *Record*, March 4, 1912. A typescript of the speech and certain sections of it in F.D.R.'s handwriting are in the Roosevelt Library. This speech is evidence that the ideas presented in Roosevelt's speeches and writings were his own: obviously composed by himself, it is a major landmark in the development of his economic thought.

42. Roosevelt's view that there is no essential conflict between capital and labor was also superficial: merely because they must cooperate in production is no reason to argue that there can be no conflicts.

43. Broadside of the New York State Wilson Conference, June 25, 1912, Roosevelt Library.

44. Broadside of the New York State Wilson Conference, undated, Roosevelt Library.

45. Resolution adopted by Empire State Democracy, July 17, 1912, Roosevelt Library.

46. F.D.R. to Thomas P. Gore, Oct. 15, 1912, Roosevelt Library.

47. Woodrow Wilson, *The New Freedom* (New York, Doubleday, Page, 1913), pp. 5-6. Quotations reproduced by permission of Doubleday and Company, Inc.

48. *Ibid.*, p. 7.

49. *Ibid.*, pp. 11-12.

50. *Ibid.*, p. 15.

51. *Ibid.*, pp. 173-76.

52. *Ibid.*, p. 187.

53. *Ibid.*, p. 180. Wilson's position was similar in many respects to that of Theodore Roosevelt. But Wilson thought of the trust as an artificial creation that could be prevented by laws outlawing predatory competition and controlling the financial operations of the trust-builders, as well as by dissolution. Theodore Roosevelt, on the other hand, considered combinations in industry "the result of an imperative economic law"; their development could not be prevented, but their activities should be controlled by a Federal Bureau of Corporations. Theodore Roosevelt, *The New Nationalism*, pp. 15-16.

54. Wilson, *The New Freedom*, p. 18.

55. *Ibid.*, pp. 229-39.

CHAPTER IV: THE NAVY DEPARTMENT

1. "First Draft of Armor Plate Statement," prepared for Secretary Daniels by Roosevelt's office, Howe Papers, Roosevelt Library.

2. Memorandum to the Press issued by Secretary Daniels, undated, Howe Papers, Roosevelt Library.

3. "Annual Report of the Secretary of the Navy," in *Annual Reports of the Navy Department for the Fiscal Year 1913* (Washington, Government Printing Office, 1914), p. 12.

4. "Annual Report of the Secretary of the Navy," in *Annual Re-*

ports of the Navy Department for the Fiscal Year 1914 (Washington, Government Printing Office, 1914), p. 12.

5. Josephus Daniels to Woodrow Wilson, April 12, 1913, Navy Archives 10580-148:3.

6. Memorandum to the Press issued by Secretary Daniels.

7. "Annual Report of the Secretary of the Navy," 1913, pp. 12-13.

8. Josephus Daniels to Senator Claude A. Swanson, March 11, 1916, Navy Archives 26256-271:3.

9. "First Draft of Armor Plate Statement."

10. Bureau of Ordnance, "Armor Plate: cost of; and probable cost of Government factory for armor plate," June 28, 1913, Navy Archives 4174-157, p. 2. The cost per ton in a government-operated plant did not include interest on investment. Midvale Steel Company estimated that the cost would be considerably higher, especially if the government included interest on invested capital in the costs of operation. House Committee on Naval Affairs, *Hearings, 1916* (Washington, Government Printing Office, 1916), III, 3702.

11. "Annual Report of the Secretary of the Navy," 1913, p. 14.

12. "Annual Report of the Secretary of the Navy," in *Annual Reports of the Navy Department for the Fiscal Year 1916* (Washington, Government Printing Office, 1917), p. 21.

13. Charles M. Schwab (Chairman of the Board, Bethlehem Steel Company) to Woodrow Wilson, July 15, 1916, Navy Archives 26256-271:9.

14. Navy Archives 28680-1. If any replies were made they are not to be found in the Navy Archives.

15. "Annual Report of the Secretary of the Navy," 1913, p. 13. The factory had hardly begun production in 1920 when the Harding administration closed it.

16. Daniels to Wilson, April 12, 1913.

17. "Annual Report of the Secretary of the Navy," in *Annual Reports of the Navy Department for the Fiscal Year 1920* (Washington, Government Printing Office, 1920), p. 71.

18. Statement by Josephus Daniels, House Committee on Naval Affairs, *Hearings, 1917* (Washington, Government Printing Office, 1917), p. 931.

19. House Committee on Naval Affairs, *Hearings, 1916*, III, 3484.

20. F.D.R. to Warren Delano, Jan. 5, 1917, Roosevelt Library.

21. Letter from the Secretary of the Navy to Members of Congress, Sept. 29, 1913, Howe Papers, Roosevelt Library; Ernest K. Lindley, *Franklin D. Roosevelt: A Career in Progressive Democracy* (New York, Blue Ribbon Books, 1931), p. 130.

22. Statement by F.D.R., House Committee on Naval Affairs, *Hearings, 1915* (Washington, Government Printing Office, 1915), p. 958.

23. *Ibid.*

24. *Ibid.*, p. 960.

25. *Ibid.*, p. 960. Two bids were $2.85 per ton and seventeen were $2.90, but the low bidders reserved the right to increase the price to $2.90 as soon as an imminent freight-rate increase was approved by the Interstate Commerce Commission.

26. *Ibid.*, pp. 959, 961.

27. *Ibid.*, p. 968; Freidel, *Franklin D. Roosevelt: The Apprenticeship*, p. 212.

28. House Naval Affairs Committee, *Hearings, 1915*, p. 968. There was considerable criticism of the new policies: Senator Chilton of West Virginia objected to the purchase of Pennsylvania coal, and some of the coal from new mines was found to be unacceptable and the mines were stricken from the approved list.

29. "Annual Report of the Secretary of the Navy," 1913, p. 14.

30. New York *Herald*, Nov. 17, 1916; New York *Sun*, Nov. 17, 1916.

31. Franklin D. Roosevelt, "The National Need of Petroleum Reserves," *Petroleum Age*, III, No. 11 (Nov., 1916), 3.

32. "Annual Report of the Secretary of the Navy," in *Annual Reports of the Navy Department for the Fiscal Year 1919* (Washington, Government Printing Office, 1920), p. 205.

33. Josephus Daniels to F.D.R., Nov. 29, 1929; F.D.R. to Josephus Daniels, Dec. 5, 1929, Josephus Daniels Papers, Library of Congress.

34. *Annual Reports of the Navy Department for the Fiscal Year 1919*, pp. 197-205.

35. "Annual Report of the Secretary of the Navy," 1919, p. 96.

36. F.D.R. to Josephus Daniels, Dec. 5, 1929.

37. *Ibid.*

38. Speech to Columbia Lodge, No. 184, International Association of Machinists, April 29, 1913, reported in Washington *Post*, April 30, 1913.

39. Speech to District of Columbia Branch, American Association of Marine Draftsmen, June 17, 1913, reported in Washington *Herald*, June 18, 1913.

40. Freidel, *Franklin D. Roosevelt: The Apprenticeship*, pp. 196-98.

41. Washington *Times*, May 18, 1913; Boston *Herald*, May 19, 1913; Boston *Advertiser*, May 20, 1913; Boston *Post*, May 20,

1913; Boston *Transcript*, May 20, 1913; Boston *Globe*, May 20, 1913; Washington *Herald*, May 22, 1913.

42. Freidel, *Franklin D. Roosevelt: The Apprenticeship*, pp. 200-201.

43. Memorandum, F.D.R. to Daniels, Sept. 25, 1917, Josephus Daniels Papers, Library of Congress.

44. The principles adopted by the War Labor Board were as follows. There were to be no strikes or lockouts during the war (but no penalties were provided if there were). Workers had the right to bargain collectively through representatives of their own choosing, and workers were not to be fired for union membership or union activities. But unions were not to use coercion to induce non-union workers to join unions or to induce employers to bargain with them. The *status quo* with regard to union and closed shops was to be maintained. The basic eight-hour day was to apply whenever existing law required it, while in other cases the decision was to be based on the needs of both the government and the workers. As for wages, union rates would be paid if they had been customary and the principle of the "living wage" was to apply to all workers; minimum rates of pay were to be established. Lewis L. Lorwin, *The American Federation of Labor: History, Policies, and Prospects* (Washington, The Brookings Institution, 1933), pp. 167-68.

45. The best account of the work of the War Labor Policies Board is United States Department of Labor, Wage and Hour Division, Economics Branch, *Wartime Policies on Wages, Hours, and Other Labor Standards in the United States, 1917-1918* (Washington, 1942, mimeographed). For an official account see Grosvenor B. Clarkson, *Industrial America in the World War* (Boston and New York, Houghton Mifflin, 1923), pp. 287-89.

46. Memorandum, Felix Frankfurter to Sir Richard Crawford, July 1, 1918, Records of the War Labor Policies Board, National Archives. Frankfurter was chairman of the Board, which met weekly from May 29, 1918 to December 20, 1918; a final meeting was held on January 24, 1919. The Board comprised representatives of the various government departments and agencies concerned with wartime labor problems, the Labor Department, an economic adviser, and representatives of business and labor.

47. Memorandum, F.D.R. to Bureau of Supplies and Accounts, "Double Time for Sunday Work—H. E. Boucher Manufacturing Company," Records of the War Labor Policies Board, National Archives; Department of Labor, *Wartime Policies*, p. 29.

48. Minutes of the War Labor Policies Board, Oct. 25, 1919, National Archives. Roosevelt had just returned from a brief trip to Europe. The Board amended its stand against night work by endorsing a system of night work permits for women in plants in which greater production was an absolute necessity (Department of Labor, *Wartime Policies*, p. 33).

49. Speaking of the labor policies of the Navy Department and Roosevelt's participation in them, Josephus Daniels said that "we both early favored the advantages to labor which came years afterwards in industry and the whole country under his 'New Deal.'" Josephus Daniels, *The Wilson Era: Years of War and After, 1917-1923* (Chapel Hill, University of North Carolina Press, 1946), p. 253.

50. Speech before the Democratic Women's Club, Syracuse, New York, Sept. 26, 1919 (undated clipping from an unidentified Syracuse newspaper, Scrapbook 9, p. 154, Roosevelt Library).

51. Speech before the Knights of Columbus, Philadelphia, Pa., Nov. 11, 1919, reported in Philadelphia *Record*, Nov. 12, 1919.

52. Commencement Address at Worcester Polytechnic Institute, June 25, 1919, typescript in Roosevelt Library, p. 3.

CHAPTER V: THE CAMPAIGN OF 1920

1. Herbert Hoover, *Memoirs* (New York, Macmillan Co., 1952), II, 5.

2. Quoted in Charles A. and Mary R. Beard, *The Rise of American Civilization* (New York, Macmillan Co., 1941), II, 664.

3. Undated draft of a statement in Roosevelt's handwriting, Roosevelt Library.

4. Quoted from an untitled and undated carbon copy of a typescript, probably written by either Louis Howe or Roosevelt, but in any case a product of Roosevelt's office, Roosevelt Library, Assistant Secretary of the Navy Papers, Box 141.

5. *Ibid.*

6. "Platform Recommendations Emphasizing Home Affairs," undated carbon copy of a typescript, Roosevelt Library, Assistant Secretary of the Navy Papers, Box 139. This document was probably the joint work of Roosevelt and Howe.

The prosperity bond idea was not original with Roosevelt. Herbert J. Davenport had suggested such a scheme in his *Outlines of Economic Theory*, published in 1896. See Joseph Dorfman, *The*

Economic Mind in American Civilization (New York, Viking, 1949), III, 379-80.

7. F.D.R. to John K. Sague, March 1, 1920, Roosevelt Library.

8. F.D.R. to Ellery Sedgwick, July 31, 1920; F.D.R. to James L. Doherty, July 17, 1920; F.D.R. to Frank H. Daley, July 22, 1920, Roosevelt Library.

9. New York *Times*, Aug. 10, 1920.

10. Speech at Chicago, Aug. 11, 1920, Roosevelt Library.

11. Speech at Minneapolis, Minn., Aug. 13, 1920, Roosevelt Library.

12. Quoted in an unidentified newspaper clipping, Roosevelt Library, Scrapbook 14, p. 138. This statement is not in the carbon copy transcript of the speech in the Roosevelt Library.

13. Speech at Fargo, N.D., Aug. 16, 1920, Roosevelt Library.

14. Statement to *The Farm Journal*, Aug. 5, 1920, Roosevelt Library.

15. Speech at Billings, Mont., Aug. 17, 1920; speech at Spokane, Wash., Aug. 19, 1920; speech at Yakima, Wash., Aug. 20, 1920, Roosevelt Library.

16. Speech at Centralia, Wash., Aug. 21, 1920, Roosevelt Library.

17. Speech at Grand Rapids, Nebr., Aug. 28, 1920, New York *Times*, Aug. 29, 1920; speech at Delphi, Ind., Aug. 30, 1920, Indianapolis *Times*, Aug. 30, 1920; speech at Butte, Mont., Aug. 18, 1920, unidentified newspaper clipping, Roosevelt Library, Scrapbook 14, p. 92.

18. Speech at Brooklyn (N.Y.) Navy Yard, Sept. 6, 1920, New York *Times*, Sept. 7, 1920.

19. F.D.R. to Luther C. Steward (President, National Federation of Federal Employees), Sept. 1, 1920, Roosevelt Library.

20. F.D.R. to Robert L. Mott, Oct. 18, 1920, Roosevelt Library. The proposal to issue prosperity bonds as a remedy for depression clearly recognized the importance of *spending* as a remedy, but the attribution of *currency inflation* as the cause of high prices did not recognize the role of spending as a cause. Roosevelt's ideas in this area of economics were not integrated into a consistent whole. The same could be said of most professional economists of the time.

21. Speech at Albany, N.Y., Sept. 20, 1920, Roosevelt Library.

22. Speech at Charleston, W.Va., Sept. 30, 1920, Roosevelt Library.

23. F.D.R. to Mrs. W. S. Benson, Nov. 15, 1920; F.D.R. to Col. Martin Archer-She, Nov. 9, 1920; F.D.R. to H. B. Baylor, Nov. 8, 1920; F.D.R. to John C. Duggan, Nov. 18, 1920; F.D.R. to William Cheatham, Nov. 9, 1920, Roosevelt Library.

CHAPTER VI: ROOSEVELT EMERGES AS A PARTY LEADER

1. For examples of this viewpoint see Frances Perkins, *The Roosevelt I Knew* (New York, Viking, 1946), p. 30, and John Gunther, *Roosevelt in Retrospect* (New York, Harper, 1950), pp. 242-43. F.D.R. was stricken by polio on August 10, 1921, and was unable to work for a year; by early fall of 1922 he was able to move about on crutches and returned to his law practice and other work.

2. Perkins, *Roosevelt I Knew*, p. 32.

3. Eleanor Roosevelt, *This Is My Story* (New York, Bantam, 1950), p. 259.

4. Perkins, *Roosevelt I Knew*, pp. 30-32.

5. List of books owned by Franklin D. Roosevelt and Anna Eleanor Roosevelt, undated longhand copy in the handwriting of F.D.R. and his wife, Roosevelt Library. The latest date on the list is 1904.

6. Hendrick W. Van Loon, "What Governor Roosevelt Reads," *Saturday Review of Literature*, IX, No. 13 (Oct. 15, 1932), 171.

7. F.D.R., "Memorandum on Leadership," July 6, 1928, Roosevelt Library.

8. F.D.R., "The Danger of Big Cities," speech before the Berkshire Bankers' Association, Lenox, Mass., June 20, 1921, (Berkshire, Mass., *Evening Eagle*, June 21, 1921).

9. F.D.R., Review of *Jefferson and Hamilton: The Struggle for Democracy in America*, New York *Evening World*, Dec. 3, 1925; reprinted in *The American Mercury*, LXI, No. 261 (Sept., 1945), 277-81.

10. Claude Bowers to F.D.R., Dec. 2, 1925, Roosevelt Library. Roosevelt's political importance at the time is indicated by his being chosen to write the review for the *World*, of which Bowers was an editorial writer. Other reviews were by John W. Davis, recently defeated Democratic candidate for the presidency, for the Sunday *World*, Senator Borah for the *New Republic*, Senator Beveridge for the Boston *Transcript*, James Truslow Adams for the New York *Sun* and Prof. Dodd of the University of Chicago for the New York *Tribune*.

11. F.D.R. to Dr. W. C. Martin, Dec. 9, 1925, Roosevelt Library.

12. Eight years later F.D.R. was able to unite all of these divergent groups. He was from upstate New York and not identified with Tammany politics—this satisfied the political heirs of Bryan. Yet he could get the votes, and this endeared him to the city machines. A Protestant, for a long time he compromised on prohibi-

tion; this, along with his ties with the South at Warm Springs, Georgia, made him acceptable to southerners. Roosevelt was an ideal candidate, and some commentators thought at the time that he could have had the nomination in 1924 if he had given the word.

13. F.D.R. to James A. Edgerton, Jan. 27, 1925, Roosevelt Library.

14. F.D.R. to Josephus Daniels, Dec. 5, 1924, Josephus Daniels Papers, Library of Congress. Identical letters were sent to hundreds of other party leaders.

15. F.D.R. to Senator Thomas J. Walsh, New York *Times*, March 9, 1925.

16. New York *Times*, March 9, 10, April 5, 9, 1925; "Premature Harmonizers," editorial, New York *Times*, April 10, 1925.

17. F.D.R. to Myron D. Kings, June 15, 1925, Roosevelt Library.

18. Fourth draft of "Confidential Memorandum by Cordell Hull," undated but probably March or April, 1927: the first draft is dated March 9, 1927, the second draft is dated March 13, 1927, Roosevelt Library.

19. Louis Howe to F.D.R., undated but probably 1928, Roosevelt Library.

20. F.D.R. to Frank R. Kent, October, 1925, Roosevelt Library.

21. F.D.R., statement written for the *Political Bulletin* of the Women's City Club of New York, 1924, Roosevelt Library; F.D.R. to Holston Bartelson, May 21, 1925, Roosevelt Library. The "scientific" tariff based on differences in manufacturing costs has the objective of protecting the American manufacturer against imports of foreign goods produced at lower costs. It is *not* designed to maximize tariff revenues. Roosevelt's equation of these two types of tariffs was incorrect. In this respect he was repeating an error common among Democratic politicians of the time.

22. Keynote speech at Democratic State Convention, Syracuse, N.Y., Sept. 27, 1926, Roosevelt Library, pp. 14-15.

23. F.D.R. to Senator Thomas J. Walsh, Feb. 22, 1926, Roosevelt Library; New York *Times*, Jan. 9, 1926. The "Lowden plan" called for farm cooperatives to purchase surplus farm products and sell them abroad. The goal was to keep prices for staple farm products above the world price. Any losses on foreign sales by the cooperatives were to be made up by an "equalization fee" paid by the farmer to the cooperative; since only a part of the crop would be sold abroad the farmer would be, in effect, obtaining higher prices only on that part of the crop consumed domestically. The "Lowden plan" was similar to the McNary-Haugen Bills of 1924 and 1925 in its basic principles, but would substitute operation of

the plan by farm cooperatives for operation by a government agency. The Dickinson Bill of 1926 embodied this idea, as did the McNary-Haugen Bills of 1926 and 1927. See John D. Black, *Agricultural Reform in the United States* (New York, McGraw-Hill, 1929), pp. 233-35.

24. Reprinted in Donald S. Carmichael (ed.), *F.D.R., Columnist: The Uncollected Columns of Franklin D. Roosevelt* (New York, Farrar, Strauss and Young, 1947).

25. *Ibid.*, pp. 33-34.

26. *Ibid.*, p. 69.

27. Henry Moscowitz (ed.), *Progressive Democracy: Addresses and State Papers of Alfred E. Smith* (New York, Harcourt, Brace, 1928), p. 51.

28. William G. Mosher, "Public Utilities and Their Recent Regulation," in *History of the State of New York* (New York, Columbia University Press, 1935), pp. 231-70; A. B. Knapp, "Water Power Problems in New York State" (Master's Thesis, Syracuse University, 1928) *passim*.

29. F.D.R. to Smith, Oct. 14, 1918, Roosevelt Library.

30. F.D.R. to Smith, Oct. 25, 1922, Roosevelt Library.

31. F.D.R., "Problems and Policies in New York State," *American Review of Reviews*, LXIX, No. 6 (June, 1924), 604-7; F.D.R., "Smith—Public Servant," *The Outlook*, CXXVII, No. 8 (June 25, 1924), pp. 390-91.

32. F.D.R. to Josephus Daniels, June 23, 1927, Roosevelt Library.

33. Eleanor Roosevelt, *This I Remember* (New York, Harper, 1949), p. 38.

34. F.D.R. to Josephus Daniels, July 20, 1928; F.D.R. to Van Lear Black, July 25, 1928, Roosevelt Library.

35. Carmichael (ed.), *F.D.R., Columnist*, pp. 114-15.

36. *Ibid.*, pp. 117-20.

37. *Ibid.*, pp. 121-31.

38. *Ibid.*, pp. 138-39.

39. *Ibid.*, p. 140.

40. Speech at Syracuse, N.Y., Sept. 27, 1926, Roosevelt Library, pp. 1-2.

41. Roosevelt's position was presented in his article "What Price Flood Relief," *National Business Review*, VI, No. 3 (Oct. 1, 1927), 6-7. Although the magazine was campaigning for a Great Lakes-Gulf waterway to be tied in with a flood control program—and Roosevelt knew it—he hardly mentioned such a project in his article. Hoover had already proposed publicly that development of inland waterways be combined with flood control (New York

Times, Aug. 28, 1927). Roosevelt favored a development program for the Mississippi Valley that would include development of waterways, flood control, and hydroelectric power development (F.D.R. to Alfred E. Smith, May 20, 1927, Roosevelt Library), although he did not advocate such a program publicly.

42. F.D.R., Address before the Schenectady County Democratic Organization, Schenectady, N.Y., March 12, 1930, *Public Papers of Governor Franklin D. Roosevelt, 1930* (Albany, J. B. Lyon Co., 1931), p. 714. Hereafter cited as *Public Papers, 1930.*

43. F.D.R., Address before the Young Men's Democratic Club, Hotel Astor, New York City, April 30, 1931, *Public Papers of Governor Franklin D. Roosevelt, 1931* (Albany, J. B. Lyon Co., 1937), p. 731. Hereafter cited as *Public Papers, 1931.*

44. F.D.R., Radio address to Thirty Luncheons in Honor of Thomas Jefferson, April 12, 1930, *Public Papers, 1930,* p. 427.

CHAPTER VII: INTERLUDE: BUSINESS AFFAIRS

1. New York *Times,* Aug. 26, Sept. 25, 30, 1920.

2. *Ibid.,* Oct. 2-22, 28-29, Nov. 1, Dec. 1-3, 8-10, 15-16, 30, 1920.

3. F.D.R. to Charles F. Abbott (Executive Director, American Institute of Steel Construction), Oct. 24, 1925, Roosevelt Library.

4. Herbert Hoover, Comments on Organization of the American Construction Council, reported in New York *Tribune,* May 5, 1922.

5. Memorandum from F.D.R. to Noble F. Hoggson (member of the board of governors of American Construction Council), May 31, 1923, Roosevelt Library.

6. New York *Times,* June 4, 1922; New York *Post,* July 1, 1922.

7. Herbert Hoover to F.D.R., June 12, 1923, Roosevelt Library; F.D.R. "The Task Ahead for Building," *Nation's Business,* January, 1923, p. 37.

8. *Ibid.,* pp. 35-37; New York *World,* June 28, 1922.

9. New York *Times,* June 4, 1922. Italics mine.

10. Speech by F.D.R. read before the Associated General Contractors of America, Chicago, Jan. 22, 1924. Carbon typescript dated Jan. 15, 1924, Roosevelt Library.

11. F.D.R. to Charles F. Abbott, Oct. 24, 1925, Roosevelt Library.

12. Minutes of the Board of Governors of the American Construction Council, May 16, 1923, Roosevelt Library.

13. *Ibid.,* pp. 41-42.

14. New York *Times,* May 9, 1923.

15. Richard H. Edmonds to F.D.R., June 15, 1923, Roosevelt Library.

16. F.D.R. to Richard H. Edmonds, June 20, 1923, Roosevelt Library.

17. F.D.R. to Johnson Heywood, Oct. 29, 1923, Roosevelt Library.

18. One reason for the inability of the Council to do any effective "planning" was F.D.R.'s infantile paralysis. Louis Howe undertook a major responsibility for the activities of the Council while F.D.R. was seeking to recover use of his legs.

19. Hoover conceived the codes of fair practice as a means of eliminating abuses and promoting higher standards in business. They were, as he saw it, to have no relationship to price-fixing. See Herbert Hoover, *Memoirs* (New York, Macmillan, 1952), II, 167-73.

20. *Public Papers and Addresses of Franklin D. Roosevelt* (New York, Random House, 1938), I, 754-55. Hereafter cited as *Public Papers and Addresses*. Reprinted by courtesy of Random House, Inc.

21. F.D.R. to Waldo Adler, May 31, 1923, Roosevelt Library.

22. Statement by F.D.R. in Minutes of the Board of Governors of the American Construction Council, May 16, 1923, Roosevelt Library.

23. Henry R. Seager and Charles A. Gulick, Jr., *Trust and Corporation Problems* (New York, Harper, 1929), pp. 337-38.

24. Don Wharton (ed.), *The Roosevelt Omnibus* (New York, Knopf, 1934), pp. 140-41, 145-46.

25. Fidelity and Deposit Company files, Roosevelt Library.

26. Earle Looker, *The American Way* (New York, John Day, 1933), pp. 130-31.

27. Telegram from Aymar Johnson to F.D.R., May 9, 1923, Montacal Oil Company file; F.D.R. to G. Hall Roosevelt, March 2, 1921, and Jan. 15, 1923, Roosevelt Library.

28. F.D.R. to E. F. Cary, May 19, 1921; F.D.R. to Commander Emory S. Land, April 4, 1922, Roosevelt Library.

29. American Investigation Corporation file, Roosevelt Library.

30. Photomaton, Incorporated file, Roosevelt Library. F.D.R. gave half of his profits to the Warm Springs Patients' Aid Fund.

31. Sanitary Postage Service Corporation file, Roosevelt Library.

32. United European Investors file, Roosevelt Library. Mrs. Roosevelt told the writer (Aug. 16, 1951) that her husband had gone into this enterprise purely as a public service venture and that he had not speculated in German marks. On the other hand, when F.D.R. sold out to Schall he owned 1,008 shares in United European Investors. If these shares had been acquired at the price at which they were offered to the public, one share for 10,000 marks, Roosevelt would have been a heavy plunger. But he may have

obtained his shares at a reduced price, or even as part of the inducement to lend his name to the enterprise. Roosevelt said: "I only went into this business because I felt that I would be rendering a very patriotic service and possibly prevent further loss to the thousands of Americans who have mistakenly bought marks at much higher prices." F.D.R. to W. S. McDonald, Sept. 19, 1922, Roosevelt Library.

33. International Germanic Trust Company file, Roosevelt Library.

34. Federal International Investment Trust file, Roosevelt Library.

35. F.D.R., *Letters*, II, 621-22.

36. F.D.R. to Peter H. Troy, March 22, 1921, Roosevelt Library.

37. Letter of resignation from F.D.R. to President of the Board of Directors of the Compo Bond Corporation, April 24, 1923, Roosevelt Library.

38. American Bankers Corporation file, Roosevelt Library.

39. General Trust Company file, Roosevelt Library.

40. Maine Lobster Fisheries file, Roosevelt Library.

41. F.D.R. to Barron G. Collier, Dec. 11, 1922, Roosevelt Library.

42. F.D.R. to Charles E. Ware, Jr., Jan. 25, 1932, Roosevelt Library.

CHAPTER VIII: THE CAMPAIGN OF 1928

1. New York *World*, Oct. 16, 1928; New York *Herald-Tribune*, Oct. 16, 1928; New York *Times*, Oct. 18, 30, 1928.

2. New York *World*, Oct. 5, 1928.

3. New York *Times*, Sept. 30, 1928.

4. The pledges included:

a. Continued support of agricultural education; appointment of a commission of experts to study distribution problems; scientific study of farm taxes; support of cooperative marketing agencies.

b. State ownership and control of power resources.

c. A complete state-wide park and parkway system.

d. Further reorganization of the state government.

e. An 8-hour day and 48-hour week for women and children in industry; consideration of old-age pensions; an advisory minimum-wage board for women and children; extension of workmen's compensation to cover all occupational diseases; prohibition of the issuance of temporary injunctions in labor disputes without notice of a hearing and trial by jury on charges of violation of such injunctions; extension of emergency rent laws.

f. Extension of health, education and highway facilities.

g. Restoration of direct primaries for state elective offices; limitation of campaign expenditures with publication of campaign receipts before and after elections.

h. Removal of unjust job discriminations against women.

i. Prohibition to be left to the individual states for decision.

New York *Times*, Oct. 2, 1928. Roosevelt had no part in the formulation of the Democratic platform, but he supported it fully in the campaign.

5. *Public Papers and Addresses*, I, 14-15.

6. "Addresses of Honorable Franklin D. Roosevelt: Campaign for Governorship, New York, October-November 1928" (bound typescript, Roosevelt Library), p. 31.

7. *Ibid.*, pp. 54-55.

8. *Ibid.*, p. 74.

9. *Ibid.*, pp. 77-78.

10. *Ibid.*, pp. 91-116.

11. *Ibid.*, pp. 152-72.

12. *Ibid.*, pp. 185-202.

13. *Ibid.*, pp. 295-318.

14. *Ibid.*, pp. 319-27.

15. *Ibid.*, pp. 364-85. Five months earlier Roosevelt had written: "There is no magic in Democracy that does away with the need of leadership. The danger of our Democracy lies in our tendency to select leaders who are similar to the rank and file of us, whereas the hope of Democracy seems to lie in our selecting leaders who are superior to the rank and file of us. . . . No man of authentic greatness of mind and character will purchase political position at the price of adjourning his own intelligence and becoming the errand boy of either Main Street or of Wall Street." F.D.R., "Memorandum on Leadership," carbon typescript dated June 7, 1928, Roosevelt Library. Mrs. Roosevelt wrote that "Franklin always felt that a president should consider himself an instrument chosen by the people to do their bidding, but that he should also consider that as president he had an obligation to enlighten and lead the people." *This I Remember*, p. 67.

CHAPTER IX: A REGIONAL PLAN FOR NEW YORK STATE

1. F.D.R., "Betterment of Agricultural Conditions," Address at the State College of Agriculture, Cornell University, Feb. 14, 1930. *Public Papers, 1930*, pp. 700-702.

2. F.D.R., "Inaugural Address as Governor," Jan. 1, 1929, *Public Papers of Governor Franklin D. Roosevelt, 1929* (Albany, J. B. Lyon Co., 1930), p. 15. Hereafter cited as *Public Papers, 1929*.

3. F.D.R., "Annual Message to the Legislature," Jan. 2, 1929, *ibid.*, p. 40.

4. Bernard Bellush, "Apprenticeship for the Presidency" (doctoral dissertation, Columbia University, 1950), Ch. 4, pp. 9-10, 15.

5. The major bills appropriated $3 million for aid to 1-3 room schools; $5,400,000 to replace the county contribution to the state highway system; and $550,000 to relieve towns of their contribution to state highway maintenance. A 2-cents per gallon gasoline tax was enacted, with the proceeds going to the local governments, while the direct tax on real estate was eliminated. *American Agriculturist*, April 13, 1929. In addition, the county contribution to grade crossing elimination was reduced from 10 percent to 1 percent and two bills to promote reforestation projects were passed. The franchise tax on farm cooperatives was removed. *American Agriculturist*, April 20, 1929.

6. *Ibid.*, May 3, 1930.

7. *Ibid.*, May 9, 1930.

8. Prepublication copy of interview with F.D.R. for *The Country Gentleman*, attached to a letter from E. H. Taylor to Guernsey Cross (secretary to the Governor), April 24, 1931, Roosevelt Library.

9. F.D.R., "Address at Dinner of New York State Press Association," Syracuse, N.Y., Feb. 1, 1929, *Public Papers, 1929*, p. 685.

10. F.D.R., "Address at Silver Lake, N.Y.," Aug. 15, 1929, *ibid.*, pp.726-27.

11. F.D.R., "Why the State Should Adopt a Scientific Land Policy," Address at Annual Dinner of the N.Y. State Agricultural Society, Albany, Jan. 21, 1931, *Public Papers, 1931*, pp. 700-701. These sentiments were repeated in a special message to the legislature five days later, *ibid.*, pp. 86-88.

12. F.D.R., "The Future of Farming in New York State," Aug. 28, 1929, *Public Papers, 1929*, pp. 729-30. Roosevelt's plan was not specific, but his listeners knew about the New York milkshed that F.D.R. wanted to use as a model. It entailed restriction of milk supplies to those provided by farmers in the state, and activities by the New York Dairymen's League to provide cost, price, and output figures to farmers in an effort to prevent overproduction. It also entailed control of milk prices by the state.

13. F.D.R., "Acres Fit and Unfit," Address before Conference of Governors, French Lick, Ind., June 2, 1931, *Public Papers, 1931*, pp. 734-38. Roosevelt was aware that a reforestation program and

industrial decentralization would have some relevance to the depression problem. He thought that a back-to-the-land movement for industry would move workers nearer to their food supply and assure farmers of a market at the same time that it would promote the development of a rural-industrial society. *Ibid.*, pp. 752-59; Radio Address, Albany, N.Y., Nov. 13, 1931, *ibid.*, pp. 480-82; "Back to the Land," *American Review of Reviews*, LXXXIV, No. 4 (Oct., 1931), 63-64; F.D.R. to Arthur B. Barret, Nov. 21, 1931, Roosevelt Library. He also thought his reforestation program would "reduce production and crops by ten to fifteen percent on the average, taking away especially the poorer qualities of fruit and other produce from the competitive market." F.D.R. to David M. Goodrich, July 19, 1931, Roosevelt Library.

14. *American Agriculturist*, April 20, 1929.

15. The purposes of the amendment were explained in a series of press releases from the State Conservation Commissioner in the months prior to the election (Conservation-Reforestation file, Official Papers); Nelson C. Brown, "Restoration of State Forests Sought by Referendum Vote," New York *Times*, Oct. 18, 1931; *Reforestation* (pamphlet published by State Reforestation Commission, Albany, no date).

16. New York *Times*, Oct. 22, 1931.

17. New York *Times*, Oct. 27, 1931.

18. The vote was 778,192 yes and 554,550 no (Bellush, "Apprenticeship for the Presidency," Ch. 4, p. 40). Of the 6 amendments voted on, the electorate approved the 3 supported by Roosevelt and rejected the 3 disapproved by him. F.D.R. could not understand Smith's actions: "What a queer thing for Al to fight so bitterly on No. 3!" he wrote. F.D.R. to John G. Saxe, Election Day, 1931, Roosevelt Library.

19. Quoted in *American Agriculturist*, Jan. 30, 1932.

20. F.D.R., Fifth Annual Message to the American Construction Council, undated, Roosevelt Library.

21. F.D.R., Address Before Rensselaer County Democratic Committee, Troy, N.Y., Jan. 8, 1930, *Public Papers, 1930*, p. 681.

22. F.D.R., Address Before the Regional Plan Association, New York, Dec. 11, 1931, *Public Papers, 1931*, pp. 783-88. This address was published, with a few editorial changes and cuts, as a magazine article, "Growing Up by Plan," *The Survey*, LXVII, No. 9 (Feb. 1, 1932), 483-85.

23. Robert M. Haig and Roswell C. McCrea, *Regional Survey of New York and Its Environs*, 8 vols. (New York, Committee on the Regional Plan, 1927-29).

24. Thomas Adams, *Outline of Town and City Planning; a Re-*

view of Past Efforts and Modern Aims (New York, Russell Sage Foundation, 1935), foreword by F.D.R. Thomas Adams to F.D.R., Nov. 11, 1932, Roosevelt Library; this letter was sent to Roosevelt via Delano.

25. When asked to comment on Stuart Chase's proposal for a National Industrial Planning Board to gather facts and advise the government, both Federal and state, and industry, F.D.R. replied: "I much like your idea of the National Industrial Planning Board as a fact-gatherer . . . . While I am very much opposed to the extension of Federal action in most economic-social problems, nevertheless the Federal Government has a very distinct function as a fact-gatherer for the whole nation." F.D.R. to Mrs. Caspar Whitney, Dec. 8, 1930. The National Resources Planning Board was to fulfill the functions proposed by Chase during the New Deal years. Roosevelt in 1931 felt that state planning provided forty-eight laboratories for the testing of new ideas that might prove to be sound or unsound. *Public Papers, 1931,* p. 788.

26. F.D.R., Inaugural Address as Governor, *Public Papers, 1929,* pp. 11-15.

27. *Public Papers, 1929,* pp. 153-54.

28. *Ibid.,* p. 156. Roosevelt defined the basis for rate-making as follows: "Operating expenses, capital outlay, representing money actually spent in plant investment and working capital, with reasonable allowance for obsolescence and depreciation." The return on the investment was to be limited to "the interest actually paid on borrowed money and dividend rates not in excess of current rates on preferred stock, and not to exceed 8 percent on all other cash capital."

29. F.D.R. to Hamilton Ward, June 29, 1929; Ward to F.D.R., July 29, 1929. Power Investigation file, Official Papers.

30. New York *Times,* July 5, 1929. Most of the other New York newspapers copied the *Times's* report of this speech. The speech was extemporaneous and no stenographer was present; there is no true copy of it.

31. New York *Post,* July 5, 1929.

32. New York *World,* July 5, 1929.

33. "Timely Topics," *New Leader,* July 13, 1929.

34. Samuel I. Rosenman, "Governor Roosevelt's Power Program," *The Nation,* CXXIX, No. 3350 (Sept. 18, 1929), 302-3.

35. F.D.R., "The Real Meaning of the Power Problem," *Forum,* LXXXII, No. 6 (Dec., 1929), 327-32. Roosevelt was a decided advocate of government enterprise as a "yardstick" with which to measure the performance of private industry. Speaking about a proposal to improve the New York State Barge Canal, he said: "We

will need it not only because of the larger volume of merchandise we will find it necessary to carry, but we will need it as an economic adjunct, to keep a check on what transportation should cost. But a little competition, even in this modern era of merger and consolidation, is a good thing." F.D.R., "Address before Convention of the New York State Waterways Association, Albany, Oct. 18, 1929," *Public Papers*, 1929, p. 747.

36. Prepublication copy of interview for *The Country Gentleman*, attached to a letter from E. H. Taylor to Guernsey Cross, April 24, 1931, Roosevelt Library.

37. Louis Howe to F.D.R., June 14, 1929, and June 24, 1929, Roosevelt Library; Floyd Carlisle to F.D.R., Jan. 10, 1930, Water Power Bill File, Official Papers.

38. *Public Papers, 1931*, pp. 591-92.

39. F.D.R. to Herbert Hoover, June 11, 1931; Walter H. Newton (secretary to President Hoover) to F.D.R., June 20, 1931; F.D.R. to Frank P. Walsh (chairman, N.Y. State Power Authority), June 23, 1931; Frank P. Walsh to F.D.R., Aug. 9, 1931; F.D.R. to Hoover, Aug. 11, 1931; W. R. Castle (Undersecretary of State) to F.D.R., Aug. 13, 1931; F.D.R. to Senator Thomas J. Walsh, Nov. 2, 1931, Power Authority file, Official Papers; Hoover to F.D.R., July 10, 1932, Homan-Hopson file, Official Papers.

40. Public Utilities Bureau file, Official Papers.

41. George R. VanNamee to F.D.R., Jan. 25, 1929, Roosevelt Library.

42. *Public Papers and Addresses*, I, 233.

43. *Ibid.*

44. Albany *Evening News*, May 9, 1929.

45. F.D.R. to J. Lionberger Davis, Oct. 5, 1929, Roosevelt Library.

46. F.D.R. to Frederic A. Delano, Nov. 22, 1929, Roosevelt Library.

47. F.D.R. to Louis Howe, Oct. 7, 1929, Roosevelt Library.

48. F.D.R., "The Real Meaning of the Power Problem," *Forum*, LXXXII, No. 6 (Dec., 1929).

49. F.D.R., "Annual Message to the Legislature," Jan. 1, 1930, *Public Papers, 1930*, p. 29.

50. F.D.R. to William A. Prendergast, Jan. 27, 1930, *ibid.*, pp. 487-88.

51. F.D.R. to Edward F. Goltra, Feb. 15, 1932, Roosevelt Library.

52. F.D.R., "Address at National Democratic Club," New York City, March 1, 1930, *Public Papers, 1930*, p. 708.

53. *Public Papers, 1930*, pp. 75-76.

54. Public Service Survey Commission file, Official Papers. Professor Bonbright modified the "prudent investment cost" concept as follows: "As to existing property, it would doubtless be necessary to compromise and to accept many if not most of the elements of value which have been accepted by the Supreme Court in past decisions. This rate base should then become final as to existing property and additions to it should be made on the basis of prudent investment only." Bonbright to F.D.R., Dec. 21, 1929, *ibid.*

55. Bellush, "Apprenticeship for the Presidency," Ch. 13, pp. 8-10.

56. *Public Papers, 1930,* p. 736.

57. Most of the basic criticisms of public utility regulation made by Roosevelt and his advisers have been accepted. Reproduction cost as the basis for rate-making is no longer the rule. It was vigorously attacked by Justices Black in 1938 and Frankfurter in 1939 (both Roosevelt appointees to the Supreme Court) and was relegated to secondary consideration in the *Hope Natural Gas Case* in 1944 (*Federal Power Commission v. Hope Natural Gas Co.,* 320 U.S. 591). In the same case the court asserted the dominance of public utility commissions in rate-making and greatly restricted the ability of utilities to appeal the decisions of regulatory commissions. It might be added that many economists now agree with Roosevelt's basic criticisms of public utility law and the weaknesses of regulation (see Horace M. Gray, "The Passing of the Public Utility Concept," *Journal of Land and Public Utility Economics,* XVI, No. 1 [Feb., 1940], 8-20, reprinted in *Readings in the Social Control of Industry* [Philadelphia, Blakiston, 1942], pp. 280-303).

58. F.D.R., "How Will New York's Progressive Proposals Affect the Investor?" *Public Utilities Fortnightly,* VII, No. 13, (June 25, 1931), 810-12.

59. *The Wall Street Journal,* July 1, 1931.

60. Francis X. Welch to the Editor, *Wall Street Journal,* July 2, 1931, Roosevelt Library. The writer believes that this letter was written by Roosevelt himself, or one of his close advisers with the Governor's knowledge, and sent under a fictitious name. Roosevelt has been known to do this on several occasions. The letter has numerous earmarks of Roosevelt's style of writing and indicates intimate knowledge of his beliefs. Roosevelt had no close acquaintance named Welch. Woodlock seems to have thought similarly, for he suggested a public discussion with the Governor on the public utilities issue. Roosevelt declined (F.D.R. to Thomas F. Woodlock, July 15, 1931, Roosevelt Library).

61. *New Leader,* Jan. 18, 1930.

62. F.D.R., to Norman Thomas, Jan. 24, 1930, Water Power Bill file, Official Papers.

63. Norman Thomas to F.D.R., Jan. 28, 1930, Roosevelt Library.

64. Herbert Hoover, *Memoirs*, II, 232.

65. Ray Lyman Wilbur and Arthur M. Hyde, *The Hoover Policies* (New York, Scribner's, 1937), pp. 317-18. The Commission was set up and after an investigation recommended that the Muscle Shoals properties be leased to a private firm, preferably a farm cooperative. "Report of the Muscle Shoals Commission", Nov. 14, 1931, Ala-Alb file, Official Papers.

66. F.D.R. to Frank P. Walsh, April 23, 1930, Muscle Shoals File, Official Papers.

At about the same time Senator C. C. Dill wrote to Roosevelt to ask his support for a state-wide referendum in Washington to decide whether rural public utility districts could be set up to buy electricity from municipal power plants. The private power companies vigorously opposed the proposal. F.D.R. favored the idea, and wrote: "What arouses my ire is the loose talk that municipal or county or district supplying of electricity is socialistic! If that is the case, it is also socialistic for a city to own and operate its own water supply, or its own sewage disposal. Some day the utility companies may cry 'wolf' just once too often." F.D.R. to Senator C. C. Dill, May 29, 1930, Public Utilities Bureau file, Official Papers.

CHAPTER X: SOCIAL WELFARE LEGISLATION, 1929-1932

1. Perkins had been trained as a social worker and had served as an investigator for the legislative commission that investigated the Triangle fire in 1911. She was appointed to the State Industrial Board in 1919 and was named chairman in 1924. The Industrial Board dealt with the judicial and legislative aspects of the work of the State Department of Labor, while the Industrial Commissioner handled the administrative affairs of the department. The former Commissioner, James A. Hamilton, had been such a weak appointee that Perkins had been given an increasing amount of his administrative work to do. Frances Perkins, *The Roosevelt I Knew* (New York, Viking, 1946), pp. 54-55.

2. F.D.R., Annual Message to the Legislature, Jan. 2, 1929, *Public Papers, 1929*, p. 44. A declaration that labor is not a commodity would mean that the anti-trust laws would not apply to labor unions. The Clayton Act (1914) had such a provision, but it had proved ineffective.

3. *Public Papers, 1929*, p. 166.

4. *Ibid.*, pp. 269, 272-73.

5. F.D.R., Annual Message to the Legislature, Jan. 1, 1930, *Public Papers, 1930*, p. 32.

6. F.D.R., Annual Message to the Legislature, Jan. 7, 1931, *Public Papers, 1931*, p. 40.

7. Dwight E. Robinson, *Collective Bargaining and Market Control in the New York Coat and Suit Industry* (New York, Columbia University Press, 1949), pp. 52-59.

8. Cloak and Suit Conference file, Official Papers, esp. Raymond V. Ingersoll to F.D.R., Dec. 4, 1929.

9. Letter framed by Lieutenant Governor Lehman for Roosevelt's signature, to be sent to the persons invited to the conference, Feb. 4, 1930, Franklin D. Roosevelt file, Official Papers of Lieutenant Governor Herbert H. Lehman.

10. Benjamin Stolberg, *Tailor's Progress* (Garden City, New York, Doubleday, Doran, 1944).

11. Cloth, Hat, Cap and Millinery Workers file, Official Papers of Lieutenant Governor Herbert H. Lehman.

12. Roosevelt also was instrumental in effecting settlement of a trucker's strike in New York City in 1929 (Bernard Bellush, "Apprenticeship for the Presidency," [doctoral dissertation, Columbia University, 1950], Ch. 9, pp. 10-11) and a strike by the Albany Typographical Union against the Albany *Times-Union* in the same year (Albany Typographical Union file, Official Papers). Lehman also had an important role in promoting the signing of a 3-year collective agreement in the ladies' garment industry in 1932 (Robinson, *Collective Bargaining*, p. 62).

13. William Green to F.D.R., Aug. 5, 1930; F.D.R. to William Green, Aug. 12, 1930, Prison Labor Committee file, Official Papers; *Public Papers, 1930*, p. 752; F.D.R. to International Association of Garment Manufacturers, Oct. 8, 1930, Roosevelt Library.

14. Prison Labor Committee file, Official Papers.

15. A study had already been made of old age insurance for wage earners by Dr. Charles H. Johnson, director of the State Board of Charities, and of the poor-farms and poorhouses in rural areas by a legislative committee headed by Assemblyman Frank X. Bernhardt of Buffalo. Old Age Pension News Release, Jan. 18, 1929, Official Papers.

16. *Public Papers and Addresses* I, 209-10.

17. *Ibid.*, p. 210.

18. *Ibid.*, pp. 212-13.

19. *Public Papers, 1930*, p. 534.

20. *Ibid.*, pp. 522-23.

21. F.D.R., Radio Address, April 16, 1930, *Public Papers, 1930,* p. 730. Many others objected to the law. The socialist *New Leader* thought the age of eligibility should be 65 (Feb. 22, 1930). The New York *Sun* said, "it is a long way from a comprehensive and satisfactory solution" (Feb. 19, 1930). The New York *Times* said, "the commission's plan is not an old age pension system" but "a modernized poor relief scheme" (Feb. 21, 1930).

22. F.D.R., Speech at Rochester, New York, Oct. 21, 1930, p. 10. "Governor Franklin D. Roosevelt's Campaign Speeches, October 18 to November 1st, 1930" (bound mimeographed press-release copies), Roosevelt Library.

23. F.D.R., Annual Message to the Legislature, Jan. 7, 1931, *Public Papers, 1931,* p. 39.

24. Frances Perkins to Miss M. A. LeHand (Private Secretary to F.D.R.) July 15, 1930, Roosevelt Library. The Socialist party had included unemployment insurance in its platform in 1928; in 1930 the national convention of the American Federation of Labor condemned it as a dole and handout; in the same year the Presbytery of Brooklyn and Nassau endorsed it (Bellush, "Apprenticeship for the Presidency," Ch. 9, pp. 20-21).

25. Bellush, "Apprenticeship for the Presidency," Ch. 9, pp. 22-23.

26. Attending the conference in addition to Roosevelt and Lehman, were Governors Ely of Massachusetts, Case of Rhode Island, Cross of Connecticut, Larsen of New Jersey, and White of Ohio. Governor Pinchot of Pennsylvania was represented by Dr. Charles Reitell. Among the experts on various phases of the unemployment problem were Frances Perkins, Leo Wolman, Paul H. Douglas, John Fahey, Bryce Stewart, William Leiserson, Joseph P. Chamberlain, and Mrs. Alexander Kohut. *Public Papers, 1931,* p. 531.

27. The proceedings of the convention are published in *Public Papers, 1931,* pp. 530-66.

28. *Ibid.,* pp. 548-49.

29. Members of the commission included Leo Wolman, Chairman, Charles R. Blunt, A. Lincoln Filene, C. A. Kulp (University of Pennsylvania), W. M. Leiserson (Antioch College), and W. J. Couper.

30. "Report of Interstate Commission on Unemployment Insurance," no date. Interstate Commission–Unemployment Insurance file, Official Papers.

31. F.D.R. to G. Hall Roosevelt, Feb. 24, 1931. Unemployment, General file, Official Papers.

32. *Public Papers, 1931,* p. 130.

33. New York *Times,* March 19, 1931.

34. *Ibid.,* March 4, 1932.

CHAPTER XI: THE ELECTION OF 1930

1. New York *Herald-Tribune*, Sept. 27, 1930.
2. New York *Times*, Sept. 29, 1930.
3. New York *Herald-Tribune*, Oct. 20, 1930.
4. F.D.R., "Address before National Democratic Club, New York City, Oct. 3, 1930," *Public Papers, 1930*, p. 769.
5. *Public Papers, 1930*, pp. 764-65.
6. "Governor Franklin D. Roosevelt's Campaign Speeches, October 18 to November 1st, 1930" (bound mimeographed press-release copies), Roosevelt Library, pp. 4-5, 10; *Public Papers, 1930*, pp. 790-99.
7. *Public Papers, 1930*, pp. 806-8.
8. *Ibid.*, pp. 811-12.
9. A comparison of the relief policies of the Hoover administration in Washington and the Roosevelt administration in Albany will be made in Chapter XII.
10. *Public Papers, 1930*, pp. 826-27. Other major measures Roosevelt pledged for his next two years in office were adequate regulation of public utilities, an improved old age security law, and a general enactment of his previous demands on the legislature.

CHAPTER XII: DEPRESSION RELIEF, 1929-1932

1. William Starr Myers and Walter H. Newton, *The Hoover Administration: A Documented Narrative* (New York, Scribner's, 1936), p. 23. On the same day the New York *American* asked Roosevelt's opinion on the state of the nation. He replied that he did not ". . . know detailed conditions but firmly believed fundamental industrial conditions sound." Bernard Bellush, "Apprenticeship for the Presidency" (doctoral dissertation, Columbia University, 1950), Ch. 8, p. 3.
2. Roosevelt wrote to a cousin in New Jersey, ". . . I wish much that the President had had the courage to state the true facts in regard to unemployment during the past winter. The facts were there and while it was a good thing for him to call various conferences to prove that the fundamentals are sound, it was silly to claim that by this time employment would be normal again." F.D.R. to Allerton D. Hitch, May 7, 1930, Unemployment—General file, Official Papers.
3. Roosevelt answered that he would ask the New York legislature for increased appropriations for hospitals and prison construc-

tion. F.D.R. to Herbert Hoover, Nov. 24, 1929, Homan-Hopson file, Official Papers.

4. Herbert Hoover, Statement of Feb. 3, 1931, quoted in Ray Lyman Wilbur and Arthur M. Hyde, *The Hoover Policies* (New York, Scribner's, 1937), pp. 375-76. As early as June 21, 1930, the governors had petitioned Hoover for a $1 billion emergency relief appropriation by the Federal government. Governor's Conference file, Official Papers.

5. Wilbur and Hyde, *The Hoover Policies*, p. 394.

6. F.D.R. wrote, "I have an idea that I am still absolutely correct in saying that the great bulk of their loans will not reach down to the individual at the bottom of the pyramid." F.D.R. to Joseph A. Broderick, April 13, 1932, Banking Department file, Official Papers.

7. F.D.R. remarked that "this is the very first effort on the part of the present administration to extend the helping hand of the United States to the bettering of world conditions. Nevertheless, I doubt much, even if his plan goes through, whether it will do much to put people back to work all through this country." F.D.R. to Senator Joseph T. Robinson, June 25, 1931, Roosevelt Library. A little later he added: "The Hoover administration apparently has no plans or program, either national or international. They jumped into this German moratorium business on twenty-four hour notice and without previous study just because they were told by the New York Bankers that if Germany went into bankruptcy, the Stock Exchange in New York would close and most of our big banks would be seriously embarrassed! I think there is no question of the authenticity of this." F.D.R. to Josephus Daniels, Aug. 1, 1931, Josephus Daniels Papers, Library of Congress.

8. The moratorium on intergovernmental debts had not solved all of the immediate problems of international finance. German and Austrian banks had issued over $10 billion of short-term bank bills at high interest rates. The bills were owned largely by other banks, especially in the United States, Britain, France, and Scandinavia. The flight of capital from central Europe continued after the Hoover moratorium and there was imminent danger that the bank bills could not be paid off. This would have involved serious financial problems in the nations whose banks held them, as well as for the central European banks. On July 17, 1931, Hoover proposed a "standstill agreement" by which the banks of the world would not press for payment when the bills fell due, with the details of the agreement to be worked out by a committee selected by the Bank for International Settlements. Hoover's proposal was ac-

cepted by a London meeting of government representatives on July 23. See Myers and Newton, *The Hoover Administration*, pp. 99-104, and Wilbur and Hyde, *The Hoover Policies*, p. 411.

9. F.D.R., speaking of Federal Reserve policies in October, 1931, wrote that he was "very happy that the plan worked out in Washington this week seems to be so well received in every part of the country." F.D.R. to Strabe V. Claggett, Oct. 12, 1931, Roosevelt Library. But in December, when the Federal Reserve Board temporarily stopped open market purchases, he wrote economist Harry Gunnison Brown: "Alas what a great change has taken place in the Board since the days of Woodrow Wilson. Apparently, today it is the tail to Secretary Mellon's kite." F.D.R. to Harry G. Brown, Dec. 22, 1931, Roosevelt Library. But in this letter Roosevelt did not specifically approve Brown's advocacy of large open market purchases by the Federal Reserve Banks.

10. *Public Papers, 1930*, p. 508.

11. *Ibid.*, p. 506.

12. *Ibid.*, p. 506 and pp. 537-38.

13. The members of the committee were Henry Bruere, Maxwell S. Wheeler, Ernest G. Draper, John Sullivan, Henry H. Stebbins, Jr., and Frances Perkins. Professor Paul H. Douglas of the University of Chicago was "technical adviser" to the committee.

14. "Preliminary Report of Committee on Stabilization of Industry for the Prevention of Unemployment," *Public Papers, 1930*, pp. 508-17.

15. "Report of Governor's Committee on Stabilization of Industry for the Prevention of Unemployment," *ibid.*, p. 591.

16. *Ibid.*, pp. 597-99.

17. *Ibid.*, pp. 600-601.

18. F.D.R. to all village presidents and mayors, Nov. 15, 1930, Housing of Unemployment file, Official Papers.

19. *Public Papers, 1930*, pp. 671-72.

20. F.D.R. to Herbert H. Lehman, Nov. 17, 1930. *Ibid.*, p. 673.

21. F.D.R. to Henry Bruere, Nov. 21, 1930, Unemployment Commission file, Official Papers.

22. State of New York Department of Public Works, *Annual Report of the Superintendent*, 1930 (Albany, J. B. Lyon Co., 1931), p. 3.

23. *Ibid.*, 1931 (Albany, J. B. Lyon Co., 1932), p. 3.

24. *Ibid.*, 1932 (Albany, J. B. Lyon Co., 1933), p. 3.

25. *Public Papers of Governor Franklin D. Roosevelt, 1932* (Albany, J. B. Lyon Co., 1939), p. 64. Hereafter cited as *Public Papers, 1932.*

26. Morris S. Tremaine to F.D.R., Dec. 18, 1931, Messages File, Official Papers.

27. "Report on Unemployment and Emergency Relief in the 59 New York Cities Exclusive of New York City. To Franklin D. Roosevelt, Governor of the State of New York by the Governor's Commission on Unemployment Problems for the State of New York, January 1931." Unemployment Commission file, Official Papers.

28. "Prospects of Unemployment Relief in 1931-32 in 45 cities of New York State," Unemployment Problem–Unemployment Suggestions file, Official Papers.

29. William Hodson to F.D.R., Aug. 19, 1931, Extra Session file, Official Papers.

30. The special session had been called ostensibly to grant immunity to witnesses testifying in the New York City graft scandals. Roosevelt's request for emergency relief legislation came as a somewhat unwelcome surprise to the Republicans, since it shifted the emphasis from Democratic corruption to Democratic welfare legislation.

31. The Temporary Emergency Relief Administration was headed by Jesse I. Strauss. His fellow committee members were John Sullivan and Philip J. Wickser. Harry L. Hopkins was Executive Director. Strauss served brilliantly for a year, and after his resignation was replaced by the equally brilliant Hopkins.

32. In May, 1932, Frances Perkins and Henry Bruere invited some twenty economists to dinner in New York City to discuss the relief situation. "The upshot of this conference was that there seemed to be of interest only two or three propositions of immediate moment which could be considered for the state:

(1) More public works,

(2) Transplanting city dwellers back to the farms,

(3) Stimulation of some housing projects."

Henry Bruere to F.D.R., May 24, 1932, Unemployment Commission File, Official Papers.

Those attending the dinner, in addition to Perkins and Bruere, were Harry Hopkins, Dr. B. M. Anderson (Chase National Bank), Prof. Elizabeth Baker (Columbia), Prof. Douglas Brown (Princeton), Robert W. Bruere, Prof. John M. Clark (Columbia), Prof. Carter Goodrich (Columbia), Prof. W. E. Hotchkiss (Pennsylvania), Virgil Jordan (McGraw-Hill Publishing Co.), Paul Mazur (Lehman Bros.), Prof. Raymond Moley (Columbia), Prof. Sumner Slichter (Harvard), Ordway Tead, Prof. Joseph H. Willitts (Pennsylvania), and Leo Wolman (Amalgamated Clothing Workers). Unemployment Commission file, Official Papers.

CHAPTER XIII: BANK FAILURES, 1929-1932

1. Robert Moses, *Report to Governor Franklin D. Roosevelt on the Investigation of the Department of Banking in Relation to the City Trust Company* (Albany, J. B. Lyon Co., 1929), pp. 10-20. Warder was later convicted of accepting a $10,000 bribe and sentenced to prison (New York *Times*, Nov. 6, 9, 15, 27, 1929).

2. Frank H. Warder to F.D.R., April 19, 1929, Banking Commission file, Official Papers.

3. F.D.R. to Warder, April 21, 1929, *ibid.*

4. Telegram, Leon Leighton to Herbert H. Lehman, no date, *ibid.*

5. Herbert H. Lehman to F.D.R., April 30, 1929, Roosevelt Library.

6. Robert Moses, *Report . . . on . . . the Department of Banking, passim.*

7. *Ibid.*, pp. 63-67.

8. F.D.R. to W. Gordon Crawford, Aug. 10, 1929, Banking Commission file, Official Papers.

9. F.D.R., Annual Message to the Legislature, Jan. 1, 1930, *Public Papers, 1930,* p. 29.

10. "Report of the Special Commission to Make Study of the Banking Law of the State," *Public Papers, 1930,* pp. 471-87.

11. *Public Papers, 1930,* p. 534.

12. Joseph A. Broderick to F.D.R., Jan. 21, 1931, April 8, 1931, July 24, 1931, Broderick, Joseph A., file, Official Papers.

13. *Public Papers, 1931,* p. 128.

14. *Ibid.*, p. 129. In a letter F.D.R. said that "the bankers so far have merely thrown cold water on every plan suggested to protect thrift accounts. I am not a proponent of any one plan but I do think something ought to be done before the legislature goes home." F.D.R. to Edmund Platt, March 24, 1931, Roosevelt Library. To his uncle F.D.R. wrote: "It is this apparent apathy on the part of the bankers to a real need which concerns me because it results invariably in stirring up a very deep feeling on the part of the average citizen against the small minority which controls finances." F.D.R. to Frederic A. Delano, April 1, 1931, Roosevelt Library.

15. *Public Papers, 1931,* p. 210.

16. *Ibid.*, p. 606.

17. *Public Papers, 1932,* p. 31.

18. *Ibid.*

19. F.D.R. to Edmund Platt, Jan. 11, 1932, Roosevelt Library.

20. *Public Papers, 1932,* p. 183.

CHAPTER XIV: WHAT CAN BE DONE ABOUT DEPRESSIONS?

1. Speech by Ralph W. Reynolds at 23rd Annual Meeting of the American Railway Development Association, Chicago, December 3-4, 1931. Unemployment Problem–Unemployment Suggestions file, Official Papers.

2. R. W. to F.D.R., June 22, 1932. *Ibid.*

3. Arthur E. Bennett to F.D.R., Aug. 19, 1931; Miss K. Owen to F.D.R., Aug. 24, 1931. *Ibid.*

4. Caleb F. Bryant to F.D.R., Aug. 17, 1931. *Ibid.*

5. George W. Sisson to F.D.R., no date. *Ibid.*

6. Sir George Paish to F.D.R., May 30, 1931, Roosevelt Library. Roosevelt did not write a foreword.

7. F.D.R. to J. Edmund Jones, May 5, 1932, Roosevelt Library. Salter wrote that "the conditions no longer exist under which a freely working competitive system can secure an automatic adjustment of the world's economic activities to changing needs," and that price inflation by "an increase in the general level of gold prices" followed by monetary management to maintain a stable level of world commodity prices was necessary. Arthur Salter, *Recovery: The Second Effort* (New York, *Century*, 1932), pp. 24-25, 86.

8. Interview with Norman Lombard, Dec. 1, 1952. The Stable Money Association was largely a creation of Irving Fisher's designed to propagate his ideas for eliminating depressions by stabilizing the general level of prices. Fisher had founded the Stable Money League in 1921, which became the National Monetary Association in 1923. In the latter year it obtained important support from business and banking circles and became largely an anti-inflation organization: there were rumblings of demand for inflation from the Middle West. The passing of that threat meant a loss of interest in stable money, and in 1925 a new organization was formed, the Stable Money Association. See Irving Fisher, *Stable Money: A History of the Movement* (New York, *Adelphi*, 1934), pp. 104-28. Frederic A. Delano, Roosevelt's uncle and a former member of the Board of Governors of the Federal Reserve System, was president of the Association in the years 1929-33.

9. Norman Lombard, "Memorandum on the Relationship between Unemployment and Business Depressions and Monetary and Credit Policies," enclosed in a letter from Lombard to F.D.R., Jan. 21, 1931, Governors' Conference file, Official Papers.

10. *Ibid.*, p. 3.

11. *Ibid.*, pp. 5-19.

12. *Ibid.*, p. 10.

13. "Suggestions for Remarks by Governor Franklin D. Roosevelt," enclosed in letter from Lombard to F.D.R., Jan. 21, 1931, Governor's Conference file, Official Papers.

Some of Lombard's supporters wrote to Roosevelt at Lombard's suggestion, and advocated measures more drastic than use of credit controls. Economist Willford I. King, for instance, suggested an increase in the volume of currency large enough to raise prices sharply. King to F.D.R., Jan. 23, 1931, Governors' Conference file, Official Papers.

14. The full name of the organization was Committee for the Nation to Rebuild Prices and Purchasing Power. Among its leading members were James H. Rand, Jr. (Remington Rand), Lessing J. Rosenwald (Sears, Roebuck), Vincent Bendix (Bendix Aviation), F. H. Frazier (General Baking), and F. H. Sexauer (Dairymen's League). See Herbert M. Bratter, "The Committee For the Nation: A Case History in Monetary Propaganda," *Journal of Political Economy*, XLIX, No. 4 (August, 1941), 537.

15. "Five Next Steps in the Program of the Committee for the Nation" (New York, Committee for the Nation, no date), third unnumbered page.

16. Fisher, *Stable Money*, p. 109. By 1932 Lombard was also advocating "reflation" of the price level (personal interview, Dec. 1, 1952).

17. Irving Fisher to F.D.R., Sept. 10, 1932; F.D.R. to Fisher, Sept. 12, 1932, Roosevelt Library.

Fisher proposed that the general price level be "reflated" at least to the 1930 level and then stabilized indefinitely at that level by the use of the "compensated dollar" plan supplemented by credit control through the Federal Reserve System and issuance of bonds to banks to increase the base for credit expansion. See Irving Fisher, *Booms and Depressions: Some First Principles* (New York, Adelphi, 1932), pp. 125-41. Under the "compensated dollar" plan the gold value of the dollar was to be changed at stated intervals as the price level changed; for example, if prices rose, the gold value of the dollar would be increased to induce a fall in prices. See Irving Fisher, *The Purchasing Power of Money* (New York, Macmillan, 1911) and *Stabilizing the Dollar* (New York, Macmillan, 1920).

18. George F. Warren and Frank A. Pearson, "Money and Prices," *Farm Economics*, No. 74 (Feb., 1932), p. 1688. Warren and Pearson contrasted their equation,

$$\text{prices} = \frac{\text{gold}}{\text{physical volume of production}}$$

with Fisher's, $P = \dfrac{MV}{T}$. See George F. Warren and Frank A. Pearson, *Prices* (New York, John Wiley, 1933), p. 81.

19. Warren and Pearson, "Money and Prices," p. 1693.

20. Warren and Pearson, "The Price Outlook," *Farm Economics*, No. 80 (May, 1933), pp. 1891, 1899.

21. Warren and Pearson, *Prices*, p. 164.

22. F.D.R. to H. R. Cox, June 8, 1932, Roosevelt Library.

23. F.D.R. to William W. Farley, May 1, 1932, Roosevelt Library.

24. *Public Papers and Addresses*, II, 138.

25. *Ibid.*, p. 425.

26. W. J. Spillman, *Balancing the Farm Output* (New York, Orange Judd Publ. Co., 1927); John D. Black, *Agricultural Reform in the United States* (New York, McGraw-Hill, 1929), Ch. 10; M. L. Wilson, *Farm Relief and the Domestic Allotment Plan* (Minneapolis, U. of Minnesota Press, 1933); "The Voluntary Domestic Allotment Plan for Wheat," Food Research Institute, Stanford University, *Wheat Studies*, Vol. 9 (Nov., 1932), pp. 23-62; "Bounty," *Fortune*, VII (Feb., 1933), 117-19.

27. F.D.R. to W. H. Harris, May 27, 1929, Roosevelt Library.

28. F.D.R. to A. N. Mathers, March 11, 1930, Roosevelt Library.

29. Prepublication copy of interview for *The Country Gentleman*, attached to a letter from E. H. Taylor to Guernsey Cross, April 24, 1931, Roosevelt Library.

30. Nevertheless, by the end of 1931, milk producers throughout the state and fruit growers west of Rochester were especially hard hit by the depression.

31. Bernard Bellush, "Apprenticeship for the Presidency" (doctoral dissertation, Columbia University, 1950), Ch. 4, pp. 43-44.

32. *Public Papers and Addresses*, I, 625-26.

33. Telegram, F.D.R. to Mr. Colbaugh, *Colliers Weekly*, May 24, 1932, Roosevelt Library.

34. F.D.R. to G. Hall Roosevelt, Feb. 24, 1931, Roosevelt Library.

35. Samuel J. Graham to F.D.R., written in Vienna, Sept. 3, 1931, mailed in Paris, Oct. 8, 1931, Roosevelt Library. Roosevelt's letter to Graham is not in the Roosevelt Library, but the form of Graham's reply is a series of answers to queries by Roosevelt.

36. Gerard Swope, "Stabilization of Industry: An Address Delivered before the National Electrical Manufacturers Association at the Hotel Commodore, New York City, September 16, 1931" (pamphlet, privately printed, 1931). "Mr. Swope's Plan Proposes"

(undated broadside distributed with copies of Mr. Swope's speech, *ibid.*).

37. New York *Times*, Sept. 18, 20, 24, 28, Oct. 4, 5, 27, Dec. 18, 1931; J. George Frederick (ed.), *The Swope Plan* (New York, The Business Bourse, 1931). The action of the Chamber of Commerce represented endorsement of the chief features of the Swope Plan by its membership.

38. New York *Times*, June 5, 1931.

39. *Ibid.*, Oct. 23-24, 27-31, Nov. 3-5, 12, Dec. 2-5, 1931.

40. *Ibid.*, March 22, 1932.

41. Herbert C. Hoover, "A Twenty Year Plan for America," *American Review of Reviews*, LXXXIV (July, 1931), 41.

42. Quoted in Ray L. Wilbur and Arthur M. Hyde, *The Hoover Policies* (New York, Scribner's, 1937), p. 310.

43. *Public Papers and Addresses*, I, 625.

44. *Ibid.*, p. 627.

45. Bernard Baruch to F.D.R., April 1, 1932. Felix Frankfurter had also written Roosevelt urging the soundness of a balanced budget. Frankfurter to F.D.R., Sept. 14, 1931, Roosevelt Library.

46. *Public Papers and Addresses*, I, 632.

47. *Ibid.*, pp. 641-46.

48. F.D.R. to Edward N. Heath, May 1, 1930, Roosevelt Library.

49. *Public Papers and Addresses*, I, 626.

50. Roosevelt knew of the work of William T. Foster and Waddill Catchings which had begun to attract attention in the late twenties and early thirties. At least two copies of their *The Road to Plenty* were sent to F.D.R. and he expressed a favorable interest in their work. R. J. Caldwell to F.D.R., July 3, 1928; F.D.R. to Caldwell, July 23, 1928, Roosevelt Library; Governor Ralph D. Brewster (Maine) to F.D.R., Dec. 4, 1928, Governors' Conference–General file, Official Papers. Foster and Catchings were of that economic "underworld" of unorthodox thinkers that never is appreciated by contemporaries. Seeking an explanation of periodic overproduction, they found it in the inability of consumption to keep pace with production: full employment could be maintained only if profits and savings were immediately spent for consumption goods—otherwise the demand for commodities would be inadequate. This was not their most important contribution, however: they developed the concept of the circuit flow of money, which emphasized that purchasing power must continue flowing from producer to consumer to producer if production were to continue at a high level. In this they anticipated a major element in the modern economics of na-

tional income. These views were worked out in *Money* (Boston and New York, Houghton Mifflin, 1924) and *Business Without a Buyer* (Boston and New York, Houghton Mifflin, 1927).

CHAPTER XV: THE "BRAIN TRUST"

1. Raymond Moley, *After Seven Years* (New York, Harper, 1939), p. 6. Reproduced by permission of Harper and Bros.

2. *Ibid.*, pp. 26-27.

3. Samuel I. Rosenman, *Working with Roosevelt* (New York, Harper, 1952), pp. 3-10. Quotations reproduced by permission of Harper and Bros.

4. *Ibid.*, p. 9.

5. *Ibid.*, p. 11.

6. *Ibid.*, p. 65.

7. Ernest K. Lindley, *The Roosevelt Revolution: First Phase* (New York, Viking Press, 1933), p. 7. Lindley did not offer an explanation of Roosevelt's political philosophy.

8. Moley, *After Seven Years*, p. 13; personal interview, Jan. 20, 1953.

9. Rosenman, *Working with Roosevelt*, pp. 10, 58.

10. Patten had studied at Halle and had been strongly influenced by German "Socialism of the Chair." He brought back a strong belief that modern industry could provide a good life to everyone. In *The Theory of Prosperity* (1902) he declared that every worker should share in the "social surplus" and had a right to comfort, recreation, and cleanliness and to relief from conditions over which he had no control, such as unemployment, crop failure, or accidents. Although he emphasized government intervention to develop natural resources and thereby increase the social surplus, he would limit government action to that role.

11. Rexford G. Tugwell, *Industry's Coming of Age* (New York, Harcourt, Brace, 1927).

12. *Ibid.*, p. 118.

13. *Ibid.*, p. 224.

14. *Ibid.*, p. 267.

15. Rexford G. Tugwell, "The Principle of Planning and the Institution of Laissez Faire," *American Economic Review*, XXII, No. 1 (March, 1932, Supplement), 75-92.

16. *Ibid.*, p. 87. Frederick W. Taylor was the originator of one of the best-known systems of scientific management in industry. See Chapter IV for F.D.R.'s early views on the subject.

17. *Ibid.*, p. 88.

18. *Ibid.*, pp. 89-90. This recommendation was repeated in a memorandum written by Tugwell for Roosevelt during the 1932 campaign. Tugwell conceived of experts on the council estimating the demand for products and then basing production programs upon those estimates. Once the council was set up the Federal government should repeal the anti-trust laws and permit each industry to form regional groups to carry out the program of coordinating production and consumption. Tugwell thought that the council should at first be advisory, but that government leadership was essential. Rexford G. Tugwell, "Economic Council" (handwritten memorandum, undated), Raymond Moley Papers, #35/1.

19. Rexford G. Tugwell, "The Theory of Occupational Obsolescence," *Political Science Quarterly*, XLVI, No. 2 (June, 1931), 171-227.

20. Rexford G. Tugwell, *The Industrial Discipline and the Governmental Arts* (New York, Columbia University Press, 1933).

21. *Ibid.*, pp. 200-216.

22. Adolf A. Berle and Gardner C. Means, *The Modern Corporation and Private Property* (New York, Macmillan, 1932), p. 345.

23. *Ibid.*, p. 336.

24. Adolf A. Berle and Victoria J. Pederson, *Liquid Claims and National Wealth* (New York, Macmillan, 1934), p. 73.

25. *Ibid.*, pp. 196-97.

26. Adolf A. Berle, "The Social Economics of the New Deal," New York *Times*, Oct. 29, 1933.

27. Moley, *After Seven Years*, pp. 21-22.

28. Among the economists and other experts who contributed material to the discussions of the brain trust were Lindsay Rogers, James W. Angell, Frederick C. Mills, Joseph D. McGoldrick, Schuyler Wallace, Howard L. McBain, M. L. Wilson, Ralph Robey, and many others. Moley, *After Seven Years, passim.*

29. *Ibid.*, pp. 20-21.

30. Rexford G. Tugwell, "The Preparation of a President," *Western Political Quarterly*, I, No. 2 (June, 1948), 138-39.

31. *Ibid.*, pp. 139-40.

32. Rosenman, *Working with Roosevelt*, p. 63.

33. *Ibid.*

34. Moley, *After Seven Years*, pp. 23-24.

35. Interview with Raymond Moley, Jan. 20, 1953.

36. Raymond Moley Papers, #52/4.

37. *Ibid.*, pp. 1-9.

38. "The Long View," fragment of a memorandum by A. A. Berle,

Jr., and Louis Faulkner, pp. 29-37. Raymond Moley Papers, #34/1. Some of the recommendations were not spelled out in detail.

39. Rexford G. Tugwell, "Notes From a New Deal Diary," typescript in the Roosevelt Library, pp. 27-29, entry for Dec. 28, 1932. This is a contemporary statement. Mr. Tugwell has not authorized direct quotation; the summary above is a close paraphrase of his statement.

CHAPTER XVI: THE CAMPAIGN OF 1932

1. *Public Papers and Addresses,* I, 677.

2. *Ibid.,* p. 832.

3. John M. Clark, *Social Control of Business* (New York, Mc-Graw-Hill, 1939), 2nd ed., p. 426.

4. Ray L. Wilbur and Arthur M. Hyde, *The Hoover Policies* (New York, Scribner's, 1937), pp. 343-44.

5. *Ibid.,* p. 347.

6. *Ibid.,* pp. 91-93.

7. William S. Myers and Walter H. Newton, *The Hoover Administration* (New York, Scribner's, 1936), p. 254.

8. F.D.R. to John A. Kingsbury, May 12, 1930, Roosevelt Library.

9. F.D.R. to William I. Sirovich, May 14, 1930, Roosevelt Library.

10. F.D.R. to Arthur B. Sherman, March 18, 1931, Roosevelt Library.

11. F.D.R. to Elizabeth Marbury, June 9, 1931, Roosevelt Library.

12. Typescript in Roosevelt Library, third unnumbered page.

13. *Public Papers and Addresses,* I, 649.

14. *Ibid.,* pp. 650-51.

15. *Ibid.,* p. 655.

16. *Ibid.,* p. 657.

17. *Ibid.,* p. 659.

18. For the official text of the platform see *Official Report of the Proceedings of the Democratic National Convention* (Chicago, Dem. Nat'l. Comm., 1932), pp. 148-49. The only major difference between the two major party platforms concerned the cause of the depression: the Republicans claimed that the depression was imported from abroad against all the defenses set up by the administration, and aggravated by the drought of 1931. As for concrete proposals, the Republicans listed most of those advocated by the

Democrats, with the same tacit assumption that the economic system was inherently sound. *Textbook of the Republican Party* (Chicago, Rep. Nat'l. Comm., 1932), pp. 87 ff.

19. *Public Papers and Addresses*, I, 648.

20. *Ibid.*, p. 663.

21. Moley, *After Seven Years*, p. 41.

22. *Public Papers and Addresses*, I, 696-97.

23. *Ibid.*, p. 699.

24. *Ibid.*, p. 702.

25. *Ibid.*

26. *Ibid.*, pp. 704-5. Roosevelt's second and third points constituted a rejection of the export debentures plan. To what extent can these points be considered as advocacy of M. L. Wilson's domestic allotment plan? Roosevelt had spoken of composing "the conflicting elements of these various plans, to gather the benefit of the long study and consideration of them, to coordinate efforts to the end that agreement may be reached on the details of a distinct policy" (*ibid.*, pp. 703-4), implying that he would accept any plan on which farm leaders could agree. However, Wilson prepared some of the material for the speech and Moley has written that the speech "outlined the Domestic Allotment Plan without mentioning it by name" (Moley, *After Seven Years*, pp. 41-43, 44-45). According to Tugwell, by the time of the acceptance speech on July 2, 1932, Roosevelt had agreed to support the Domestic Allotment Plan (Tugwell, "Notes From a New Deal Diary," pp. 39-40). After the election Morgenthau and Tugwell met with a group of farm leaders in Washington on December 12-13, 1932, and came out with agreement on the voluntary domestic allotment plan (*ibid.*, pp. 54-55; "Bounty," *Fortune*, III (Feb., 1933), 117-18). It is quite possible that Roosevelt's Topeka speech was intended to give two impressions: that he supported domestic allotment and that he would accept any plan on which farm leaders could agree. Just before the speech was given Roosevelt did not feel he had committed himself: "The chief difficulty is that as a general proposition the farm leaders themselves are not agreed on the details of handling the surplus . . . . In any event the chief thought to get across is that I have a deep and very practical and personal interest in the farm problem and that I am willing to try things out until we get something that works" (F.D.R. to Governor Floyd B. Olson of Minnesota, Sept. 5, 1932, Roosevelt Library).

27. Quoted in Joseph S. Davis, *Wheat and the AAA* (Washington, Brookings Institution, 1935), p. 33.

28. Myers and Newton, *The Hoover Administration*, p. 255.

29. Wilbur and Hyde, *The Hoover Policies*, p. 171.

30. Myers and Newton, *The Hoover Administration*, p. 256.

31. *Public Papers and Addresses*, I, 813.

32. *Ibid.*, pp. 763-67.

33. *Ibid.*, p. 785. Roosevelt had first outlined his advocacy of reciprocal trade agreements in Seattle on September 20.

34. *Ibid.*, pp. 835-36.

35. New York *Times*, Nov. 5, 1932.

36. F.D.R., Speech at Wheeling, W.Va., Oct. 19, 1932. Typescript in Roosevelt Library, p. 3.

37. *Public Papers and Addresses*, I, 679.

38. *Ibid.*, pp. 682-83.

39. *Ibid.*, pp. 716-20.

40. *Ibid.*, p. 731.

41. *Ibid.*, pp. 737-40. The pledge to proceed with these four great power developments was repeated several times in the campaign, particularly in a speech at Hollywood, California, on Sept. 24.

42. *Ibid.*, pp. 749-54.

43. *Ibid.*, p. 782.

44. *Ibid.*, p. 784.

45. *Ibid.*, pp. 787-88, 791-92, 852.

46. Typescript with penciled notes by F.D.R., Roosevelt Library, pp. 8-9.

47. *Public Papers and Addresses*, I, 790-91.

48. *Ibid.*, pp. 847, 851-52.

49. *Ibid.*, pp. 795-811. In the 1936 campaign Roosevelt wanted to make another speech at Pittsburgh explaining his 1932 stand in the light of the huge Federal deficits of the succeeding years. Samuel I. Rosenman re-read the 1932 speech and then told F.D.R. that "the only thing you can say about that 1932 speech is to deny categorically that you ever made it." Rosenman, *Working with Roosevelt*, pp. 86-87.

50. Herbert C. Hoover and Calvin Coolidge, *Campaign Speeches of 1932* (Garden City, N.Y., Doubleday, Doran, 1933), p. 167.

51. *Ibid.*, p. 171.

52. *Ibid.*, p. 190.

Bibliography

SOURCE MATERIAL

Most of the source material for this study is to be found at the Franklin D. Roosevelt Library, Hyde Park, N.Y. The most important papers consulted there were the Personal Papers of Franklin D. Roosevelt, grouped in the follow categories:

New York State Senator, 1911-13
Assistant Secretary of the Navy, 1913-20
Relating to Political Activities, 1913-20
Relating to Political Activities, 1920-28
Governor of New York, 1929-32
Relating to Family, Business, and Other Personal Affairs, 1882-1945

Items cited as "Roosevelt Library" are from this collection.

Other papers at the Roosevelt Library that were consulted include Papers of Members of the Roosevelt Family, 1715-1863; Collected Manuscripts Pertaining to Franklin D. Roosevelt and His Times; Papers of Louis McHenry Howe, 1913-36 (consulted for the period 1913-33); Papers of Frances Perkins, 1932-44 (consulted for 1932-33); Records of the Roosevelt Headquarters of the Democratic National Campaign Committee, 1920; Records of the Democratic National Committee, 1928-40 (consulted for the 1932 presidential campaign); Papers of Charles W. Taussig, 1932-36.

The Roosevelt Library has a typewritten copy of Rexford G. Tugwell's "Notes From a New Deal Diary," which has been consulted, but which cannot be directly quoted.

Also at the Roosevelt Library the Official Papers of Governor Franklin D. Roosevelt (cited as "Official Papers") and the Official Papers of Lieutenant Governor Lehman were extensively used. These papers cover the period 1929-32 and are files of material from the offices of the Governor and Lieutenant Governor. They are the property of New York State and are normally stored in the State Archives at Albany.

Use was made of the Woodrow Wilson Papers and the Josephus Daniels Papers at the Library of Congress, Washington, D.C. The

Papers of Robert F. Wagner at Georgetown University, Washington, D.C., were consulted, but not much pertinent information was found.

At the National Archives, Washington, D.C., the General Correspondence files of the Secretary of the Navy contain much material relating to Roosevelt as Assistant Secretary of the Navy and were particularly useful as a source for material on Roosevelt's dealings with the armor plate and coal contractors. Also consulted at the National Archives were the records of the War Labor Policies Board.

A very valuable body of information on Roosevelt's career at Harvard was obtained from student notebooks and other material in the Harvard Archives, Harvard University Library, Cambridge, Mass.

Raymond Moley made available to me two memoranda written by Rexford G. Tugwell and one written by Adolf A. Berle, Jr., and Louis Faulkner. They are the only memoranda written by members of the brain trust in 1932 that I have been able to find.

Several persons have helped to fill in gaps by personal interviews or correspondence: Mrs. Eleanor Roosevelt, Raymond Moley, Norman Lombard, Adolf A. Berle, Jr., Samuel I. Rosenman, Rexford G. Tugwell, and Langdon P. Marvin.

NEWSPAPERS

The New York *Times* was extensively used to follow Roosevelt's career from 1910 to 1933. From time to time it was supplemented by files of other New York City newspapers, particularly the *Tribune, Post,* and *World* for the period 1928-32.

The Albany *Knickerbocker Press* provided additional background material for Roosevelt's career as State Senator and Governor.

The Washington newspapers—*Star, Times, Post,* and *Herald*— were consulted for particular incidents in Roosevelt's career in the Navy Department, and the Boston newspapers—*Post, Advertiser, Transcript, Globe,* and *Herald*—provided information on Roosevelt's trip to the Charlestown Navy Yard in 1913.

Background material on Roosevelt's campaign trips in the 1932 election was obtained by consulting major newspapers from cities along the route.

Local newspapers in Dutchess County, N.Y., and the surrounding area were not consulted directly. The stories cited are from a series of scrapbooks of newspaper clippings in the Roosevelt Library.

Two periodicals were useful in obtaining background material on Roosevelt's governorship: *American Agriculturist* (1928-32) and *The New Leader* (1929-32).

BOOKS AND ARTICLES

Adams, Charles Francis, and Adams, Henry. Chapters of Erie and Other Essays. Boston, J. R. Osgood, 1871.

Adams, Thomas. Outline of Town and City Planning: A Review of Past Efforts and Modern Aims. Foreword by F.D.R. N.Y., Russell Sage Foundation, 1935.

Allen, Robert S. Why Hoover Faces Defeat. N.Y., Brewer, Warren & Putnam, 1932.

Alsop, Joseph, and Kintner, Robert. Men around the President. N.Y., Doubleday, Doran & Co., 1939.

Annual Reports of the Navy Department for the Fiscal Year. 1913-19. Washington, Govt. Printing Office, 1914-20.

Ashburn, Frank D. Fifty Years On: Groton School, 1884-1934. N.Y., privately printed, 1934.

—— Peabody of Groton: A Portrait. N.Y., Coward McCann, 1944.

Bagehot, Walter. Lombard Street: A Description of the Money Market. 11th ed. London, Kegan, Paul, 1899.

Beale, Joseph H., and Wyman, Bruce. Cases on Public Service Companies, Public Carriers, Public Works and Other Public Utilities. Cambridge, Harvard Law Review Publ. Assn., 1902.

Beard, Charles A. Economic Origins of Jeffersonian Democracy. N.Y., Macmillan, 1915.

Beard, Charles A., and Beard, Mary R. The Rise of American Civilization. N.Y., Macmillan, 1941.

Bellush, Bernard. Apprenticeship for the Presidency. Doctoral dissertation, Columbia University, 1950.

Berle, Adolf A., Jr. "The Social Economics of the New Deal," New York Times, Oct. 29, 1933.

Berle, Adolf A., Jr., and Means, Gardner C. The Modern Corporation and Private Property. N.Y., Macmillan, 1932.

Berle, Adolf A., Jr., and Pederson, Victoria J. Liquid Claims and National Wealth. N.Y., Macmillan, 1934.

Binkley, Wilfred Ellsworth. American Political Parties, Their Natural History. N.Y., A. A. Knopf, 1943.

Black, Harold G. The True Woodrow Wilson, Crusader for Democracy. Introduction by F.D.R. N.Y., Fleming H. Revell, 1946.

Black, John D. Agricultural Reform in the United States. N.Y., McGraw-Hill, 1929.

—— "The McNary-Haugen Movement," American Economic Review, Vol. XVIII (Sept., 1928).

—— "The Progress of Farm Relief," American Economic Review, Vol. XVIII (June, 1928).

—— "Plans for Raising Prices of Farm Products by Government Action," *Annals of the American Academy of Political and Social Science*, CXLII (March, 1929), 380-90.

Black, Ruby A. Eleanor Roosevelt, a Biography. N.Y., Duell, Sloan & Pearce, 1940.

Bornet, Vaughn D. Labor and Politics in 1928. Doctoral dissertation, Stanford University, 1951.

"Bounty," *Fortune*, VII (Feb., 1933), 117-19.

Bowers, Claude. Jefferson and Hamilton: The Struggle for Democracy in America. Boston and N.Y., Houghton Mifflin, 1925.

Brandeis, Erich. Franklin D. Roosevelt, the Man. N.Y., American Offset, 1936.

Bratter, Herbert M. "The Committee For the Nation: A Case History in Monetary Propaganda," *Journal of Political Economy*, XLIX, No. 4 (Aug., 1941), 531-53.

Brockway, Archibald Fenner. Will Roosevelt Succeed? A Study of Fascist Tendencies in America. London, G. Routledge & Sons, Ltd., 1934.

Brogan, Denis W. The Era of Franklin D. Roosevelt: A Chronicle of the New Deal and Global War. New Haven, Yale University Press, 1950.

Brown, Bernard E. American Conservatives: The Political Thought of Frances Lieber and John W. Burgess. N.Y., Columbia University Press, 1951.

Brown, Rollo Walter. Harvard Yard in the Golden Age. N.Y., Current Books, 1948.

Bryan, William J., and Bryan, Mary B. Memoirs of William Jennings Bryan. Philadelphia, United Publishers, 1925.

Burgess, John W. Political Science and Comparative Constitutional Law. Boston, Ginn and Co., 1902.

Busch, Noel. What Manner of Man? N.Y., Harper & Bros., 1944.

Cameron, Turner C., Jr. The Political Philosophy of Franklin Delano Roosevelt. Doctoral dissertation, Princeton University, 1940.

Campaign Addresses of Governor Alfred E. Smith, Democratic Candidate for President, 1928. Washington, Democratic National Committee, 1929.

Carmichael, Donald S. (ed.). F.D.R., Columnist: The Uncollected Columns of Franklin D. Roosevelt. Chicago, Pellegrini and Cudahy, 1947.

Carter, John Franklin (Unofficial Observer). The New Dealers. N.Y., Simon & Schuster, 1934.

Chapman, Charles C. From the New Democracy to the New Deal. Doctoral dissertation, Fordham University, 1934.

Childs, Marquis. They Hate Roosevelt. N.Y., Harper & Bros., 1936.

Clare, George. A Money Market Primer and Key to the Exchanges. London, Effingham, Wilson, 1891.

Clark, John M. "Possible Complications of the Compensated Dollar," *American Economic Review*, III, No. 3 (Sept., 1913), 576-88.

—— Social Control of Business. N.Y., McGraw-Hill, 1939.

Clark, Wesley. Economic Aspects of a President's Popularity. Philadelphia, University of Pennsylvania Press, 1943.

Clarkson, Grosvenor B. Industrial America in the World War: The Strategy Behind the Line, 1917-1918. Boston and N.Y., Houghton Mifflin, 1923.

Cobb, William T. The Strenuous Life: The "Oyster Bay" Roosevelts in Business and Finance. N.Y., William E. Rudge's Sons, 1946.

Columbia University Bulletin of Information: School of Law. N.Y., Columbia University, 1904, 1905, 1906.

Commager, Henry. The American Mind: An Interpretation of American Thought and Character Since the 1880's. New Haven, Yale University Press, 1950.

Committee for the Nation. Five Next Steps in the Program of the Committee for the Nation. N.Y., privately printed, no date.

—— Interim Report and Immediate Recommendations. N.Y., privately printed, no date.

Commons, John R., and associates. History of Labour in the United States. N.Y., Macmillan, 1926-35.

Conant, Charles A. History of Modern Banks of Issue; with an Account of the Economic Crises of the Present Century. N.Y., G. P. Putnam's Sons, 1902.

Consecration of St. John's Chapel, Groton School. Boston, T. R. Marvin, 1900.

Cox, James M. Journey through My Years. N.Y., Simon & Schuster, 1946.

Crane, Milton. The Roosevelt Era. N.Y., Boni & Gaer, 1947.

Creel, George. Rebel at Large. N.Y., G. P. Putnam's Sons, 1947.

Daniels, Jonathan. Frontier on the Potomac. N.Y., Macmillan, 1946.

Daniels, Josephus. Editor in Politics. Chapel Hill, University of North Carolina Press, 1941.

—— Tar Heel Editor. Chapel Hill, University of North Carolina Press, 1939.

—— The Wilson Era: Years of Peace, 1910-17. Chapel Hill, University of North Carolina Press, 1944.

—— The Wilson Era: Years of War and After, 1917-23. Chapel Hill, University of North Carolina Press, 1946.

Davis, Joseph S. Wheat and the AAA. Washington, Brookings Institution, 1935.

Day, Donald. Franklin D. Roosevelt's Own Story. Boston, Little, Brown, 1951.

Delano, Daniel W., Jr. Franklin Roosevelt and the Delano Influence. Pittsburgh, Pa., James S. Nudi Publications, 1946.

Dorfman, Joseph. The Economic Mind in American Civilization. N.Y., Viking, 1946, 1949.

Dows, Olin. Franklin Roosevelt at Hyde Park. N.Y., American Artists, 1949.

Dunbar, Charles F. Chapters on the Theory and History of Banking, 2d ed. Ed. by O. M. W. Sprague. N.Y., G. P. Putnam's Sons, 1901.

Edmunds, Sterling. The Roosevelt Coup d'Etat of 1933-40. Charlottesville, Va., Michie, 1940.

Ely, Richard T. Monopolies and Trusts. N.Y., Macmillan, 1900.

Farley, James A. Behind the Ballots: The Personal History of a Politician. N.Y., Harcourt, Brace, 1938.

—— Jim Farley's Story. N.Y., McGraw-Hill, 1940.

Fay, Bernard. Roosevelt and His America. Boston, Little, Brown, 1933.

Fetter, Frank W. The New Deal and Tariff Policy. Chicago, University of Chicago Press, 1937.

Filler, Louis. Crusaders for American Liberalism. N.Y., Harcourt, Brace, 1939.

Fisher, Irving. Booms and Depressions: Some First Principles. N. Y., Adelphi, 1932.

—— The Purchasing Power of Money. N.Y., Macmillan, 1911.

—— "A Remedy for the Rising Cost of Living: Standardizing the Dollar" and Discussion, *American Economic Review*, III, No. 1 (March, 1913), Supplement, 20-51.

—— Stabilizing the Dollar. N.Y., Macmillan, 1920.

—— Stable Money: A History of the Movement. N.Y., Adelphi, 1934.

Flynn, Edward J. You're the Boss. N.Y., Viking, 1947.

Flynn, John T. Country Squire in the White House. N.Y., Doubleday, Doran & Co., 1940.

Foster, William T., and Catchings, Waddill. Business without a Buyer. Boston and N.Y., Houghton Mifflin, 1927.

—— Money. Boston and N. Y., Houghton Mifflin, 1924.

—— The Road to Plenty. Boston and N.Y., Houghton Mifflin, 1928.

Frederick, J. George (ed.). The Swope Plan. N.Y., Business Bourse, 1931.

Freidel, Frank. Franklin D. Roosevelt. Vols. 1-2. Boston, Little, Brown, 1952-53.

Gosnell, Harold F. Champion Campaigner. Vols. 1-2. N.Y., Macmillan, 1952.

Gray, Horace M. "The Passing of the Public Utility Concept," *Journal of Land and Public Utility Economics*, XVI, No. 1 (Feb., 1940), 8-10, reprinted in Readings in the Social Control of Industry (Phila., Blakiston, 1942), pp. 280-303.

Gunther, John. Roosevelt in Retrospect: A Profile in History. N.Y., Harper & Bros., 1950.

Haber, Paul. The House of Roosevelt. Brooklyn, privately printed, 1936.

Hacker, Louis M. A Short History of the New Deal. N.Y., F. S. Crofts, 1934.

Hadley, Arthur T. Economics: An Account of the Relations between Private Property and Public Welfare. N.Y., G. P. Putnam's Sons, 1899.

—— Railroad Transportation. N.Y., G. P. Putnam's Sons, 1885.

Haig, Robert M., and McCrea, Roswell C. Regional Survey of New York and Its Environs. N.Y., Committee on the Regional Plan, 1927-29.

Hardy, Charles O. The Warren-Pearson Price Theory. Washington, Brookings Institution, 1935.

Hargreaves, H. Walter. Federal Fiscal Policy and the Guaranteed Debt, 1932-1940. Doctoral dissertation, Duke University, 1940.

Hatch, Alden. Franklin D. Roosevelt: An Informal Biography. N.Y., Holt, 1947.

Herrick, Genevieve F. The Life of William Jennings Bryan. Chicago, Stanton, 1925.

Hibben, Paxton. The Peerless Leader, William Jennings Bryan. N.Y., Farrar and Rinehart, 1929.

Hinshaw, David. Herbert Hoover, American Quaker. N.Y., Farrar, Straus, 1950.

Hobson, John A. Evolution of Modern Capitalism. N.Y., Scribner's, 1894.

Hofstadter, Richard. The American Political Tradition and the Men Who Made It. N.Y., Knopf, 1948.

Hoover, Herbert C. The Challenge to Liberty. N.Y., Scribner's, 1934.

—— Memoirs (Vols. 1-3). N.Y., Macmillan Co., 1951, 1952.

—— "A Twenty Year Plan for America," *American Review of Reviews*, LXXXIV (July, 1931), 41.

Hoover, Herbert C., and Coolidge, Calvin. Campaign Speeches of 1932. Garden City, N.Y., Doubleday, Doran, 1933.

Hoover, Irwin H. Forty-Two Years in the White House. Boston and N. Y., Houghton Mifflin, 1934.

Hopkins, Harry. Spending to Save: The Complete Story of Relief. N.Y., Norton, 1936.

Hull, Cordell. Memoirs. N.Y., Macmillan, 1948.

Husted, William. Bott, The Story of a Schoolmaster. Introduction by F.D.R. N.Y., Coward-McCann, 1936.

Jenks, Jeremiah W. The Trust Problem. Rev. ed. N.Y., McClure, Phillips, 1901.

Johnson, Alvin. Franklin D. Roosevelt's Colonial Ancestors: Their Part in the Making of American History. Boston, Lothrop, Lee & Shepard, 1933.

Johnson, Emory R. American Railway Transportation. N.Y., Appleton, 1903.

Johnson, Gerald W. Roosevelt: Dictator or Democrat? N.Y., Harper & Bros., 1941.

Johnson, Hugh S. The Blue Eagle from Egg to Earth. Garden City, N.Y., Doubleday, Doran, 1935.

Kerr, Peyton. The Economics of Work Relief: A History and an Analysis. Doctoral dissertation, George Washington University, 1939.

King, Clyde L. "What a Federal Farm Board Can Do," *Annals of the American Academy of Political and Social Science,* CXLII (March, 1929).

Kinley, David. "Objections to a Monetary Standard Based on Index Numbers," *American Economic Review,* III, No. 1 (March, 1913), 1-19.

Klein, Henry H. From "Rags to Riches" a la Alfred E. Smith. Privately published by the author, N.Y., 1936.

Knapp, A. B. "Water Power Problems in New York State." Master's thesis, Syracuse University, 1928.

Knapp, Sally E. Eleanor Roosevelt: A Biography. N.Y., Crowell, 1949.

Knox, Franklin. We Planned It That Way. N.Y., Longmans, Green, 1938.

Knox, John. The Great Mistake. Washington, National Foundation Press, 1930.

Lapp, John A. The First Chapter of the New Deal. Chicago, J. A. Prescott, 1933.

Lasky, Joseph. Our President, Franklin Delano Roosevelt, a Biography. N.Y., Walters and Mahon, 1933.

Lawrence, Richard W. The New York State Gubernatorial Campaign of 1930. N.Y., privately printed, no date.

Lewis, A. B. "Present and Probable Future Uses of Land in Tompkins County," *Farm Economics*, No. 77 (July, 1932), pp. 1772-88.

Lindley, Ernest K. Franklin D. Roosevelt: A Career in Progressive Democracy. N.Y., Blue Ribbon Books, 1931.

—— Half Way with Roosevelt. N.Y., Viking Press, 1936.

—— The Roosevelt Revolution: First Phase. N.Y., Viking Press, 1933.

—— "Two Years of Franklin Roosevelt," *The Nation*, CXXXI, No. 3402 (Sept. 17, 1930), 289-91.

Long, John C. Bryan, the Great Commoner. N.Y., Appleton, 1928.

Looker, Earle. The American Way: Franklin Roosevelt in Action. N.Y., John Day, 1933.

—— This Man Roosevelt. N.Y., Brewer, Warren & Putnam, 1932.

Lord, Russell. The Wallaces of Iowa. Boston, Riverside Press, 1947.

Lorwin, Lewis L. The American Federation of Labor: History, Policies, and Prospects. Washington, Brookings Institution, 1933.

Ludwig, Emil. Roosevelt, a Study in Fortune and Power. N.Y., Viking, 1938.

Lyons, Eugene. Our Unknown Ex-President, a Portrait of Herbert Hoover. Garden City, N.Y., Doubleday, Doran, 1948.

McAdoo, William G. Crowded Years. Boston and N.Y., Houghton Mifflin, 1931.

McCombs, William F. Making Woodrow Wilson President. N.Y., Fairview, 1921.

Maine, Basil. Franklin Roosevelt, His Life and Achievement. London, J. Murray, 1938.

Manual for the Use of the Legislature of the State of New York, 1911, 1912, 1913. Albany, J. B. Lyon Co., 1911, 1912, 1913.

Meade, Edward S. Trust Finance. N.Y., Appleton, 1903.

Mill, John Stuart. Principles of Political Economy, with Some of Their Applications to Social Philosophy. Boston, Little and Brown, 1848; London, Longmans, Green, 1896.

Moley, Raymond. After Seven Years. N.Y., Harper & Bros., 1939.

Montague, Gilbert H. The Rise and Progress of the Standard Oil Company. N.Y., Harper & Bros., 1903.

Moody, John. The Truth about the Trusts: A Description and Analysis of the American Trust Movement. N.Y. and Chicago, Moody Publ. Co., 1904.

Moses, Robert. Report to Governor Franklin D. Roosevelt on the Investigation of the Department of Banking in Relation to the City Trust Company. Albany, J. B. Lyon Co., 1929.

Mosher, William G. "Public Utilities and Their Recent Regulation," in History of the State of New York, VIII, 231-70. N.Y., Columbia University Press, 1935.

Moskowitz, Henry. Alfred E. Smith: An American Career. N.Y., Thomas Seltzer, 1924.

Moskowitz, Henry (ed.). Progressive Democracy: Addresses and State Papers of Alfred E. Smith. N.Y., Harcourt, Brace, 1928.

Mowry, George. Theodore Roosevelt and the Progressive Movement. Madison, University of Wisconsin Press, 1946.

Myers, William S., and Newton, Walter H. The Hoover Administration: A Documented Narrative. N.Y., Scribner's, 1936.

Nations, Gilbert O. The Political Career of Alfred E. Smith. Washington, The Protestant, 1928.

Neuberger, Richard L., and Kahn, Stephen B. Integrity: The Life of George W. Norris. N.Y., Vanguard, 1937.

Newton, Edward P. Historical Notes of St. James Parish. Poughkeepsie, A. V. Haight, 1913.

Norris, George W. Fighting Liberal. N.Y., Macmillan, 1945.

Official Report of the Proceedings of the Democratic National Convention. Chicago, Democratic National Committee, 1932.

Oliver, Alfred C. This New America: The Spirit of the Civilian Conservation Corps. Foreword by F.D.R. N.Y., Longmans, Green & Co., 1937.

Paish, George. The Way to Recovery. N.Y., G. P. Putnam's Sons, 1931.

Paris, James D. Monetary Policies of the United States, 1932-1938. N.Y., Columbia University Press, 1938.

Parrington, Vernon L. Main Currents in American Thought. N.Y., Harcourt, Brace, 1927.

Partridge, Bellamy. The Roosevelt Family in America: An Imperial Saga. N.Y., Hillman-Curl, 1936.

Peek, George N. "Equality for Agriculture with Industry," *Proceedings of the Academy of Political Science*, XII (January, 1927), 564-75.

Peek, George N., and Crowther, Samuel. Why Quit Our Own. N.Y., Van Nostrand, 1936.

Peek, George N., and Johnson, Hugh S. Equality for Agriculture. Moline, Ill., privately printed, 1922.

Perkins, Frances. The Roosevelt I Knew. N.Y., Viking, 1946.

Pringle, Henry F. Alfred E. Smith: A Critical Study. N.Y., Macy-Masius, 1927.

—— The Life and Times of William Howard Taft. N.Y., Farrar and Rinehart, 1939.

Rauch, Basil. The History of the New Deal, 1933-1938. N.Y., Creative Age, 1944.

Regier, Cornelius C. The Era of the Muckrakers. Chapel Hill, University of North Carolina Press, 1932.

Ripley, William Z. Main Street and Wall Street. Boston, Little, Brown, 1927.

—— Railroads: Finance and Organization. N.Y., Longmans, Green, 1915.

—— Railroads, Rates and Regulations. N.Y., Longmans, Green, 1912.

Ripley, William Z. (ed.). Trusts, Pools and Corporations. Boston and N.Y., Ginn and Co., 1905.

Robinson, Dwight E. Collective Bargaining and Market Control in the New York Coat and Suit Industry. N.Y., Columbia University Press, 1949.

Rodgers, Cleveland. Robert Moses: Builder for Democracy. N.Y., Holt, 1952.

Roos, Charles F. NRA Economic Planning. Bloomington, Ind., Principia Press, 1937.

Roosevelt, Eleanor. This I Remember. N.Y., Harper & Bros., 1949.

—— This is My Story. N.Y., Harper & Bros., 1937.

Roosevelt, Elliott (ed.). F.D.R.: His Personal Letters. N.Y., Duell, Sloan and Pearce, 1947, 1948. Cited as: Letters.

Roosevelt, Franklin D. "The Age of Social Consciousness," *Harvard Graduates Magazine*, XXXVIII, No. 149 (Sept., 1929), 1-7.

—— "Back to the Land," *American Review of Reviews*, LXXXIV, No. 4 (Oct., 1931), 63-64.

—— "A Debt We Owe," *Country Home*, LIV, No. 6 (June, 1930), 12-14.

—— Government—Not Politics. N.Y., Covici-Friede, 1932.

—— "Growing Up By Plan," *The Survey*, LXVII, No. 9 (Feb. 1, 1932), 483.

—— The Happy Warrior: Alfred E. Smith. Boston, Houghton Mifflin, 1928.

—— "How Will New York's Progressive Proposals Affect the Investor?" *Public Utilities Fortnightly*, VII, No. 13 (June 25, 1931), 810-12.

—— "Is There a Jefferson on the Horizon," *American Mercury*, Vol. LXI, No. 261 (Sept., 1945). Originally published in the New York *Evening World* for December 3, 1925.

—— Looking Forward. N.Y., John Day, 1933.

—— "The National Need of Petroleum Reserves," *Petroleum Age*, III, No. 11 (Nov., 1916), 3.

—— "A Newly Discovered Fragment From a Voyage to Lilliput," *Harvard Advocate*, LXXIV, No. 10 (Feb. 28, 1903), 133-34.

—— On Our Way. N.Y., John Day, 1934.

—— Our Democracy in Action: The Philosophy of President Franklin D. Roosevelt as Found in His Speeches, Messages and Other Public Papers. Washington, National Home Library Foundation, 1940.

—— Power Views of Franklin D. Roosevelt. Washington, National Power Policy Committee, 1934.

—— "Problems and Policies in New York State," *American Review of Reviews*, LXIX, No. 6 (June, 1924), 604-7.

—— Public Papers and Addresses of Franklin D. Roosevelt. Vols. 1-2. N.Y., Random House, 1938. Cited as: Public Papers and Addresses.

—— Public Papers of Governor Franklin D. Roosevelt, 48th Governor of New York, 1929-1932. Albany, J. B. Lyon Co., 1930-31, 1937, 1939. Cited as: Public Papers.

—— "The Real Meaning of the Power Problem," *Forum*, LXXXII, No. 6 (Dec., 1929), 327-32.

—— "Smith—Public Servant," *The Outlook*, CXXVII, No. 8 (June 25, 1924), 309-11.

—— "A State Helps Its Farms," *National Farm Journal*, LIV, No. 3 (March, 1930), 7-8.

—— "The Task Ahead for Building," *Nation's Business*, Jan., 1923, p. 37.

—— "What Price Flood Relief," *National Business Review*, VI, No. 3 (Oct. 1, 1927), 6-7 and 38-39.

—— Whither Bound? Boston and N.Y., Houghton Mifflin, 1926.

Roosevelt, Mrs. James (Sara Delano). My Boy Franklin. N.Y., Long and Smith, 1933.

Roosevelt, Theodore. An Autobiography. N.Y., Scribner's, 1912.

—— The New Nationalism. N.Y., *Outlook*, 1910.

Roper, Daniel C. Fifty Years of Public Life. Durham, N. C., Duke University Press, 1941.

Rosenman, Samuel I. "Governor Roosevelt's Power Program," *The Nation*, CXXIX, No. 3350 (Sept. 18, 1929), 302-3.

—— Working with Roosevelt. N.Y., Harper & Bros., 1952.

Saloutos, Theodore, and Hicks, John D. Agricultural Discontent in the Middle West, 1900-1939. Madison, Wis., University of Wisconsin Press, 1951.

Salter, Arthur. Recovery: The Second Effort. N.Y., Century, 1932.

Schlesinger, Arthur M. The New Deal in Action, 1933-1939. N.Y., Macmillan, 1940.

—— New Viewpoints in American History. N.Y., Macmillan, 1922.

Schriftgiesser, Karl. The Amazing Roosevelt Family. N.Y., Wilfred Funk, 1942.

Seager, Henry R., and Gulick, Charles A., Jr. Trust and Corporation Problems. N.Y., Harper & Bros., 1929.

Seidman, Joel. The Needle Trades. N.Y., Farrar and Rinehart, 1942.

Sherwood, Robert. Roosevelt and Hopkins, an Intimate History. N.Y., Harper & Bros., 1948.

Smith, Alfred E. Up to Now: An Autobiography. N.Y., Viking, 1929.

Smith, Rixey, and Beasley, Norman. Carter Glass: A Biography. N.Y., Longmans, Green, 1939.

Spahr, Walter E. The Monetary Theories of Warren and Pearson. N.Y., Farrar and Rinehart, 1934.

Spillman, William J. Balancing the Farm Output: A Statement of the Present Deplorable Condition of Farming, Its Causes, and Suggested Remedies. N.Y., Judd, 1927.

Sprague, Oliver M. W. Banking Reform in the United States. Cambridge, Harvard University Press, 1911.

—— History of Crises Under the National Banking System. Washington, Govt. Printing Office, 1910.

—— Recovery and Common Sense. Boston and N.Y., Houghton Mifflin, 1934.

State of New York Department of Public Works, Annual Report of the Superintendent, 1930. Albany, J. B. Lyon Co., 1931.

Steeholm, Clara, and Steeholm, Hardy. The House at Hyde Park. N.Y., Viking, 1950.

Steffens, Lincoln. Autobiography. N.Y., Harcourt, Brace, 1931.

Stimson, Henry L. On Active Service in Peace and War. N.Y., Harper & Bros., 1948.

Stolberg, Benjamin. Tailor's Progress. Garden City, N.Y., Doubleday, Doran, 1944.

Swope, Gerard. "Stabilization of Industry: An Address Delivered Before the National Electrical Manufacturers Association at the Hotel Commodore, New York City, September 6, 1931." Pamphlet, privately printed, 1931.

Tannenbaum, Frank. Osborne of Sing Sing. Introduction by F.D.R. Chapel Hill, University of North Carolina Press, 1933.

Tarbell, Ida M. The History of the Standard Oil Company. N.Y., McClure, Phillips, 1904.

Textbook of the Republican Party. Chicago, Republican National
Committee, 1932.
Timmons, Bascom N. Garner of Texas: A Personal History. N.Y.,
Harper & Bros., 1948.
Trombley, Kenneth E. The Life and Times of a Happy Liberal:
A Biography of Morris Llewellyn Cooke. N.Y., Harper & Bros.,
1954.
Tugwell, Rexford G. "The Agricultural Policy of France," *Political Science Quarterly*, XLV, Nos. 2, 3, 4 (June, Sept., Dec.,
1930), 214-30, 405-28, 527-47.
—— The Battle for Democracy. N.Y., Columbia University
Press, 1935.
—— "Experimental Economics," in The Trend of Economics.
N.Y., Knopf, 1924.
—— "Experimental Roosevelt," *Political Quarterly*, XXI, No. 3
(July-Sept., 1950), 239-70.
—— "Farm Relief and a Permanent Agriculture," *Annals of the
American Academy of Political and Social Science*, CXLII
(March, 1929), 271-82.
—— The Industrial Discipline and the Governmental Arts. N.Y.,
Columbia University Press, 1933.
—— Industry's Coming of Age. N.Y., Harcourt, Brace, 1927.
—— Mr. Hoover's Economic Policy. N.Y., John Day, 1932.
—— "The New Deal in Retrospect," *Western Political Quarterly*,
I, No. 4 (Dec., 1948), 373-85.
—— "The New Deal: The Available Instruments of Government
Power," *Western Political Quarterly*, II, No. 4 (Dec., 1949),
545-80.
—— "The New Deal: The Decline of Government," *Western
Political Quarterly*, IV, No. 2-3 (June-Sept., 1951), 295 ff., 469 ff.
—— "The New Deal: The Progressive Tradition," *Western Political Quarterly*, III, No. 3 (Sept., 1950), 390-427.
—— "The Preparation of a President," *Western Political Quarterly*, I, No. 2 (June, 1948), 131-53.
—— "The Principle of Planning and the Institution of Laissez
Faire," *American Economic Review*, XXII, No. 2 (March, 1932,
Supplement), 75-92.
—— "The Protagonists: Roosevelt and Hoover." *The Antioch
Review*, Winter 1953-54, pp. 419-42.
—— "The Source of New Deal Reformism," *Ethics*, LXIV, No. 4
(July, 1954), 249-76.
—— The Stricken Land, the Story of Puerto Rico. Garden City,
N.Y., Doubleday, 1947.

—— "The Theory of Occupational Obsolescence," *Political Science Quarterly*, XLVI, No. 2 (June, 1931), 171-227.

Tugwell, Rexford G., and Hill, Howard. Our Economic Society and Its Problems. N.Y., Harcourt, Brace, 1934.

Tugwell, Rexford G., Munro, Thomas, and Stryker, Roy E. American Economic Life. 3d ed. N.Y., Harcourt, Brace, 1930.

Tully, Grace G. F.D.R., My Boss. N.Y., Scribner's, 1949.

Turner, Frederick J. The Frontier in American History. N.Y., Holt, 1920.

U.S. Bureau of the Census. Historical Statistics of the United States, 1789-1945. Washington, Govt. Printing Office, 1949.

U.S. Dept. of Labor, Wage and Hour Division, Economics Branch. Wartime Policies on Wages, Hours, and Other Labor Standards in the United States, 1917-1918. Washington, 1942, mimeographed.

U.S. House of Representatives, Committee on Naval Affairs. Hearings, 1915, 1916, 1917. Washington, Govt. Printing Office, 1915, 1916, 1917.

Van Loon, Hendrik Willem. "What Governor Roosevelt Reads," *The Saturday Review of Literature*, IX, No. 13 (Oct. 15, 1932), 169-71.

Wallace, Henry A. New Frontiers. N.Y., Reynal and Hitchcock, 1934.

—— "Stabilization of Prices and the McNary-Haugen Bill," *Annals of the American Academy of Political and Social Science*, CXLII (March, 1929), 402-5.

Wallace, Schuyler C. The New Deal in Action. N.Y., Harper & Bros., 1934.

Warburg, James P. Hell Bent for Election. Garden City, N.Y., Doubleday, Doran, 1936.

—— The Money Muddle. N.Y., Knopf, 1934.

Warren, George F., and Pearson, Frank A. "Adjusting Agriculture to the Probable Price Level," *Farm Economics*, No. 74 (Feb., 1932), pp. 1700-1702.

—— "A Business Panic," *Farm Economics*, No. 73 (Nov., 1931), pp. 1610-11.

—— "Commodity Prices," *Farm Economics*, No. 74 (Feb., 1932), pp. 1659-71.

—— "The Decline in Commodity Prices," *Farm Economics*, No. 66 (June, 1930), pp. 1298-99.

—— "Duration of Major Panics in the United States," *Farm Economics*, No. 75 (May, 1932), pp. 1719-28.

—— "Money and Prices," *Farm Economics*, No. 74 (Feb., 1932), pp. 1685-99.

—— "Physical Volume of Production in the United States," *Farm Economics*, No. 74 (Feb., 1932), pp. 1678-85.

—— "The Price Outlook," *Farm Economics*, No. 80 (May, 1933), pp. 1879-1900.

—— Prices. N.Y., Wiley, 1933.

—— "Prices in the United States Since Suspension of the Gold Standard," *Farm Economics*, No. 81 (June, 1933), pp. 1914-27.

—— "Prices of Farm Products," *Farm Economics*, No. 79 (Feb., 1933), pp. 1822-35.

—— "Relation of Gold to Prices," *Farm Economics*, No. 76 (June, 1932), pp. 1742-51.

—— "Relation of the Supply of Gold to the Value of Gold," *Farm Economics*, No. 77 (July, 1932), pp. 1766-71.

—— "Wages," *Farm Economics*, No. 74 (Feb., 1932), pp. 1671-77.

—— "Wholesale Prices in the United States for 135 Years," *Farm Economics*, No. 72 (Sept., 1931), pp. 1579-89.

—— "Wholesale Prices of All Commodities," *Farm Economics*, No. 68 (Nov., 1930), pp. 1418-40.

Werner, Morris R. Bryan. N.Y., Harcourt, Brace, 1929.

Wharton, Don. The Roosevelt Omnibus. N.Y., Knopf, 1934.

"What's to Become of Us?" *Fortune*, VIII, No. 6 (Dec., 1933), 112. Reprinted in Wharton, Don, The Roosevelt Omnibus, as "The Enigma," 92-124.

Wilbur, Ray L., and Hyde, Arthur M. The Hoover Policies. N.Y., Scribner's, 1937.

Williams, Wayne C. William Jennings Bryan. N.Y., G. P. Putnam's Sons, 1936.

Wilson, Milburn L. Farm Relief and the Domestic Allotment Plan. Minneapolis, University of Minnesota Press, 1933.

—— "The Voluntary Domestic Allotment Plan for Wheat," in Food Research Institute, Stanford University, *Wheat Studies*, IX (Nov., 1932), 23-62.

Wilson, Woodrow. The New Freedom: A Call for the Emancipation of the Generous Energies of a People. N.Y., Doubleday, Page, 1913.

Wolman, Leo. Ebb and Flow in Trade Unionism. N.Y., National Bureau of Economic Research, 1936.

Index

Abbott, Charles F., 201

Adams, James Truslow, 275 (n.10)

Adie, David S., 148

Adirondack forest preserve, 131

Agricultural Adjustment Administration (AAA), 248, 255, 256

Agricultural Advisory Commission, formed, 125; major recommendations of, 125-26, 282 (n.5); recommends land-use survey, 127; recommendations to F.D.R., 198-99

Agricultural Credit Banks, 174

Agriculture, 97, 123; F.D.R. advocates planning in, 50; plans for relief of, 90, 248; problem in New York state, 119; causes of decline of agricultural prosperity, 124; *see also entries beginning* Farm

Airways Corporation of America, 111

Altgeld, John P., 17

Aluminum Company of America, 44

American Agriculturist, 131

American Anti-Trust League, 59

American Association for Labor Legislation, 46

American Bankers Corporation, F.D.R.'s connection with, 115

American Construction Council, 253, 256; F.D.R.'s connection with, 101-6; objectives of, 102-3; forerunner of the N.R.A., 106-7; basic idea behind, 107

American Federation of Labor, 46, 68, 70, 157; opposes unemployment insurance, 289 (n.24)

American Individualism (Hoover), quoted, 121

American Investigation Corporation, F.D.R.'s connection with, 110-11

American Legion, 79

American Mining Congress, 64

American Review of Reviews, 202

American Sugar Refining Corporation, 41

Anderson, B. M., 293 (n.32)

Andrew, A. Piatt, 25; teaches Harvard economics course, 23-25; quoted on competition, 23; quoted on monopoly, 24; on labor unions, 24; Harvard course on Money, 30-31, 263 (n.33); advocate of economic reform, 33-34; later career of, 261 (n.15)

Angell, James W., 300 (n.28)

Anti-trust laws, 201, 287 (n.1); and trade association codes, 106, 107

Armor plate, problem of bids on, 58-61; government-owned plant, 60-62, 270 (n.10, n.15)

Astor, John Jacob, 108

Ayrault, Guy, F.D.R.'s economics instructor at Groton, 17, 261 (n.3)

Baker, Elizabeth, 293 (n.32)

Bank for International Settlements, 291

Banking Law, Commission on Revision of the, appointed by F.D.R., 185; recommendations of, 186-87; disagrees with Moses report, 186

Bank of England, 32

Bank of the United States, failure of, 183, 187

Banks and banking, 24; Harvard course on banking, 32-33, 263-64 (n.35); bank failures, 183-89; protection of thrift accounts, 186, 187, 188; F.D.R. proposes more rigid supervision of banks, 238

Barnum, Jerome D., 128

Baruch, Bernard M., 216; advises F.D.R. that a balanced budget is necessary for recovery, 203

Beacon (N.Y.) *Standard,* 96